VOYAGERS TO THE NEW WORLD

By the same author

The Aztecs
The Toltecs

Voyagers to the New World

NIGEL DAVIES

WILLIAM MORROW AND COMPANY, INC.

NEW YORK   1979

CONTENTS

LIST OF ILLUSTRATIONS

Between pages 178 and 179

Maps

PREFACE

THE excellent reception which *The Aztecs* was accorded so encouraged me that I decided to write another book on Ancient America for the general reader.

The political history of the Aztecs had been rather neglected in recent decades. This time, however, I have chosen a subject which might almost be thought to have received more than its due share of attention: the whole problem of Man's origins in America, and of transoceanic contacts between the Old World and the New before Columbus.

I feel, however, that a major gap still remains to be filled. The reader at present has to make his choice between two types of writing on the subject that differ radically: either he must plough through the works of anthropologists, written in technical jargon and published in professional magazines, or alternatively he must content himself with the outpourings of writers intent on providing the simplest but not necessarily the most correct solution to a most complex question.

My object has been to try to sum up the general state of knowledge on the contentious but fascinating problem of Old World influences on American cultures and to produce a work that is both readable and in conformity with the latest scientific evidence on the subject. I have made a special effort to make available the most recent data, and a considerable proportion of the references are taken from books and papers written in the 1970s, giving information not previously available and which in many instances has transformed the whole picture. In the obtaining and ordering of this material I have had invaluable help from Antoinette Nelken, close collaborator of Richard MacNeish, whose work figures so prominently in the early chapters of my book.

I first became deeply interested in the possibility of transoceanic contacts between the Old World and the New when I attended the heated discussion which took place at the 35th International

Congress of Americanists in Mexico City in 1962. Since then some of my colleagues have begged me to steer clear of such a burning topic, going so far as to suggest that I might ruin my reputation if I had the audacity to enter the fray! I have ignored their advice, and here is the result. I feel entitled to add that the most distinguished anthropologists of recent times were not afraid to become involved, including my revered master Dr Paul Kirchhoff, as well as the two most outstanding Mexican archaeologists of this century, Alfonso Caso and Pablo Martínez del Río, who wrote a book entitled *American Origins*.

Nowadays the public tends to prefer categoric answers to any question. But to many problems science has no single and simple solution, and theories are subject to rapid change. Where contact between the Old World and the New is concerned, more is now known of prehistoric times, and of the last phase before the Spanish Conquest, concerning Vikings and Polynesians; much of what happened, however, in the intervening millennia remains obscure, and it is impossible to give an answer that is both honest and categoric, though I have tried to express my personal opinions as clearly and concisely as possible.

I hope sincerely that this modest contribution to the problem will help to enlighten the reader – so avid for information on every aspect of pre-Columbian America – and give him a clearer picture of what we know and what we don't know on a subject of worldwide interest.

NIGEL DAVIES

Ice-age land bridge between Siberia and Alaska
(approx. 34000 - 30000 B.C.)

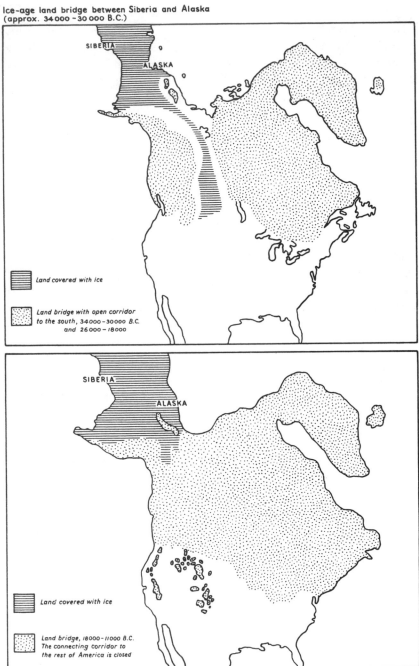

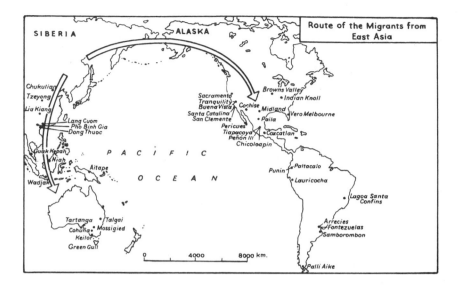

Route of the Migrants from East Asia

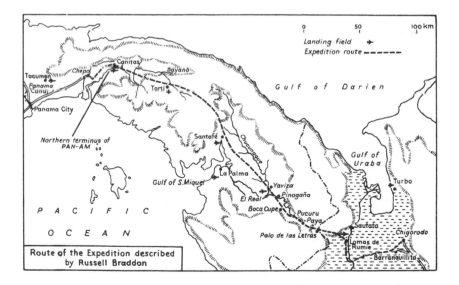

Route of the Expedition described by Russell Braddon

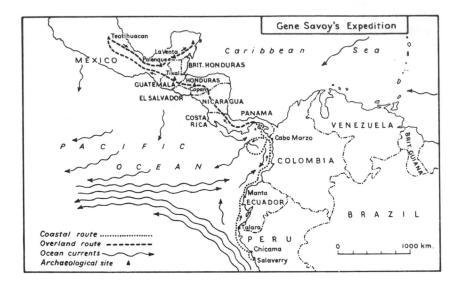

Gene Savoy's Expedition

Coastal route ....
Overland route - - - - - -
Ocean currents
Archaeological site ▲

0   1000 km.

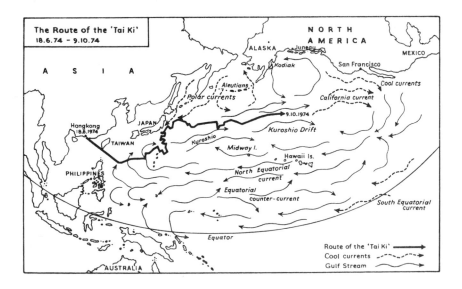

The Route of the 'Tai Ki'
18.6.74 – 9.10.74

Route of the 'Tai Ki' ———————▶
Cool currents - - - - - -▶
Gulf Stream

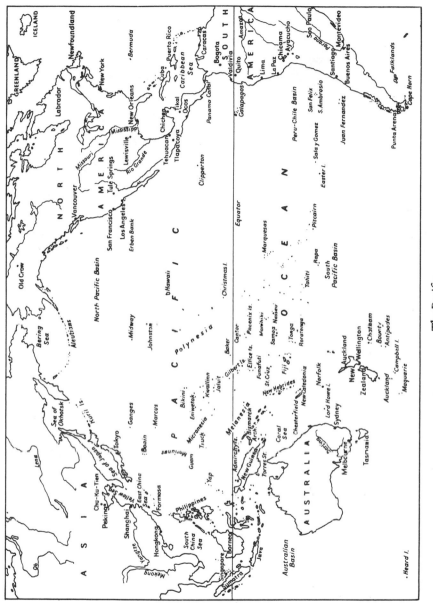

The Pacific

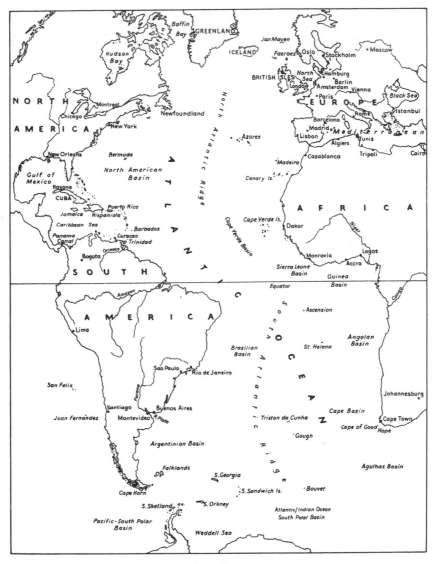

The Atlantic

VOYAGERS TO THE NEW WORLD

CHAPTER ONE

A PERENNIAL PROBLEM

'ELOI, Eloi lama sabachthani?' were the last words of the dying Christ, spoken in Aramaic and rendered in English as 'My God, my God, why hast thou forsaken me?'

But the French antiquarian, Augustus Le Plongeon, writing a hundred years ago, denied that our Lord had spoken in such plaintive tones and maintained that He had really said: 'Helo, helo, lamah zabac ta ni.' These were Maya words, signifying 'Now, now, sinking, black ink over my nose,' to be interpreted as meaning: 'Now I am sinking, darkness covers my face.' The writing on the wall of the Chaldean banquet hall, reported in the Book of Daniel as spelling out the doom of Belshazzar's kingdom, was also Maya, according to Le Plongeon, who regarded this tongue as a kind of Near Eastern lingua franca! The self-styled doctor maintained that Maya colonies had long been established on the banks of the Nile, later to be visited by Queen Moo, exiled ruler of Chichén Itzá; driven from her Mexican kingdom, she had been received with open arms in Egypt and made Queen, after a brief but eventful sojourn in the lost continent of Atlantis.*

In contrast, modern scholars write with caution about early migrations across the oceans. Typical of the sceptics is Dr John H. Rowe, an outstanding authority on Ancient Peru:

> In all too many courses on New World archaeology, diffusionist fantasies are being presented as a substitute for archaeological theory. But any innocent archaeologist who comes away from one of those sessions convinced that transpacific contacts are the wave of the future is sadly deluded. Diffusionism is the wave of the past. It was the favourite theory used by sixteenth-century travellers to explain odd similarities that struck

* Source-references are fulfilled in the List of Sources on p. 269, indicated by the page number of the text.

I

their notice, and it has remained ever since the favourite recourse of Western folk-belief in dealing with such problems.*

Is Le Plongeon correct when he treats Ancient Mexico and Egypt as a single culture; or should we trust the scholar who denounces such notions as a snare and a delusion? The whole controversy is charged with emotion, and for Mormons and Theosophists the origins of American Man are an article of faith. The search for solutions to the riddle has unleashed floods of speculation and has become a major industry; the quest is sustained by millions of readers, avid for bold theories, suitably gift-wrapped and seemingly novel. A few writers offer a serious approach, but the works of many others are more suited to the fiction than to the non-fiction section of the best-sellers list.

The subject is topical but far from new. Even before Columbus, Aztec emperors liked to speculate on their ancestry; one Aztec ruler even sent an official expedition, complete with sixty magicians, to seek the place of origin of his tribe. These emissaries had an easier passage than later explorers; legend relates that they were changed into birds by an obliging demon; they flew nonstop to remote shores, where they discovered people who spoke their own language, and shared a common past.*

For Columbus the problem never arose since he remained convinced that he had discovered the eastern extremity of Asia. He accordingly dubbed the people of those lands 'Indians', and so they have remained. Once, however, the Spaniards realized that they were in a different hemisphere, they naturally wanted to know where these 'Indians' had come from. Either American Man had originated in the new continent, or he had arrived there from somewhere else. A dual creation, complete with a duplicate Adam and Eve in a transatlantic Garden of Eden, was an unthinkable heresy, alien to the teachings of the Old Testament. American Man must have derived from the Old World, as a descendant of Adam and Eve. This theory was established only after initial doubts had been resolved as to whether the Indian was a human being at all, and fit to receive the sacraments of the Church; the debate was settled in 1537 by a Bull of Pope Paul III, though the task of conversion was still beset by uncertainties.

Ill-intentioned people continued to insist that the Indians, even if they were human, were unfit for baptism; they were not genuine converts but lapsed believers. This insistence was due to an odd conviction that the New World had already been visited in pre-Hispanic times by St Thomas. The Apostle's reputation for long-distance travel embraced the Old World as well as the New and in the Late Middle Ages he was widely believed to have travelled to India, where he made many converts and suffered martyrdom.

Once the American Indian had been accepted as a member of the human race, a host of suggestions was advanced by Spanish friars as to his origins. Anticipating the Mormons, Padre Durán in the late sixteenth century proposed that the Mexicans were Israelites because of their propensity for infant sacrifice (small children were the favourite fare of the Mexican Rain God, Tlaloc; in the Bible they are 'passed through the fire' to propitiate the Canaanite god Moloch). Fray Juan de Torquemada, writing a generation later, cites Romans and Carthaginians as possible ancestors of the Indians; he even questions whether they might not be Irish, on the dubious grounds that they ate human flesh. The Lost Tribes of Israel theory never lacked supporters: in his *Origin of the Americans*, the Amsterdam rabbi Menasseh ben Israel, writing in 1650, told of a Jewish traveller in South America who became convinced that his Indian guide was an Israelite, and greeted him with the words 'Shema Israel', 'Hear, O Israel'. Rabbi Menasseh was a man of considerable standing: he came to London in 1655, and was invited to dine by the Lord Protector Cromwell.

As early as 1590, long before the Bering Strait was explored, Padre Joseph de Acosta first proposed that the Indians had crossed from Asia to America in Arctic latitudes. This view gained further adherents in the seventeenth and eighteenth centuries and was later supported by Thomas Jefferson.

In the nineteenth century the triumphs of early archaeologists created a new interest in prehistory and produced a bumper harvest of speculation on the ancestry of American Man; as a result of the spectacular re-creation of the Egyptian past that followed Napoleon's expedition, Israel yielded first place to Egypt, and New World origins were increasingly sought on the banks of the Nile.

This book is mainly concerned with modern theories and recent discoveries. However, before viewing the present situation, the leading contenders who joined battle on the issue in the past century deserve mention. For information on these early combatants, I am much indebted to Dr Robert Wauchope, the distinguished Americanist and

3

editor of the fifteen-volume *Handbook of the Middle American Indians*, who in *Lost Tribes and Sunken Continents* succinctly summarizes so many divergent, if far-fetched, theories.*

Augustus Le Plongeon, whom I quoted above, wrote in the second half of the nineteenth century, at a time when talk of pyramids, tombs or ancient texts automatically conjured up visions of the monuments of the Nile Valley. Le Plongeon, however, by a unique feat of mental gymnastics, managed to link the Maya not only with Egypt, but simultaneously with Atlantis, the Lost Tribes of Israel, the Indian Rig Veda, the Chinese books of the Chou King, and even with the birth of Christianity: 'It is on this story of the courting of [the Mayan] Queen Moo by Prince Aak, the murderer of her husband . . . that rests the whole fabric of the Christian Religion.' Le Plongeon claimed that the Maya Indians had told him of their 'secret' history, linking Mexico with Egypt and the god Quetzalcóatl with Isis. Such tales are mere figments of a fertile imagination, since few Maya of the 1880s would have heard of Egypt, let alone of Isis.

Not only did Le Plongeon invent princes and deities quite freely, he even found a niche for himself in the Maya pantheon. In *Queen Moo of the Egyptian Sphinx* the author, having unearthed a buried Chacmool (a peculiar type of reclining figure in stone), pointed to the resemblance between his own features and those of the image; from that moment onwards, his every word was faithfully obeyed by his workers, who proclaimed: 'Thou too wast a companion of the Great Lord Chacmool. . . . His time to live again on earth has arrived.' Le Plongeon firmly believed that the Maya had invented the electric telegraph and waxed indignant if anyone queried his statements. Even so, his knowledge of Maya lore and language was deficient. In a letter written a few weeks before he died, Sir Eric Thompson, the leading Maya scholar of his time, told me that the Mayanized version of our Lord's words on the cross was nonsense: *zabac*, for instance, simply means 'to write', and cannot conceivably be twisted into signifying 'black ink' and hence 'darkness'.

Edward King, Viscount Kingsborough, 1795–1837, was a man of different calibre. When still at Oxford this English nobleman became a passionate student of American antiquities and soon convinced himself that the Mexican Indians were descended from the Lost Tribes of Israel. He devoted his entire fortune to his Mexican research; to provide proof of his theories, he financed the production of nine volumes of the Mexican codices, then virtually unknown. Modern scholars still use this edition, which was republished by the Mexican government in 1964, with a foreword by the Minister of Education.

Kingsborough's endeavours landed him heavily in debt. He was sued for £508 10s 6d by a paper manufacturer and in 1835 was consigned to the common debtors' prison. But the indefatigable peer would not learn his lesson: he died during a third spell in jail for his debts, at the age of forty-two.*

Another prominent nineteenth-century figure is the Abbé Brasseur de Bourbourg, who spent some time in Boston and later became a parish priest in Guatemala. In the earlier part of his career, the learned Abbé was a foremost pioneer in the study of Ancient America, producing the first translations and commentaries of Maya documents, and publishing a Maya grammar and dictionary. For decades, Brasseur continued to shed light on these hitherto unknown topics; then suddenly the scholar suffered a brainstorm. This was partly triggered by his astonishing discovery that the Indians used words of seemingly Germanic origin, such as the Quiche word for 'book', *Vuh*, that he judged equivalent to the German form, *Buch*. He became persuaded that his beloved Mayan texts were allegories, without historical foundation, and that, together with the scrolls of Egypt, they merely reflected the history of Atlantis, true mother of all civilizations: Horus was the same as the Mexican Plumed Serpent god, who had annihilated Atlantis and caused her to sink beneath the waves.

According to Brasseur, the Phoenician Votan had built the Maya city of Palenque and founded the Empire of Xibalba that covered all Mexico and part of the United States. The Nahua tribes, who were the ancestors of the Aztecs, had passed from Asia to Europe and then migrated to America; the word *Nahual* came from the English 'know-all', and implied a British sojourn. At this time Brasseur was strongly influenced by another extraordinary figure, Jean Frédéric de Waldeck, a Napoleonic soldier, who received his baptism of fire at the siege of Toulon in 1794, when Napoleon first attracted wide attention. However, Waldeck's career as a Mayan scholar did not begin until twenty-eight years later, in 1822; ultimately he came to believe that the New World civilizations were more ancient than those of the Near East, with which they were linked by Atlantis – already looming large on the horizon as a staging post between the two hemispheres. It is said that Waldeck died in Paris just after his 109th birthday, as the result of an accident suffered when he turned his head to look at a pretty girl.

Of the nineteenth-century Americanists whom I have mentioned, Kingsborough is remembered not for his theories on the Tribes of Israel, but for those fine editions of the Mexican codices. Brasseur was among the leading scholars of his day; neither he nor Kingsborough was an amateur, and every student of American anthropology has heard, or should have heard, of both, though he may be less familiar with Le Plongeon's fantasies. The three have much in common: for each the struggle for a cause lay closer to the heart than the mere advancement of science; all three led difficult if not tragic lives and died disconsolate, having enjoyed scant praise and endured harsh ridicule.

Most earlier writers on American origins erred on the side of boldness, claiming that Indian culture derived from such a medley of peoples as Israelites, Egyptians, Assyrians, Koreans, Trojans, Etruscans, Scythians, Greeks, Tartars, Chinese, Irish, Welsh, and Norsemen, to name only a few. Passing references were made to Cretans, less known at the time but perhaps a more obvious choice, in view of their maritime skills. The Hittites have also been rather neglected in this respect, since they only came into public view after bold claims had already been made on behalf of the other candidates.

But speculation on Indian origins was not the exclusive preserve of eccentrics. The nineteenth century also produced serious studies of Ancient America. Between 1839 and 1841 John Lloyd Stephens, the American traveller, diplomat, and amateur archaeologist, visited the Maya area and later wrote his *Incidents of Travel*. Published in two volumes, the work was magnificently illustrated by the English artist, Frederick Catherwood, who had accompanied Stephens. The books were very popular and were chiefly responsible for making the great cities of the Maya civilization known to the outside world. Thereafter, the main archaeological sites were mapped and illustrated, and by the turn of the century the father of Andean archaeology, Max Uhle, was already at work in Peru.

Nowadays there is a rich annual harvest of books advancing audacious

6

theories on American origins for a wide reading public, while the work of those who are cautious about Old World contacts reaches a limited audience since it usually appears in professional publications. The controversy cannot, however, be treated simply as a battle between daring amateurs and stuffy scholars, who scornfully deny that America was exposed to outside influences and claim the conception of New World culture was immaculate.

Professional opinion is far from united, and bitter controversy has been the order of the day within academic circles as well as outside. The first International Congress of Americanists was held at Nancy in 1875; the location reflected the early pre-eminence of French and German scholars in the field. The august gathering, far from attaining a consensus, became the scene of verbal battles over the proposal that the Chinese had reached America in the early centuries of our era. By a masterpiece of understatement, the official report described the discussion as 'a courteous but fierce struggle' ('une guerre courtoise mais acharnée').

The arguments have, in fact, developed into a hundred years' war, with no end in sight. At the 35th International Congress of Americanists, held in Mexico City in 1962, the experts were once more locked in combat over precisely the same problem, and again tempers became frayed. Since then, discussion has continued unabated. However, attitudes have changed since 1875. Nowadays many anthropologists prefer to keep an open mind about pre-Columbian contacts between the two hemispheres. Some scholars search actively for new evidence, among them most of the participants in a symposium held in Santa Fé, New Mexico, in 1968; the proceedings, published in book form, were entitled *Man across the Sea: problems of pre-Columbian contacts*. Significantly, specialists who seek Old World contacts with America tend to turn towards Asia, while links with the Near East attract the amateur.

But although professionals unite in rejecting those wilder theories whose theme is more emotional than scientific, they seldom bother to examine in any detail the propositions with which they are supposedly locked in combat. Moreover, many experts simply steer clear of the treacherous shoals of transoceanic contacts and treat them as irrelevant to their subject. Even the German Edward Seler, perhaps the greatest of all investigators of the American past, makes scant mention of the issue in his voluminous writings. Yet Seler's works, published in the early part of the century but re-edited comparatively recently, are basic reading for modern students and his research on ancient American religion has never been surpassed.

A small but strident body of writers may still see America as peopled uniquely by a mass influx of Israeli tribes or Greek navigators but science can now demonstrate that Man's original route into America lay across a vast land bridge that once united Siberia and Alaska. The question of whether this migration took place 20,000 or 50,000 years ago is at this stage immaterial.

Two serious possibilities, therefore, confront the investigator: having entered America via north-east Asia, either primitive man was left to his own devices on the new continent, forging a separate culture with little or no outside influence; or, since human civilization was too rare a plant to be engendered more than once, the ascent of American Man was inspired by one single 'cradle of civilization', obviously situated in the Old World. According to this latter theory, even if primitive man reached America during the Ice Age, his progress was minimal until enlightenment came from some Old World centre, such as Egypt or Mesopotamia.

The notion of a single genesis of higher cultures still held the field in the latter part of the nineteenth century, at a time when comparisons between America and Egypt were greatly in vogue. The belief that civilization could be invented only once owed much to the then current teachings of the German anthropologist Friedrich Ratzel, reinforced by the German and Austrian *Kulturkreis* groups; different cultures were seen to develop as 'bundles' or 'complexes' of traits that spread out from one heartland, like ripples from a stone dropped in a pond. However, in the first decades of the twentieth century, the wheel took a full turn, as the views of Franz Boas came to dominate American anthropology. A more go-it-alone attitude was then in fashion, and American culture was regarded as an independent achievement.

Regardless of whether Boas or Ratzel is right, similarities between customs and art forms of the two hemispheres are undeniable. Parallels range from pyramid-building and other general features to finer details, such as the suggested presence in Mayan reliefs of elephants and lotus flowers, then unknown in America. On a more utilitarian level, the use in South America and East Asia of very similar star-shaped mace heads is often cited, or the hafting by identical methods of stone axes in places as remote one from the other as Portugal and the north-west coast of North America.

To put the question in its simplest form: were such likenesses the outcome of unrelated development in the two worlds; or were they the direct result of Old World contacts with America, long after the main population of the latter had already passed through Alaska?

No appraisal of Old World contacts with the New is meaningful without firm notions as to what kind of evidence is valid and what irrelevant. The tendency exists — by no means confined to the layman — to list a few traits shared by peoples of America and Eurasia and then leap to the conclusion that contact between the two regions is thereby proved beyond doubt. But the belief that similarity denotes contact is false. Countless examples may be quoted of likenesses that must have arisen by sheer coincidence; only by adopting stricter criteria can a relevant case for pre-Columbian incursions into the New World be established. Discussion is futile unless known similarities can be measured by certain yardsticks.

To fix such guidelines, the evidence has to be divided into separate categories, whose usefulness can then be assessed. First and foremost, some physical link between two regions, say, Cambodia and Peru, would be established beyond dispute if objects made in one place were discovered in the other. For example, the presence of Cretan pottery throughout the Mediterranean and even in northern Europe demonstrates contact. The discovery in many places of Roman coins may be cited as indicating either dominion or trade. A single object, such as the proverbial twentieth-century umbrella that is likely to turn up in excavations, proves little, but if a whole series of eleventh-century Khmer objects, made in Cambodia, were found in a Chimu-period tomb in Peru, then no scientist would deny that contact, direct or indirect, had taken place. Someone had to transport such treasures across the Pacific.

In particular, the architecture of two cities may bear such an identical stamp as to rule out coincidence. The hypothetical discovery of a Gothic cathedral in the Central Australian desert may serve as an example; such a find, implying a direct tie, would have wider implications than, say, the numerous Buddhist figures located in Scandinavia, which were not brought there by Buddhist monks but were acquired by Norse visitors to Arab lands.

Only on rare occasions have objects of Old World provenance been reported in a pre-Columbian context, and these may have been imported by the Spaniards. A handful of Roman coins from Costa Rica do not prove that the Romans crossed the Atlantic; the pieces of Roman glass on my own desk may be unearthed by a future archaeologist alongside my few pre-Columbian pieces although the glass was acquired in Crete and brought to Mexico in 1962. Even if Roman coins were found in an impeccably pre-Columbian context, one instance would not provide absolute proof. I recall that in Zacatenco, near Mexico City, an almost fresh watermelon rind was unearthed accompanied by sherds some three thousand years old, having mysteriously penetrated to that level through some cleft. Highly trained archaeologists are sometimes at pains to determine whether objects from one layer have not become confused with those of another. Only if the coins had been discovered in an unviolated stone tomb, of a kind that exists in north-west Mexico, would the picture be dramatically altered.

In the absence of concrete archaeological evidence, other yardsticks exist, of which the most valid are languages or plants common to two areas. The study of Old and New World fauna is most relevant to their history, but is far from being an ideal weapon in the armoury of those who have a case to prove, since present evidence is too ambiguous.

It is unknown in science for the same plant to originate twice in two unconnected regions. If, for instance, the sweet potato − of patently American origin − was demonstrably present in Polynesia before the Europeans arrived, then previous visitors must have brought it there; the sweet potato is reproduced not from seeds but from tubers that could scarcely be carried by birds. But while the early Polynesians are *assumed* to have cultivated this plant, its presence in Ancient Oceania still requires to be proved by modern techniques, such as the study of fossilized human excreta.

Languages, like plants, can offer absolute proof of contact; but equally, false conclusions may be drawn through oversimplification. The science of linguistics has made vast strides since the time when the great Oxford scholar, the German Max Müller, once famous and now almost forgotten, unravelled the complexities of Sanskrit, establishing the common origin of the whole Indo-European family of languages, including such improbable cousins as English, Hindi, and Russian.

Languages can be compared with plants: usually a number of variants spring from a common trunk and come to form a family of related tongues. Equally, just as occurs with plant or animal species, a single language cannot be born twice; a linguistic group must have one place of origin and one only, regardless of its subsequent spread. Thus, if two languages, current in two widely separated regions, can be shown to belong to the same family, then a close connection existed between the ancestors of their respective speakers. Polynesian, for instance, belongs to the same group as Malay and Indonesian, a fact of far-reaching implications.

With certain exceptions, such as Basque, all the world's languages can be divided into such families or groups, not by the study of superficial likenesses, but by profound analysis of basic structure. In surveying a building, not the top floor but the foundations need first to be examined. Related tongues may best be identified by delving for common roots since all languages of a given group follow similar laws of phonetic change; for instance, if p changes to f in the course of centuries in one language of a group, the same process occurs in all its cousins. While the study of current vocabularies of, say, Polish and English would yield scant results, common origins can be demonstrated beyond doubt by examining roots and structure.

With the exception of a few mavericks, the two thousand five hundred languages of America have been divided into groups in this manner, although much detailed work remains to be done to complete the process. Unfortunately, however, authors seeking signs of transoceanic contacts pay scant attention to such findings and confine themselves to viewing the mere tip of the linguistic iceberg. A single American language, not its parent group, is seized upon as an example, and its relationship to some Asiatic or European tongue 'proved', not on the basis of common structure, but of similarities between a few words in everyday use.

The word-list game, as I prefer to call this practice, is riddled with pitfalls despite its popularity, and its value is slight since it relies on superficial likenesses. A virtual identity may be immediately apparent between the word for 'god' in Ancient Greek (*theos*) and its equivalent in classical Mexican Nahuatl (*teotl*); *mati* means 'eye' in both Greece and

Malaysia (*mati* in Nahuatl also means 'to know' and, therefore, in a sense, 'to perceive' or 'to see'). But words offer infinite scope for chance coincidence, and Robert Wauchope has admirably stressed this point by making up his own list of near-duplicates between English and Maya.

No book that seeks a single Old World source for American culture, whether in the Near or Far East, is complete without its list of common words, designed to clinch the matter. The game appeals to the beginner and the initiate alike: it was played by the eminent anthropologist Paul Rivet, in order to prove the common origin of South American Indians and Australian aborigines. In the 1920s Professor Leo Wiener of Harvard collected no less than three thousand Mayan and Nahuatl words and sought to show that both were derived from the Mandingo language of Africa. But, apart from loan-words, no competent linguist nowadays admits serious links between Mayan and Nahuatl, which belong to two distinct Mexican language groups, let alone between these tongues and Mandingo.

Plants and languages accordingly are part and parcel of the study of transoceanic contacts, and their study may offer concrete evidence if analysed correctly. In addition, peoples on different continents may share somatic traits such as pigmentation, shape of skull, blood group, colour and type of hair. Such factors sometimes help to denote common descent, though the use of outward signs in tracing tribal origins has lost force as science has discovered ever more unseen variants in the human body. Moreover, American Man is such a hybrid creature that his origins cannot easily be traced to a single Old World race.

In their search for the fountainheads of American culture, writers also draw heavily upon surviving myths and sagas – especially upon the appealing legend of the pre-Columbian presence of white, bearded supermen, in both North and South America. I shall devote a chapter to the doubtful derivation of such tales, of which some may be genuinely native, while others are Spanish inventions, designed to enhance the image of the Conquistadores themselves. But whether false or authentic, the story of the white god underpins many stock theories as to American origins.

Irrefutable proof of pre-Columbian contacts is therefore elusive: Old World artefacts are conspicuous by their absence; Old World plants and languages offer little that is hard and fast; somatic evidence conflicts and myths confuse. Some of these pointers, such as legend and language, may be often cited as an indication of oceanic interchange, but the more cogent theories tend to rely upon two other factors: the sharing of tribal customs and the use of similar art forms. The evidence arising from art and custom is often related: for instance, the presence of near-identical panpipes in Bolivia and the Solomon Islands involves both tribal practice and artistic design.

The validity of such parallels is never easy to assess, and each case has to be judged on its merits in the light of certain general principles. To take an example of the problem, cyclindrical tripod jars with conical tops were made by both Chinese and Mexicans around A.D. 200; but no one can say for sure whether the Mexican jars developed independently or were copied from a Chinese model. Many theories rest heavily upon such comparisons of style, but a few casual similarities prove nothing; the evidence must be judged by stricter standards. Where only one like form or custom appears in two places, independent invention is the obvious explanation. For example, the practice of tonsure not only prevails among European monks, but also in certain Amazonian tribes. Equally, the Roman dome (built of coursed stone) is unlikely to have inspired that of the Eskimo igloo (made out of spirally laid snow blocks).

As firmer evidence of contact, not single traits, but a whole complex of similarities is needed. The odds on likenesses arising from pure chance then diminish dramatically. Suppose that the probability of trait 'X' being twice independently developed were one in two (fifty-fifty), and that the same odds applied to trait 'Y'. Now if both trait 'X' *and* trait 'Y' are shared between two places, the chances that they were separately invented is reduced to one in four. The presence of a third common element reduces the odds to one in eight, and so forth.

A complex of traits shared between two peoples is, therefore, more meaningful. However, where customs are concerned, rather than art forms, long lists can be compiled in which rather banal items outnumber more peculiar similarities of a kind that are unlikely to be invented twice. For instance, one list of elements shared between South-East Asia and Peru includes eight such everyday traits: the use of cotton and copper, litters, irrigation, terraced land, organized clans, plant domestication and mound construction.*

Sometimes mere necessity leads to the dual invention of a given type of artefact. The hammock, for instance, is an obvious solution to a special problem and is found in both worlds. The ordinary knife offers an even more striking example: its function is constant in any culture and, therefore, its form does not automatically evolve from simple to more complex designs. The Eskimo knife has hardly varied since the days of the first proto-Eskimos, four thousand years ago, and is basically little different from our standard table knife. Eskimos, until very recently, would not use scissors: if offered a pair, they would separate the two blades for use as ordinary knives, to which they were accustomed.

Between two peoples supposedly in contact, traits that are *not* shared have also to be taken into account. If the Chinese indeed brought pottery designs to America, their failure to introduce the potter's wheel becomes an awkward and inescapable snag. Equally, if the Chinese were responsible for introducing plant cultivation, it is far from clear why they did not also bring the plough, whose absence severely limited New World agriculture. Nor can anyone explain why the Chinese did not import into America the domestic pig, which later spread from Asia and became an untold blessing to innumerable Pacific Islanders.

Adoption of inventions and styles is admittedly selective; countries will take to Coca-Cola without embracing American democracy. Sometimes, moreover, a reason exists for rejecting a specific item: the usefulness of the wheel was limited in America because of the absence of draught animals. The potter's wheel, however, would have come in very handy, and the spindle-whorl (involving the same principle) was known and put to some good use. Other items may be present in two continents, but serve a different purpose. For a European, the use of a laxative for ritual cleansing would be a novelty; for an Indian, the idea of its employment for routine secular health would seem peculiar.

Specimens of an unusual type of African stirrup-spout bottle are displayed in New York in the Brooklyn Museum, and in Berkeley in the Museum of Anthropology of the University of California. These Magbetu bottles, made barely a generation ago in A.D. 1930, are virtually indistinguishable from others from the north coast of Peru dating from 800 B.C. Rafael Larco Hoyle, leading authority on Peruvian pottery, once even questioned whether the African vessels had been correctly catalogued. These confusing bottles illustrate the dangers of judging the issue on the basis of one similar item and underline the key role of dating in making true comparisons. Near-identical art forms mean little if one derives from the time of Homer and the other from the age of the aeroplane. Nowadays, the interval needed for any novelty to spread across the globe has been reduced almost to zero although in former times inventions travelled slowly, and in the Stone Age innovations such as the bow and arrow took millennia to pass from one continent to another.

Certain pieces of evidence pass the test of chronology with flying colours, while others fail. For instance, the Han Dynasty tripod jars mentioned above are between 100 and 200 years earlier than those of central Mexico, an ideal interval to allow for their introduction by sea, which takes less time than by overland route. But the suggested parallels between Chou Dynasty scroll patterns and those of Tajin in Mexico fall foul of dating problems: Chou ended in the third century B.C., but the comparable Mexican forms appear some six centuries later and attempts to explain away such differences are unconvincing.

Quite apart from the dating problem, suggestions of contact mean more when the peoples in question have reached a similar stage of development. For instance, possible links between Ecuador and Japan in about 3000 B.C. fulfil this condition; those proposed between Mexico and Egypt do not. If the builders of the Great Pyramids had really set foot in Mexico, they would have encountered people still living in caves, who had a long road to tread before they built their own pyramids.

Furthermore, similarities in style and custom become more credible if it can be shown just how they passed from one place to another. Many authors happily overlook this problem; they argue persuasively that two peoples were in contact, but leave the question of transportation to look after itself, on the grounds that too little is known about ancient boat-building and that the matter therefore lies beyond our ken. I reject this line of thought: enough data are now at hand to permit judgment as to whether certain voyages were feasible. Obviously, for instance, a Chinese junk stood a far better chance of surviving the perils of the boundless ocean than an early Japanese dugout canoe, even if the junk in its turn was far less apt for the task than the Portuguese caravel.

If we merely scratch the surface, startling likenesses between the civilizations of the two hemispheres emerge, even if proof of contact eludes our grasp. Concrete evidence may never come to light unless the entire Pacific Ocean were drained in an exhaustive search for the remains of the first Chinese junk to reach American shores. Accordingly, where proof is not absolute, judgment cannot be entirely objective, and the data are open to many interpretations. Instances do arise where evidence of contact is very strong, more particularly between North and South America than across wider ocean barriers. The affinity between certain styles of the Andean region and Mexico is so striking that some kind of connection is hard to deny.

Moreover, new techniques may offer a helping hand in deciding what evidence is valid. By making a comparative series of detailed illustrations known as a scalogram, the imperceptible changes in a given style can be pinpointed in precise terms and the steps by which object A was slowly transformed into object B can be scientifically charted. Using this method, French scholars have been able to illustrate in twenty-eight drawings the step-by-step modification of Chinese bronzes from the Shang to the Chou pattern.* Conversely, a scalogram should be capable of showing that a resemblance between our stirrup-spout jars from ancient Peru and modern Africa is superficial and owes nothing to common origins. In the United States Jon Muller and W. C. Watt have developed 'generative grammars' for art styles with the aid of computers.*

Nevertheless, the genealogy of art forms remains harder to unravel than that of animals and plants. Techniques are still in their infancy, but may serve in the long run to determine if one culture has derived from another. Even so, studies like this cannot solve many borderline cases that will remain subject to the caprice of personal opinion – or of mere guesswork.

Moreover, nothing is ever proved to everyone's satisfaction, however clearcut the data may be. The shape of the world was officially settled long ago, once and for all; but surprisingly, the notion that the earth is flat can still boast of an organized body of twentieth -century supporters. The Catholic Apostolic Church of Zion was founded in 1895 by a Scotsman, John Dowis; its original concern was with 'clean' or 'pure' foods: oysters were banned as well as alcohol. But in 1905 the Church was taken over by Wilbur Glen Voliva, who was more interested in cosmic matters. For thirty years the doctrine was then propounded that the North Pole was the centre of the world and that the South Pole represents the circular circumference, surrounded by a wall of snow and ice to keep ships from sailing off the edge. According to Voliva, the moon shines with its own light, and the sun is only thirty-two miles in diameter.*

By the same token, in the field of transoceanic contacts, theories are hard to prove, and harder still to disprove. For instance, a statement that people from Heligoland once visited Peru can never be categorically disproved. Children sometimes used to be told that the moon was made of cheese; thus far, we possess rock samples taken from only an infinitesimal part of the total surface, yet to maintain that the rest of our satellite is nothing but a huge Gruyère and that the astronauts have deliberately distorted the facts could hardly be more far-fetched than some of the theories advanced on American origins. If the derivation of Culture B from Culture A seems wildly improbable, then similarities between the two must be put down to coincidence. And in studying transoceanic contacts, the extraordinary lengths to which sheer coincidence can run must always be borne in mind; often not one, but a whole chain of close parallels may be involved between two unrelated sets of circumstances. The case of Presidents Kennedy and Lincoln provides a good example: President Lincoln was elected in 1860, Kennedy in 1960; their successors were both named Johnson. Andrew Johnson was born in 1808, Lyndon Johnson in 1908. John Wilkes Booth, Lincoln's killer, was born in 1839, and Lee Harvey Oswald in 1939; both were assassinated before their trials. Lincoln's secretary, whose name was Kennedy, advised him not to go to the theatre; Kennedy's secretary, who was called Lincoln, pressed him not to go to Dallas. John Wilkes Booth shot Lincoln in a theatre and ran into a warehouse; Oswald shot Kennedy from a warehouse and ran into a theatre.

The war of words still rages between those who attribute all human culture to a single source and others who favour parallel development in more than one continent. The problems of Old World contacts, therefore, become a contest between the disciples of evolution and of diffusion. Evolution in this context implies that the peoples of the world are fated to follow the self-same path, though they find themselves at different stages on the same route. But, like individuals, peoples are dissimilar and cannot be treated as automatically bound for identical goals. The countries of the Third World are often resentful when lectured by the developed nations and urged to copy their path to progress. New states may prefer to show their preceptors and paymasters that they are different and intend to remain so. Accordingly, the discovery of a novel technique, whether an art form or a mode of living, cannot always be classified as 'inevitable', like the passing of a given milestone on the same road entitled 'evolution', inescapable to all. The argument between evolution and diffusion is itself another oversimplification. And if peoples do not all follow an identical path, though their courses often lie parallel, the urge to borrow from one another can never be taken for granted. A do-it-yourself attitude, relying only partially, if at all, on borrowed techniques, becomes possible and many halfway houses can be found between pure evolutionism and diffusionism. Equally, *proved* or *unproved* cannot always serve as the ultimate touchstone. Subjective judgment is involved as much as pure science, and a layman willing to study the details and assimilate the known facts may be just as well-qualified to pass judgment as the specialist.

Between America and Eurasia, so many unexplained likenesses exist that no hard-and-fast dividing line can be set between what (if anything) was copied and what was independently invented. Similarities may have arisen not through physical contact but as the product of some kind of common heritage from Man's remote past. Many facets of human civilization can be traced back to the hunters of the Ice Age, and – as will later be made clearer – American and Asian Man possessed a common, if distant ancestry. It seems likely, therefore, that East Asians and Americans shared a certain cultural or artistic potential, which caused them to react in like manner under a given set of circumstances. Though living on different continents for many millennia, the two peoples at times tended to adopt similar customs and to invent similar things.

At times the reasoning of both those who see American culture as imported and those who do not fails to satisfy. Proof of contact may be lacking, but the sceptics also leave many facts unexplained; they may be right to insist that a king must naturally wear a crown upon his head, should necessarily sit upon a throne, be protected from the sun by a parasol, and be kept cool by fans placed on poles, and so deduce that such customs developed independently in the New World and the Old.

But suppose Man one day discovers other sentient beings on the planet of a distant star. Can it be taken for granted that those astronauts will also find kings seated upon their thrones, complete with crowns, courtiers, parasols and fans? Would the human visitors expect to repeat Cortés' experience and encounter scenes as reminiscent of their own world as the court of Moctezuma, complete with his attendant dwarfs, elaborate cuisine, and exotic menagerie? If the people of the new planet had by then reached a later stage in their development, would the space travellers be privileged to attend a special session of Congress or Parliament convened in their honour? Had they landed in a more turbulent corner of their new-found world, might they arrive in the wake of a military *coup d'état*? Or are such institutions and events peculiar to Earth and unrepeatable in other spheres?

An inhabited region of outer space might well be ruled by beings so different from ourselves that they were incapable of wearing crowns or mounting thrones. All civilizations of our planet are in some ways alike, and, in spite of arguments to the contrary, some particularly *human* heritage may be shared and account for so many similarities between the worlds of Cortés and Moctezuma, who knew much less of each other than we now know of outer space.

But first, before considering the nature of any ties between the two hemispheres in recent millennia, the latest evidence on prehistoric migration from Asia into the New World must be reviewed. For all except a lunatic fringe, the crucial question is no longer where the first migrants to the New World came from, but whether they were later joined by other voyagers before Columbus arrived.

CHAPTER TWO

THE NORTHERN TRAIL

WHEN I took a plane from Hong Kong to Mexico City, the flying time totalled seventeen hours. Between stopovers in Tokyo and Vancouver, the aircraft skirted the shores of Alaska, and the view of the majestic peaks of Alaska's southern coastline reminded me that approximately the same route had led Ancient Man into the Americas. By modern standards, a seventeen-hour flight is considered wearisome, but the early hunters' trek over the frozen tundra took millennia to complete. By comparison with this epic of endurance, visitors who supposedly came to America later in spaceships or Chinese junks enjoyed an easy passage.

Early Man did not come in quest of gold, like the Spaniards; nor like later migrants did he seek religious freedom. Slowly but unsurely, he simply edged forward into an unknown world; the animals that he hunted had made the journey long before, and Man merely followed in pursuit of his accustomed prey.

Originally nurtured in the tropics and lacking protective fur, Man was among the last of the beasts to proceed from north-west Asia into America, whose temperate latitudes are divided from those of Eurasia by three thousand miles of territory still today sparsely populated and hard to cross. Before the animals could migrate there, the New World had first to be created; for America and the other continents have existed in their present form for a tiny fraction of the lifespan of our planet, totalling about four thousand five hundred million years. The great single continent of Pangaea split into its northern and southern portions, Laurasia and Gondwana, a mere fifteen million years ago.

In 1915 the German meteorologist, Alfred Wegener, was ridiculed by fellow scientists for his contention that the existing continents had gradually moved apart, and that South America once lay alongside Africa as two complementary parts of a single landmass. But new facts about Earth's development have now come to light that scarcely a decade ago would have been treated as sheer fantasy, and which vindicate Wegener. Computer calculations have shown beyond doubt that South America did indeed fit into Africa; different continents of the planet are not moored to the ocean bed, but glide majestically if imperceptibly across the seven seas, and their annual drift can now be measured with the aid of new techniques, including laser beams aimed at reflectors landed on the Moon's surface.*

For millions of years after the continents first separated, the northern, or Laurasian, portion consisted of one landmass. And even after the Atlantic Ocean opened up a chasm between them, Eurasia and America still formed a single continent, since an ample territory joined Siberia to Alaska at the opposite end of the globe. This land bridge has been periodically opened and closed during the last ten million years of the world's history. Long before the ocean first submerged the connecting link and gave separate existence to America, the era of the mammals had dawned, the successors of those giant reptiles whose exotic shapes adorn our textbooks. Because the continents were then less well-defined, the primaeval mammals were free to roam throughout lands that only later became divided into two worlds, the Old and the New. Typical of such mammals is the monkey; bred from common ancestors, the Old and New World forms diverged markedly, as a result of eons of separate evolution (the American varieties, among other differences, all possess 36 teeth, while Old World monkeys – and Man – have 32). The elephant developed in both Africa and Asia, and from there his first cousin, the mastodon, wandered into America over the Siberia–Alaska land bridge millions of years ago.

Like the elephant, most of the more familiar animals are not native to the American continent. Two exceptions to this rule deserve mention, the horse and the camel. The horse, among the best documented of all the animals, can boast of a long history. The earliest fossil specimens (known as Eohippus), unmistakable from certain peculiarities of mouth and foot, have been found in both Europe and North America; Eohippus was a tiny creature, about eleven inches high, and equivalent in size to a fox terrier. Fossil remains, mainly located in North America, establish the stages by which this proto-horse evolved into the animal we know today. The modern horse then emigrated into Asia, where he was much later domesticated, and from there spread throughout the Old World, but in his native American habitat became extinct!

22

The ancestors of the camel family surprisingly originated not in the desert sands of Arabia, but on the grassy plains of North America, from which, like the horse, they later vanished. But, unlike the horse, which started life as a pigmy, the early cameloids that reached Siberia from America were giants; in the New World the species survived only in South America and in much reduced form as the llama, vicuña and alpaca, which were to become the principal domestic animals of the Incas, and continue to roam in herds in the High Andes, providing essential means of transport, food and clothing to the modern inhabitants.

While Man is, therefore, a product of the Old World, by an odd paradox the horse and camel, his main means of locomotion before the automobile, derived from the New and crossed the Bering bridge into Asia millions of years before the first humans migrated in the opposite direction.

Undeniably Man first entered America via Alaska, regardless of whether other pre-Columbian migrants came later from Europe, China or elsewhere. Early Man's approach to the New World therefore revolves around the history of the land bridge from Siberia to Alaska, now known to have existed for specific periods of time.

In the sixteenth century, seeking an escape from the heresy of a separate genesis for the American Indian, Fray Joseph de Acosta proposed that a land corridor joined Asia to America. And not until one hundred and thirty years later, on a foggy August day in 1728, did Vitus Bering, in the service of the Russian Emperor, sail northwards through the Strait that bears his name to show that the Old and New Worlds were now entirely separate. Had the mists barring his view cleared, Bering would have seen a different continent on either side of his ship. Both coasts are often visible from the Diomede Islands in the middle of the Strait, of which the larger belongs to the USSR, while the smaller is US territory; from the mountainside behind Wales Village in Alaska, the East Cape on the Soviet shore can be viewed on clear days. Animals hunted by local Eskimos, such as lemmings, white fox and caribou, visit the Diomede Islands during the winter, and about once every ten years the ice between the continents can bear dog sleds; the Eskimos often also cross to the islands in their kayaks. The Strait in its present form presents only a minor physical obstacle to the passage of men and animals.

However, political barriers have been raised, and an old Eskimo in Kotzebue asserted that, although a few of his friends possessed relatives on the Soviet side, all contact had now been lost.

No land bridge such as Fray Acosta envisaged had in fact existed for ten thousand years, when the fourth glacial period, or glaciation – the last of the series which constituted the Great Ice Age – ended, approximately. This fourth glaciation, known in America as Wisconsin and in Siberia as Sarstanske, had begun in about 70,000 B.C. Except when the ice receded during warmer intervals, the glaciation covered large parts of Europe and North America with huge ice-caps, sometimes as much as fifteen thousand feet thick.

Four times in the past million years the ice had advanced and retreated, and in the interval between each glaciation important climatic changes had taken place, affecting man and beast. Vast quantities of water had been periodically stored on the land in the form of ice-caps and glaciers, and these accumulations affected the ocean level. At times the sea fell as much as four hundred and sixty feet, while at others it rose three hundred feet above today's level. These changes left their mark on the coasts of Alaska and Siberia in the form of fossil-bearing sediment, though only in very recent years have scientists learned to interpret these marine profiles. As a result, fluctuations in sea level can now be charted to give a much clearer picture of when the Bering bridge was open or closed.

It is the last three periods during which crossings could be made that are relevant to Man's arrival. The first of these occurred between seventy thousand and forty thousand years ago: the second, some thirty-five thousand years ago; the bridge was then finally re-established from about twenty-five thousand until ten thousand years ago and is unlikely to emerge again unless there is a fifth Ice Age.*

The term 'land bridge' conveys the impression of a narrow causeway over which at best one man or a single mammoth could pass without wetting his feet in the sea. But even before the recent scrutiny of sea-levels clarified the issue, it was known to have been a broader passage. The Western Hemisphere became the New World not only for Man but for countless animals and plants, and this diffusion of fauna and flora required an ample avenue of approach open for long periods.* Indeed the stretch of land which the sea laid bare was more like a continent than a corridor. The ocean floor to the south of the Bering Strait is one of the flattest and smoothest in the World; when the water level fell, a landmass measuring over one thousand miles at its widest point from north to south was exposed. It was in fact a sub-continent stretching from the present-day Aleutian Islands in the south right up to the northern margin of the Arctic Ocean. Now once more engulfed by a shallow sea, this territory could have housed many permanent residents and provided plant food for a host of those animals which Man hunted.

This land, best referred to as Beringia, consisted mainly of a featureless but slightly undulating plain, studded with bogs and swamps, and covered by tundra vegetation of sedges, grasses and low shrubs. The term *tundra* lacks an exact definition, but may be described as country with short-stemmed arctic vegetation, sometimes including shrubs, but never trees.

An obvious objection now arises: the continental ice-caps which caused the sea-level to sink, exposing Beringia, must surely have spread to those bleak latitudes and blocked the approaches to the great land bridge. But, strange as it may seem, neither western Alaska nor north-eastern Siberia — except for their mountain ranges — were ice-covered, mainly because of their low rainfall. The climate was then even drier than today, when parts of Alaska still form an arctic desert, and in other respects conditions were not dissimilar to the present, though the temperature might have been a few degrees lower.

The ice-caps created another problem, however: Man was able to reach Alaska from Siberia during certain glacial periods, but then found himself bottled up there, his exit totally barred by a forbidding ice-shield, literally miles high, which loomed ahead and covered much of Canada, stretching far down into the United States. This barrier probably existed from about 21,000 to 11,000 B.C. Before and after this date, ice-free roads lay open from Alaska to the south, either along the west coast or through the Valley of the MacKenzie River. Even so, during most of the Ice Age, Man was able to enter Alaska more easily than he could leave it to pursue his southward journey. Accordingly Alaska, once a Russian possession until its purchase by the United States in 1867, was in pre-historic times also more a projection of Asia than a gateway to the American continent, from which it was effectively sealed by ice-caps and glaciers.

Though eastern Siberia remained relatively ice-free, in contrast to

European Russia, the climatic conditions were extremely severe. The appalling rigours to which early Man was exposed are well illustrated by the fact that today (when the climate is warmer) no Siberian station north of 59 degrees of latitude reports a mean monthly temperature of more than 6 degrees Fahrenheit between the months of December and March. In the inland part of the Chukchi Peninsula, facing Alaska, the temperature can drop even in April to −22 degrees F. and the average temperature in May is 17 degrees F. Vegetation is consequently very sparse; scattered and scrubby bushes grow only on the banks of the larger streams, grasses only on the southern shore of Lake El'gytkhin. But neither the scant plant life nor the fierce climate deter reindeer, mountain sheep, polar foxes and brown bears from inhabiting the region, where Soviet archaeologist Nekrasov found them roaming in herds.*

Beringia abounded in Arctic game, and its extension was so great that Man did not enter the New World at any precise point on his journey. His progress, and that of the animals that preceded him, represented a kind of overspill across a contiguous territory. The first human visitors simply followed their prey, little aware that their descendants, countless generations later, would eventually reach the tropics, where their own species had originated.

As a visitor to the Bering Strait today, one may in the month of July bask in a Mediterranean sun that continues to shine throughout the night. This balmy interlude is brief, however, and the sea is frozen for nine months of the year. In these summer months, migratory birds lay eggs upon the shore and thousands of seals come to breed; in the countryside berries and roots that are still eaten by the Eskimos abound. But for eight months of the year, Ancient Man would have depended on game, such as the caribou and reindeer.

What tempted Man to enter this region of tundra and permafrost in preference to more hospitable latitudes? His journey was certainly not a brief one; by the shortest route the trek from the temperate zones of Asia to those of America measured three thousand miles. Man was now entering a region which has since been inhabited only by the Eskimo, specially adapted to the climate and protected by the most elaborate clothing, including a snug suit of caribou hide with fur turned inwards and a looser outer garment with fur turned outwards.

The first step to America was the occupation of the north-eastern limits of Asia. It was hardly deliberate; Man just stumbled onwards towards ever greater extremes of winter cold. The reindeer and other wild animals of eastern Siberia tend to move north in the warmer summer, fleeing from the clouds of mosquitoes further to the south. Human migrants perhaps moved in the same direction, partly to follow their prey, and partly to avoid the mosquitoes on their own account. Furthermore, the continuous variations of climate during the Ice Age were an added incentive to northward migration; animals, as well as human beings, became adapted to a given range of temperature during a glacial period and then had to go farther north to retain those same conditions during a warmer interlude.

Such factors partly explain what occurred; but did some deeper urge underlie Man's conquest of the kingdom of the caribou? The final period of the Old Stone Age, known as the Upper Palaeolithic, began some forty to fifty thousand years ago and was fundamental to Man's progress from ape to astronaut. This was first and foremost an age of great technical change, marked by the advent of new skills in the making of stone instruments. In place of crude rounded tools, little more than glorified pebbles, sharp blades and projectile points were now developed that could be fitted to darts, javelins and eventually to arrows. Previously the hunter had been limited to the pursuit of prey that could be caught in traps and clubbed to death with coarse stone axes. With improved arms, the range of action was extended and faster-moving and bigger animals could be pursued at less risk; moreover Man was now better equipped to pierce the coarse hide of his victims and carve them up, once he had killed them.

Little by little these techniques spread throughout the inhabited parts of the Old World. But any process of change acquires a momentum of its own; new skills created new needs and as larger supplies of food became available, the population grew – a development which spurred the human race towards ever remoter and grimmer corners of the globe. The urge to expansion arose because, despite better methods of tackling his quarry, Man still required vast tracts of hunting ground just to keep alive. Tribes living north of 60 degrees latitude and armed with rifles to this day need between two hundred and three hundred square miles per capita even though 40 per cent of their diet comes from fishing, not practised to the same extent by their early forebears.*

Stone Age Man may at some point have reached a stage where

Malthus' teachings applied, or their implications may have been avoided only by breaking new ground. Writing specifically of the North American Indian, Malthus stated: 'Misery is the check that regresses the superior power of population and keeps its effects equal to the means of subsistence.'* Such views are nowadays apt to be challenged; Marshall Sahlins, for instance, portrays the Palaeolithic as the original affluent society.* But if life was easier in temperate climes, in Siberia and Alaska it remained precarious. During the bitter and interminable winters game became even scarcer: under such conditions, the all-the-year-round situation counts less than the ability to keep alive during the worst season.

Radical advances in hunting skills were part and parcel of a process by which Man himself became transformed; and at this point, some fifty thousand years ago, *Homo sapiens*, true precursor of Modern Man, appeared upon the scene. Early *Homo sapiens*, if dressed in suit and tie, could probably pass unnoticed in a present-day social gathering, but the same could hardly be said of the more brutish and beetle-browed Neanderthalers who had dominated the world stage for many millennia. In the past prehistorians believed that the new species quickly superseded and eliminated the Neanderthalers but the takeover processss is now seen as more gradual. In many instances Neanderthal and *Homo sapiens*, or sometimes even intermediate specimens, lived side by side; *Homo sapiens* looked different, being taller and slimmer, but he was not necessarily much more intelligent than his forerunners, whose cranial capacity was similar. He merely knew more because there was more to know.

Man's sum of knowledge continued to grow, and this closing phase of the Old Stone Age witnessed epic advances which paved the way to the first move into America: the adoption of clothing, for example, and of primitive dwellings. In Russia archaeological sites situated above the Arctic Circle are first found in this period; but the main evidence derives from recent work in the Ukraine, where winters were then of arctic severity. These sites, unlike others of the USSR, have yielded ample radiocarbon dates, and I. K. Ivanova has demonstrated that, thirty-five to forty thousand years ago, proper protection against extremes of cold began to be devised.*

During the fourth and last glacial period, the Ukraine was not ice-covered, but the climate deteriorated far more than in east Siberia because of the proximity of the great ice-caps. The Ukraine then consisted of periglacial steppe, surrounded by ice-covered areas, which has no parallel on our planet now. The ground was overlain with permafrost and the average air temperature was some 15 degrees Centigrade lower than today. The harsh climate did not drive away all the animals, however, and the periglacial steppe supported a varied fauna, including wild horse, woolly rhinoceros and reindeer.

Ivanova and her colleagues made one discovery crucial to New World prehistory: skeletons of wolf, arctic fox and hare were found to lack paws, which were separately located, indicating that the carcasses had been skinned and the pelts used to provide warmth for their hunters. Furthermore certain bone artefacts were very suggestive of needles, which might have been used for sewing hides to make up skin garments. Other Ice Age skeletons from regions east of Moscow were girdled with string beads that must have been sewn on to close-fitting clothing. More-over, in the Ukraine, along with the evidence of clothing, primitive forms of man-made shelter were found; the quantities of charcoal present suggest that the shelters were even heated.

The reader may protest that the Ukraine, though situated in the USSR, lies closer to London than to the Bering Strait and that this information is therefore irrelevant to the issue. But these new skills were destined to spread slowly but surely to regions such as east Siberia, where they were crucial to human survival; for the trek into America, the improvements in dress and shelter made by *Homo sapiens* were a decisive step. Even if minibands of hunters had approached America before this time, their sufferings would have been unimaginable, and most if not all would surely have succumbed to the rigours of bare Beringia before they reached Alaska. This featureless territory which joined the continents could offer few caves, the invariable refuge of primitive Man in milder but hillier surroundings. Accordingly, any full-scale invasion of America can hardly have predated the advances in clothing and shelter made about forty thousand years ago. One invention led to another, and once the new hunting techniques had prompted the population to multiply and spread into new territory, other inventions in their turn became indispensable as the price of survival in conditions of extreme cold.

Man, when he eventually reached America, preyed upon the typical cold-climate game that then ranged over much of the Northern

Hemisphere, from western Russia through Siberia to Alaska and beyond: the reindeer, moose, wild sheep, horse, fox, dog, together with the giants of this animal kingdom, the mammoth, mastodon and bison. These animals would have thrived on the sparse low vegetation of Beringia. Conspicuous by their absence, however, were other beasts that had formed part of the standard fare, such as musk deer, whose ancestors had frequented warm wooded areas, and that standby of the Asian hunter, the woolly rhinoceros. These were both forest animals and shunned the treeless expanse that led to America. The squirrel did not even penetrate as far as the Kamchatka Peninsula, much farther to the south, since he was unfitted to the open tundra that separated Kamchatka from the Siberian mainland. Distinctive to America, however, and therefore new to Man, was the giant sloth, which had originated in South America though he later migrated northwards and then, like the horse, became extinct in the New World.

American Man did not enjoy an exclusive diet of mammoth steak, a delicacy whose procurement bristled with hazards, nor did he dine daily off the bulky bison or the swift-moving horse. Like present-day hunting tribes in Africa, these early migrants preferred to supplement their calory intake by gathering plants and fruits. But in northern latitudes the range of vegetable food was meagre and, therefore, when no larger animals were available, Man devoured the smallest, including rodents: the guinea-pig (originally present in South but not North America) is still a staple element in the diet of the High Andes; and grubs, as among the Australian Aborigines, were also prized as a source of extra protein.

As C. W. Ceram points out, small groups of hunters were ill-equipped to confront a herd of mammoths in open country and had to rely on the skilful use of terrain to achieve their objective. Animals have to drink and game was easiest to track down at springs and other watering-places, particularly if they were situated in canyons that could be blocked by stones and tree-trunks; an attack could then be launched from a safe distance, preferably from above. Perhaps with the help of fire, the quarry was sometimes driven over a cliff – as archaeological finds demonstrate – to lie helpless at the bottom of the chasm with limbs shattered. Any final chances of escape could be removed by cutting the hind leg tendons, a custom still practised by African hunters.

The flesh of one victim was ample for many a feast, and specimens have been found of single beasts with primitive missiles implanted in their sides. However, a direct hit only marked the beginning of a struggle between hunter and hunted, since it would be optimistic to assume that one stone javelin or one boulder could cause a mastodon to expire; special bullets are currently used against his first cousin, the elephant. A preferred tactic was to separate one victim from his companions, wound him with a hail of projectiles, and engage in gruelling pursuit until he finally bled to death.

Ceram gives a picture of how a small band of weary, footsore hunters might have cautiously approached a few bison, which they had stampeded away from the main herd:

> Ten in number, the bison had finally paused to drink at a small spring in a rincon of the canyon wall and to graze upon the thick, tall grass. For a day and a half, the hunters had carefully followed the large, hairy mammals, hoping the beasts would lose their sense of danger and allow themselves to be boxed into a place where the hunters could approach close enough to kill them.
>
> At last the moment was at hand! Warily, two hunters crawled along the slope of the canyon wall from opposite sides, seeking places from which they could throw large rocks upon the animals or hurl their spears with devastating force. Patiently, five more hunters waited below, concealed by the tall grass or behind convenient boulders. When the first two were in place, the leader gave the signal. Rocks came tumbling down on the startled bison; spears whistled through the air and thudded into soft flesh; one or two missed, but most found their targets. Shouts and cries filled the air. The bison, caught by surprise, whirled and milled around the waterhole for a moment, then several broke for the open country. One was wounded, the spear in its flank bobbing like a wave-tossed spindle. On this animal the hunters concentrated; three more spears found their target, and the great beast went down thrashing wildly. Two other animals lay maimed at the waterhole; one young calf, hobbling painfully, tried to get away to the open country but was quickly dispatched. The remaining six bison disappeared through the thickets and tall grass to the west.*

This description relates to a period long after Man's first entry into America but the scene had not greatly varied since earlier times, when more use was made of boulders and less of javelins. At Dent, Colorado, at the mouth of a small gulley archaeologists found the bones of twelve mammoths that had apparently been stampeded over the edge of a cliff.

Some of them would have been killed by the fall, and others stunned by rocks before they were finally dispatched. In certain mammoth-kill sites in North America, the animals had been bogged down in marshy land into which they had been driven.

The wild rejoicing following a major kill is easy to picture: the hunters with their wives and children gathered round their prey and gorged themselves on perishable parts such as liver and kidneys, before the rest of the carcass was hacked up. The preservation of the remaining store of flesh depended on latitude: in parts of Alaska, for instance, the permafrost offered natural means of refrigeration. Big-game hunting required groups of seven to ten. Such corporate action, whether in America or Asia, entailed a rudimentary social organization and brought in its train certain religious observances. In this respect, the study of peoples remaining at a similar stage of development, such as the African Bushmen or the Australian Aborigines, serves to complement our knowledge.

The genial cave paintings which followed the rise of *Homo sapiens* go back as far as thirty thousand years. Examples of the same art in the New World, many situated in the farthest extremity of South America, are less old. However, the American specimens depict scenes of the chase strangely reminiscent of those found throughout the Old World and are clearly rich in religious significance.

Hunting may have led not merely to an enhanced degree of social cohesion, but also to the first manifestations of violence, and the earliest types of warfare on a minute scale. But if the Australian Aborigines can offer any guidance, hunting also engendered a complex tribal lore, together with a special concern for the lives of the quarry. Magic rites brought luck to the hunter, and the tribes themselves would become associated with animal spirits, leading to a form of totemism whereby each group had its patron or protector which it never killed.

Magic ensures success, but also springs from fear, and from the urge to dominate the spirits of evil; it therefore brings forth an elaborate ceremonial whose origins are obscure. Magic was intimately linked with every phase of life and death and led to strange practices, nowadays considered repellent, such as the eating of human flesh in order to absorb the strength of the dead man. Such embryonic religions already entailed the presence of shamans to preside over ceremonies and to perform healing rites.

*

This brief digression may offer an idea of how the first Americans lived, but not of when they arrived. On this opinions have fluctuated between two extremes: before the 1890s, Man was generally believed to have reached America some one hundred thousand years ago. Then, for lack of archaeological evidence, the fashion developed in the early decades of this century to maintain that the first migration took place a few thousand years before the present time. But in the early days of radiocarbon after World War II, proof of human presence in the New World for at least twelve thousand years was discovered. In the 1970s, important finds have pushed the date much farther back, and authenticated radiocarbon figures in excess of thirty thousand years now exist for both north-eastern Siberia and north-western America.

The underlying principle of radiocarbon dating scarcely needs to be recalled: in brief outline, the process rests upon the discovery that all *organic* material during its lifetime absorbs from the atmosphere tiny quantities of the isotope Carbon 14, which it loses again at a set pace after death. A laboratory measurement of the quantity of Carbon 14 remaining in, say, an ancient beam accordingly tells us how long ago the tree in question was cut, a date not automatically corresponding to the building of the structure from which the beam was taken.

In recent years, new methods have been developed, such as the collagen technique, which depends on the measurement of the protein content of bones. Means are in process of development for the dating of non-organic materials, including obsidian and even pottery, but their application is not yet universal. Therefore the figures that I shall give derive from radiocarbon dating unless otherwise stated.

The accuracy of the radiocarbon method has been enhanced by close cross-checking with other systems, in particular the technique of dating by tree-rings, used to good effect in the western United States and in Scandinavia; and for dates of comparative antiquity, radiocarbon figures have been shown to be often too low. But, far from casting doubts on the principle involved, refinements in radiocarbon technique only serve to prove its overall validity – a key factor in weighing the relevance of many ideas about New World migrations. For theories are often advanced by authors who carelessly cast established dating systems to the winds whenever it suits their purpose to do so and are happy to treat Ancient Egyptians and Maya as contemporaries, in the face of irrefutable evidence to the contrary.

The earliest reliable dates for human occupation of the Western Hemisphere were secured in the last few years from the site of Old Crow in the Yukon territory in north-western Canada, and range from twenty-five thousand to thirty thousand years ago. Other dates of approximately thirty-four thousand years, not yet fully confirmed, derive from Hugues Complex, also in the Canadian north-west. Figures in a somewhat lower time-range come from places farther south, such as twenty-one thousand five hundred for Scripps Campus Site in California (known as La Jolla) and twenty-three thousand for Tlapacoya near Mexico City.*

When they were first claimed, dates in excess of thirty-seven thousand years for Lewisville, near Dallas, Texas, aroused great interest, although doubts were expressed as to whether the material tested was genuinely associated with human remains. But the figure of thirty-seven thousand becomes more plausible in the light of the new and fully authenticated Canadian dates. Even so, reports in early 1977 in newspapers in the United States and other countries of human remains over forty thousand years old on Santa Rosa Island, a hundred miles west of Los Angeles, must still rank as unconfirmed. In late 1975 geologist John Wooley discovered a burned-out area on that island that has been dated by radiocarbon and is without any doubt over forty thousand years old. On the perimeter of this area Dr Rainer Berger, of the Institute of Archaeology at UCLA, found dwarf mammoth bones and man-made chopper tools. Berger insists that the tools and mammoth bones are associated with the burned-out area, which must therefore be a human hearth. But judgment should surely be suspended until a more detailed report is published, together with photographs.

Evidence from Peru tends to favour an early rather than a late occupation of America. Peru lies many thousands of years' travelling distance from Texas, in terms of the stately pace of Early Man's migrations. Stone tools have now been found at Ayacucho, some two hundred miles south-east of Lima, whose antiquity is certainly twenty thousand years, and which their discoverer, Richard MacNeish, puts at twenty-three thousand. In Brazil, new finds at Alice Böer Site are dated to fourteen thousand years before the present and *may* go back as far as twenty thousand.*

Near the Bering Strait the situation is less clear, despite an abundance of material stemming from much later arrivals, such as the Eskimos. The earliest tentative figures for Alaska come from sites belonging to the British Mountain Tradition that began twenty to twenty-five thousand years ago, though no radiocarbon dates are yet available.*

More concrete signs are now beginning to emerge of early human occupation of America's arctic gateway. Some of the evidence stems from Onion Portage, excavated by Douglas Andersen and lying about one hundred and twenty-five miles upstream from the point where the Kobuk River enters the sea near the Bering Strait. Onion Portage is almost exactly on the present-day treeline: to the north of the site stretches the bleak tundra, so familiar to the first immigrants, while to the south the countryside is dotted with patches of spruce, willow and even birch in sheltered places. As in other Alaskan haunts of early migrants, a sandy knoll dominates the landscape, serving as a lookout for the herds of caribou which cross the river at this point as they move north in the spring and south in the fall. Hunters both ancient and modern have used this hillock to watch for their prey.* Andersen insists that the oldest tools recall those of the Lake Baikal region, far away to the other side of the Bering bridge; he considers that the site is between seven thousand five hundred and fifteen thousand years old. During the earlier part of this period, Beringia was still dry land, and no major obstacle divided Siberia from Alaska, although a forbidding wall of ice blocked the way southwards until the MacKenzie River Valley corridor opened up an ice-free passage to the Great Plains.

Neither in Alaska nor in the adjacent parts of Siberia do the newest finds provide dates as early as places located farther inland. Two good explanations exist for this: first, early migrants are unlikely to have crossed the Chukchi and Seward Peninsulas, which now face each other across the Strait, but probably kept farther south and passed through territory that is now submerged, missing the eastern extremity of Siberia. Furthermore, since the sea-level constantly rose and fell, ancient coastal settlements have disappeared; sites on the shore are normally the easiest to identify and often the oldest, since life in the barren tundra of the interior was harder than on the game-rich coast, where birds laid their eggs, seals were easy to catch and even the climate was somewhat less harsh. Moreover, if Man moved inland, he tended to camp on river banks where animals congregated, and traces of early occupation were then washed away whenever the stream changed its course. Existing inland sites in Alaska usually take the form of mounds where the hunter lay in wait for caribou and other prey; the ground frequently has little or no soil and the archaeologist's efforts to date his finds become futile when spearpoints many thousands of years old simply lie on the surface, indistinguishable from those made a century ago. The permafrost adds to the problem: in summer the ground beneath remains frozen, while the top layer becomes saturated with water and resembles a huge sponge, in which ancient artefacts can literally 'float' from one layer of occupation to another. The terrain is therefore no more welcoming to the modern archaeologist than to those primitive migrants whose past he seeks.

However, more news may be expected in the not-too-distant future from Alaska, where one of the biggest archaeological projects ever mounted in the United States is about to be launched. The project will cost $600,000, to be provided by the National Geographic Society and the National Park Service, and its very size shows how scientific interest in man's entry into the New World has grown. Work will be centred upon Dry Creek, just north of Mount McKinley National Park; this site was discovered in 1973 by Charles Holmes, then a graduate student in archaeology and now with the Alaska State Park System.

Known traces of Early Man in Siberia comparable in age to those of Alaska, let alone of the Canadian Yukon, are confined to places far removed from the western tip of America. The first finds of real antiquity were made in the region of Lake Baikal, situated more than half-way from the Strait to the Ural Mountains that divide Europe from Asia. The site of Malta, about sixty miles north-west of Lake Baikal, and others in the same area yielded remains that were long regarded as the earliest examples of a human presence in Siberia, dating from about twenty-six thousand years ago. Finds included bone needles suggesting that sewn clothing had by then spread from the Ukraine. The dating of Malta corresponds to that of the British Mountain Tradition in Alaska, and the two cultures share specific traits. Farther to the north, signs of human occupation twenty-one thousand years old have been found on the banks of the Lena River, which flows into the Arctic Ocean, but at points some fifteen hundred miles from the nearest part of Alaska.

Malta was discovered as long ago as 1929, but not until 1968 did Soviet archaeologists, led by Y. A. Mochanov, discover traces of Siberian Man which were both older and more closely related to America. Throughout a wide region of eastern Siberia a common

culture was found which Mochanov designated Dyuktai, after a place
three hundred miles from the town of Okhotsk, on the shore of the
Okhotsk Sea. Radiocarbon tests show that this culture existed from
thirty-five thousand to ten thousand years ago; the Dyuktai people, like
the earliest Americans, were hunters, and many bones of horses and
mammoth were located.* Mochanov stresses that Dyuktai Man
resembled the earliest Americans in his implements, way of life and
physical appearance. But the Soviet archaeologist looks towards
northern China and in particular towards the Peking area for Dyuktai
origins.* Equally Okhladnikov, the father of Soviet archaeology in
Siberia, and other scientists who have worked in the Soviet Far East are
unanimous in regarding northern China as the birthplace of these
cultures.

Northern China has ranked among the earliest known homes of the
human race ever since the discovery at Chu-Ku-Tien of the famous
Pekin Man, usually considered to have lived five hundred thousand
years ago, although in 1975 archaeologist Richard E. Leakey, director of
the National Museum of Kenya, discovered in the northern part of the
country a skull, almost identical to the Pekin fossils, which he estimates
to be one and a half million years old (exact comparison surely cannot be
easy because the Pekin bones have long since been lost).* Between the
era of Pekin Man and that of his first descendants, huge gaps in our
knowledge persist, only partially filled by finds at Ting Ts'un suggestive
of an intermediate period. Traces of a human presence in the Ordos
Desert, also situated in northern China, date from about 50,000 B.C. and
include primitive stone implements and remains of meals from the flesh
of animals also found much nearer to Beringia, such as wild horse,
mastodon and woolly rhinoceros. Much more recently, the Chinese
archaeologist Chiu Chung Kang has made other discoveries at Yuan
Chu, comparable in antiquity to those of Ordos.* This whole area, lying
just within the Great Wall of China, still awaits a closer study and better
dating to shed more light on the origins of American and east Siberian
Man. Situated between Siberia and north China, Manchuria and
Mongolia are also virgin territory for the archaeologist and may conceal
within their soil many a secret affecting the first migrations into
America.

Though lying east rather than north of the Pekin region, Japan has to
be taken into account. During certain phases of the Ice Age, much of the

Sea of Okhotsk was dry, and studies of ancient beaches and maritime platforms reveal that Japan was linked to the Asiatic mainland. Until 1949, no one had thought of investigating pre-pottery cultures; since that date, however, the work has been carried forward with an energy characteristic of modern Japan. Primitive tools were found within the site of Iwajuku, believed to date from about 70,000 B.C., the beginning of the last glacial period; in one of the latest reported Japanese finds, the leading Japanese archaeologist Masso Suzuki describes cultures twenty-five thousand years old, as calculated by recent methods for dating obsidian. Suzuki, moreover, thinks that the most primitive tools found there are very much older than this.*

These Asian discoveries are most significant, but hard to link directly with any American counterpart. Early American Man's equipment is so diverse and varied that its development cannot yet be related step by step to that used in Siberia, while certain cruder implements continued to be made in parts of the New World when they had already been largely superseded in Asia.

Man's existence in America before he invented pottery can best be traced by his stone implements, which offer an overall view of his past. For this purpose, the classification of Richard MacNeish, whose work in that field is both recent and comprehensive, may be used. As a result of his latest finds in Ayacucho, Peru, MacNeish identified four different stages in the evolution of the American hunter. The first is the core-tool tradition, consisting of primitive artefacts that are really stones fashioned to serve as choppers or scrapers. Only an expert can distinguish them from ordinary pebbles and identify traces of work by human hands. In Peru this core-tool phase lasted from 23,000 to 13,000 B.C.

After a second phase when progress was more limited, a third ensued when true blades were fashioned, as opposed to mere choppers; in South America this stage ran from about 12,000 to 8,000 B.C. (the North American equivalent phase would be earlier), and its traces are more evident in Chile and Venezuela than in Peru. Then finally more sophisticated projectile points came into use, worked on both sides and ideal for fitting on lances or spears.* Similar missiles were found in North America, actually embedded in the flanks of a mastodon; that such tools were not extracted for re-use suggests that they were comparatively easy to make.

This fourth phase of refined toolmaking was first identified in 1929 in North America at Folsom, New Mexico, where typically grooved projectile points were found, linked with the remains of bison. At Sandia, another cave in New Mexico, a slightly different type of point was found, associated with camels, mammoths and sloths; the hunters made their camps on the shores of lakes, now dried up, to which numerous animals were then attracted in search of water. These weapons caused a sensation at the time, for they had no strict Old World parallel; in North America the earliest prototypes were dated to about 13,000 B.C., and at the time were believed to have belonged to the first people to set foot on the new continent. Since then our ideas have been transformed as different and more primitive tools have been unearthed.

So the implements of MacNeish's later Peruvian stages have their parallels in Mexico and the United States; however, he doubts whether his earliest and crudest Ayacucho artefacts will ever be located in North America, where they may have been simply blotted out by time. In order to allow a sufficient interval for these users of rough core-tools to reach South America, MacNeish thinks that they originally crossed Beringia between sixty thousand and one hundred thousand years ago, when certain peoples in China shared the same chopping-tool traditions.* These estimates of dates do, however, present certain problems: at such an early period, the species of Homo sapiens was not yet in existence, while Soviet archaeologists insist that Homo sapiens' predecessor, Neanderthal Man, could not have survived the extremes of climate of north-east Siberia, where the mean January air temperatures can reach —25–30 degrees C. lower than in the coldest parts of Eurasia inhabited by the Neanderthalers. Soviet scientists therefore consider that a comparatively early version of Homo sapiens passed through north-eastern Siberia, say, thirty-five to forty thousand years ago, and crossed from there into America.*

The argument may be advanced that Man is such an adaptable animal that – in his primeval state – he could have adjusted himself to any extremes of climate. The inhabitants of Tierra del Fuego, though they are now on the point of extinction, have for timeless centuries survived the rigorous conditions of this extremity of South America virtually without clothing. But Tierra del Fuego lies at a latitude of approximately 55 degrees and is not comparable to the Bering Strait region, situated almost on the Arctic Circle above the 65 degree parallel and washed by a sea that is frozen for nine months of the year. Admittedly not the present-day Strait, but the former Beringia landmass has to be considered: by skirting its southern coast, early migrants would have journeyed at an average latitude nearer to that of Tierra del Fuego. However, they could not have avoided territory situated as far north as 60 degrees, at points where Beringia did not stretch any farther to the south. A dilemma therefore arises: if Man entered America seventy thousand years ago, then the first migrants would have been not *Homo sapiens* but Neanderthalers, who, according to Soviet archaeologists, developed few defences against extreme cold. Yet the Soviet solution presents equal problems. The oldest known remains in east Siberia are almost contemporary with those of north-western Canada and allow practically no time for the slow pace of migration characteristic of that age. Moreover, the Siberian sites are situated at a great distance from Alaska.

But no hard-and-fast rule can be established to the effect that the southward move in America averaged about seventeen miles per generation, as MacNeish considers likely. Man could have come later and moved a little faster, particularly since he was advancing towards climatic conditions that were more tempting. Even if the first arrival *did* take place seventy thousand years ago, such tiny bands, ill-adapted to the conditions, would probably have been extinguished.

Both MacNeish and his Soviet colleagues unite in viewing China as the birthplace of east Siberian and American Man. But the sea of Okhotsk was at times partly dry and finds have been made in Japan of greater antiquity than those of east Siberia. Accordingly I consider that the first Americans might have followed a route leading through Japan and then over a partially dry Okhotsk Sea, roughly by way of the present-day Kurile and Aleutian Islands – richer in resources than the tundra farther north – and thence into the lower part of Alaska. I incline to the opinion that the main migrations began not more than fifty thousand years ago and perhaps less than forty thousand, at a moment when the Bering Bridge was again open. The migrants would have avoided north-eastern Siberia, and the settlement of this region then becomes not previous to but contemporary to that of Alaska. A penetration into America and eastern Siberia in 40,000 B.C. corresponds more closely to the first invasion of Australia, where the oldest human traces are now known to be about thirty-six thousand years old;

significantly, the earliest Australian dates derive from the south, or the part that lies farthest from Asia, and present data on Australian prehistory call in doubt the notion that Man needed many tens of thousands of years to spread from one end to the other of a large landmass.*

Expansion into two new continents followed *Homo sapiens'* development of better tools and better ways of resisting extremes of climate, and the ensuing age of flux led to the great overspill into remoter parts of the globe. Data may be hard to recover from the bottom of the Okhotsk and Bering Seas, but much that is still dry land remains unexplored and new discoveries by American, Japanese, Soviet and Chinese archaeologists may one day lead to a recasting of current views.

Finally, the questions of how and when Man reached America having been considered, the problem remains: who was he? Was he Caucasian, the prototype that created the legend of the white bearded god, or did he have the negroid nose and lips portrayed in some of the earliest sculpture? Was he perhaps more like the North American Indian, or did he have Mongoloid features, typical of the Chinese and Japanese? Alternatively, was he a primitive-looking being, reminiscent of the Australian aboriginal?

The question is hard to answer. In the Old World ethnic divisions are often more clearcut, but the medley of physical types existing in aboriginal America defies generalization. In the early part of this century the conviction that the earliest American descended directly from Egyptians or Israelites waned, as his ancestry came under closer scrutiny. Anthropologists, however, still thought in terms of an overall racial unity, a notion reflecting the eighteenth-century adage that whoever had seen one American Indian had seen them all, since they were so alike.

Admittedly a kind of Mongoloid veneer overlays the majority, with their straight black locks and their relatively hairless bodies, often combined with slanting eyes and high cheekbones. These rather striking characteristics may prove dominant when mixtures occur between Mongoloids and others; and within this broad framework, American Man displays a marked variety of physical appearance. To illustrate the fallacies of sweeping generalizations, I asked a Peruvian collector to point to one true Mongoloid from among his pieces, which included many Mochica 'portrait' heads. My friend was unable to do this, confining himself to the remark that in early Peruvian ceramics the eyes were sometimes prolonged by slits cut at the extremities, as if to create an *artificially* Chinese look. The Mochica heads uniformly possess noses recalling a North American Indian brave, never a Chinese sage.

The earliest studies of blood groups, starting in about A.D. 1900, reinforced oversimplified conclusions concerning the American Indian: with his very high percentage of O group, and relative absence of A and B, he clearly formed a race apart, distinct from the peoples of Europe and even from those of East Asia, where the B frequency is also quite high. The obvious deduction was made, that the first migrants had come from Asia but had left that continent before members of blood groups A and B had arrived.

But suddenly, as often occurs, the pendulum took a full swing: in the face of physical differences so marked as to be apparent to any casual observer between, say, the dwellers of the Bolivian Andes, the Mayan jungles and the North American plains, ancient skeletons were examined more closely and uniformist views began to be questioned. The Argentinian anthropologist, Imbelloni, now proposed that successive waves of people comprised of distinct races had come separately from Asia. While conceding that the Indians belonged to the Mongol branch of the human family, Imbelloni drew a distinction between two types of skull he had found: the short-headed (brachycephalic) and the long-headed (dolicocephalic). The short-headed represented the Mongol element, while the long-headed belonged to individuals defined as Australoids, because of resemblances between their skeletons and those of the Australian Aborigines: Australoids had been the first to reach America but had later been pushed by Mongoloid migrants into the extremities of the continent, such as Patagonia, Lagoa Santa on the coast of Brazil and the Lower Californian Peninsula in Mexico, where these long-heads had been found. They survive in Patagonia today.

Imbelloni envisaged eight 'waves' of immigrants in all: the first three consisted of Australoid or related stock, dark-skinned and long-headed; the five following waves were basically Mongoloid. According to the Argentinian scholar, the long- and short-headed peoples at times intermarried. Typical of such blends are the tribes of the high Bolivian Andes, who present a mixture of the two physical types.

The eminent French Americanist, Paul Rivet, was greatly struck by the recognition of these Australoid elements. The prevalence of long-headed types in the extreme south of the American Continent led Rivet to the startling proposal that Man had reached Patagonia about ten thousand years ago by walking across the Antarctic Continent from Australia. This theory was reinforced by a list of words seemingly common to certain Australian and South American tongues; the French scientist also pointed to similarities between the Malayo-Polynesian language family (in which he included the Australians) and Hoka, spoken on the coast of North America.

Colleagues who still remember Rivet invariably speak of his endearing and brilliant qualities; nevertheless his view of American origins, to which he stuck through thick and thin, gained few adherents at the time and is now viewed as irrelevant. When Rivet first formulated his theory, scientists had already established that after the end of the last Ice Age, which would have totally blocked transit across Antarctica, this landmass was divided both from Australia and from South America by broad expanses of open sea. Moreover, to the south of Australia the currents nowadays run consistently from east to west and would inevitably carry canoes not to Antarctica but to South Africa. Even if Man *had* reached Antarctica from Australia, he would have faced a trek of some three thousand miles over the high Antarctic Plateau, a journey beside which the crossing of Beringia would have been a mere summer stroll.

At one time Man was thought to have reached Australia long before America, and when Rivet wrote this view still prevailed. However, ideas on American Indian origins have since changed with startling rapidity and many cherished theories have been consigned to the waste-paper basket – sometimes prematurely. Imbelloni's concept of waves of immigrants itself requires redefinition. The notion of compact bodies of newcomers crossing a narrow isthmus at set intervals, before pressing southwards in search of sustenance, has to be discarded. It seems that people just seeped into America across Beringia if the passage was open. The original idea of separate squads of long-heads followed by short-heads has lost its relevance, while earlier claims that Australoid types arrived first are now hard to substantiate, as remains have been found of equal or greater antiquity that are Mongoloid in type. Not long ago Antoinette Nelken and Richard MacNeish visited Lagoa Santa in

Brazil, where a much-discussed discovery of long-headed skulls was made (they are now preserved in Denmark). The two archaeologists observed that the skulls were found in a very humid grotto and under such conditions special problems arise that make correct dating hard to achieve.

Like cranial forms, blood groups can no longer be treated as providing simple solutions to complex questions: the identification of a vast array of different combinations has made it well nigh impossible to use this method to consign people to clearcut ethnic pigeon-holes. Blood types are now seen to be capable of more rapid mutation than was previously held possible and, if subject to recent changes, can reveal little about distant generations.

Not only are the hazards of defining American Man by a single physical trait, such as the shape of his skull or the colour of his skin, now patent but the very notion of race as a scientific concept is under heavy challenge. On a purely practical level, well-defined groups contain physical types that vary visibly: for instance, Mongoloids are not all flat-nosed or Europeans long-nosed. In Sweden people exist with rather snub noses and sensuous lips; but for their rosy complexion and ash blond hair such individuals could be taken as part-Negro. Alternatively, the Japanese are typically Mongoloid and notably homogeneous, having been unaffected by intermarriage during many centuries; but certain members of the Imperial Family have a profile undeniably different from that of the average Japanese and that was described to me by a distinguished diplomat as 'Aztec'. In other countries, such as India or Hawaii, the aristocracy have tended to be fairer in complexion than the common people; for many generations its members were shaded by parasols and protected by verandahs, while the remainder toiled in the open sun. Precisely because it implied a freedom from manual work, the possession of a fairer skin became a status symbol among many non-Caucasian peoples. Even for the White Man, pallor was formerly prized as synonymous with virtue and beauty. In the jet age, a suntan is no longer the hallmark of the labourer, but the afterglow of an expensive winter holiday. But at the turn of the century English ladies shunned exposure to the sun, and girls working as millhands in the north of England drank vinegar, which they believed gave them a whiter skin.

Even if racial groups really were uniform in outward appearance, firm conclusions could not be drawn on this basis. Using the latest techniques, the whole biochemical make-up of the individual can now be measured and the countless enzymes in the human blood separated and identified. Vast strides in the science of genetic analysis prove that features such as aquiline and flat noses, or black and white skins, account for a tiny fraction of the innumerable ways in which human beings differ: science has demonstrated that variations *within* any given group far outnumber those outward signs that distinguish that group from others.

Racial sub-divisions still serve as a convenient form of label: the straight-haired yellow-skinned Oriental; the woolly-haired black African; the fair and lank Caucasian. These images are so ingrained that people who rage at notions of Black Power or White Supremacy still take them for granted; they are significant simply because they are visible, though they arise from a mere handful among countless gene combinations present in the human body.

Genes are themselves hard to distinguish, but give rise to variations in enzymes and proteins whose separate functions are easier to determine. By random sampling, enzyme and protein differences between any two Caucasoids or any two Africans have been found to number as many as three hundred thousand, of which very few are related to genes producing outward racial characteristics. Race therefore becomes nothing more than an additional factor among the countless biochemical variations between two human beings; such differences increase only marginally when the enzymes of a Caucasian are compared with those of a Black, instead of comparing one Caucasian with another.*

Whatever doubts the scientists may cast upon the very notion of race, the average person will nonetheless want to know how the first American really looked. For this purpose, his East Asian homeland has to be taken into account. Among early skeletal remains from that region, proto-Mongoloid traits are naturally in evidence, but the Australoid element is also present. In Chu-Ku-Tien, where the Pekin Man was discovered, later finds in the vicinity were suggestive of the future Australian Aboriginal and of Neanderthal Man; these bones were associated with others that were Mongoloid in type. If in China ancient remains of proto-Mongoloids lie side by side with proto-Australoids, it is small wonder that both turn up in the New World.

It has been suggested that the earliest arrivals in America were more like Europeans, being related to the Caucasoid Ainus still existing in reduced numbers in the north of Japan. The people of this tribe are more heavily bearded than the Japanese and are sometimes even blue-eyed, though to judge from such photographs as I have seen, they would hardly be confused with a modern European. The Ainus, who form a distinct racial enclave, are a well-known object of curiosity. But, most significantly, other people with Caucasoid traits survive in East Asia – in that very part of Siberia which lies closest to America, and to which they were driven by Mongoloid intruders, a fate that also befell the people of Patagonia. In eastern Siberia, both in the Kamchatka Peninsula and in the Chukchi Peninsula facing Alaska, tribes exist that are Caucasoid in type and speak languages with affinities traceable not only to Eskimo, but to certain tongues of north-western Canada. These long-headed Caucasoids were also present in the Ice Age cultures of Lake Baikal far to the west, but nowadays live only in the eastern extremity of Eurasia.*

Early migrants across the Bering Strait are also thought to have included people of Negroid stock, possibly pigmies. This theory presents no special problems, since people with broad noses, black skin and woolly hair still predominate in the islands of Melanesia and were also to be numbered among the aboriginal inhabitants of Indonesia, the Philippines and Malaysia, where they still exist. However, other aboriginal Malays are more Caucasoid and therefore akin to the Palaeo-Siberians already mentioned. Accordingly, among an East Asian people of mainly Mongoloid stock, some of the aboriginal inhabitants are Caucasoid and others are Negroid.

It is likely that the Australian aboriginals descended from some of these Proto-Malays; hence the name Australoid has been given to the species, wherever it is found. In Australia proper, people of this kind remained in sole possession of the field, but in order to enter Australia the Torres Strait, which never became dry, had to be crossed. A once-and-for-all, and perhaps accidental, immigration by canoe is more likely to have occurred, not strictly comparable to the peopling of America, which was of easier access to pedestrian groups entering at different times. A medley of racial types was present in Asia, and all tended to be on the move during the period of flux following the emergence of *Homo sapiens*.

Some writers may still be tempted to search for traces of Alexander the Great's fleet every time they see portrayed a man with a beard;

others jump to conclusions about black Phoenician slaves at the mere sight of an old statue with thick lips. In reality, however, these very elements, as well as Mongoloids, are to this day present in East Asia, which at the time of the main migrations into America was no Nazi paradise of racial purity. So ancient America also became a melting pot for people of varied stock.

CHAPTER THREE

MAN AND MAIZE

FOR modern Americans, technical advance grew to be an end in itself; the premise that no problem was insoluble accelerated the march of progress to a point where its benefits became open to question. In marked contrast, Early American Man preferred to leave things as they were and, if changes occurred, the pace was leisurely. During the first forty thousand years of his presence in America, Man's existence probably altered less than during the present century; he went on doing much the same things, even if he learned to do them rather better. In due course stone instruments were improved, and specialized tools were devised of types unknown in Asia. But no epoch-making advance took place; human beings spread and multiplied while life went on much as before.

However, after this long gestation period, about ten thousand years ago, America suffered its first economic crisis, occasioned by the extinction of most of those very mammals whose pursuit had brought Man to the new continent. After this hiatus the rate of progress began to quicken: agriculture first appeared, and much later pottery. Towards the end of this chapter, evidence of early maritime contacts between the two hemispheres will be reviewed. But the possibility of contacts across the ocean can only be seen in the light of happenings in America itself during this crucial period that ran from about 8000 to 3000 B.C. Events tended to run parallel from one end of that great territory to the other, and their course must be traced before attempting to detect Old World influences in any particular area.

Inexplicably, the large mammals of the western hemisphere one by one became extinct. The mammoth breathed his last, as well as the original bison, though other varieties survived; the giant American camel disappeared, leaving in his place in parts of South America the modestly proportioned llama; the swift-moving antelope and the

49

ponderous sloth were equally affected. The American horse existed until about 6000 B.C., and the mastodon roamed for a further one thousand years on the coast of Peru, where his last remains are to be found. The gravity of the situation defies exaggeration: it was as if the modern world's staple crops were all smitten by an indestructible pest and could never be grown again. Equally serious, smaller mammals such as the wild pigs that had made their way across Beringia also disappeared without leaving any descendants that could later be domesticated. This absence affected the course of history, leading to solutions to New World social and economic problems that were different from those prevailing in the Old, with its greater range of domestic animals. Lacking the cow, the sheep and the pig, the population in the larger centres faced a deficiency of animal protein that left its mark on their way of life; the taming of the turkey and the dog was a poor consolation. Moreover, the absence of the horse left the cities as they expanded with inadequate means of communication with the countryside, though the great civilizations were at least spared that scourge of the Old World, the incursions of nomad horsemen.

The causes of the extinction in America of the larger mammals, most of which survived in Europe, have been hotly debated. Prehistorians never cease to remind us that Man did not feed mainly on big animals such as mammoths and horses. However, their meat must have provided the more succulent part of his fare, and without the occasional addition of a choice cut of mastodon, the human diet became rather meagre. A double crisis occurred: at a moment when the population was rising, the supply of food declined. For his daily sustenance Man relied on humbler creatures, such as gophers, squirrels and rabbits, but he can hardly be absolved from his share of the blame for the disappearance of the monarchs of the American animal kingdom. Even if the killing of a mammoth was a major event, Man surely made inroads into the herds as he spread and multiplied and his hunting skills improved. In some respects, however, the very imperfections of technique increased the damage since one of the best ways to kill large beasts was to drive them over a cliff; though a single carcass sufficed for a banquet, a whole herd might be wantonly destroyed to meet this necessity. In Czechoslovakia remains have been found of ninety mammoths slaughtered simultaneously. Climatic changes also played their part; the world warmed up after the Ice Age, and the animals had to migrate to different latitudes in order to find climate and pasture to suit their established tastes, as the borders of desert, grassland and forest fluctuated. The need to move could upset the reproductive cycle of the beasts concerned, and in addition human activities tended to impede these migrations necessary for survival.

Nevertheless, in such expanses of territory, space was sufficient for both Man and mammal if these had been left to their own devices; the puzzle remains unsolved as to why many such beasts continued to thrive in the Old World.* Besides, after the extinction of the larger beasts, many smaller animals survived, such as wild dogs and cats, hares, tortoises, foxes, iguanas and even deer, of which some species had outlived the holocaust. (The Indians later used the word deer for the Spanish horses, having no word of their own for that long-extinct animal.)

Long before the extinction of the mammals, Man had already modified his daily fare in other respects. In the frozen north, he had been mainly limited to a diet of flesh, consuming animals that could live off the tundra grasses and bushes. Only in midsummer were supplies of berries available, of a kind still eaten by Eskimos. But as the bands of hunters progressed southwards, they had a rich abundance of plant life at their disposal; the flora of tropical America is most varied, though it was then quite different from that of Eurasia. Plant gathering, therefore, came to be a major source of food; much less effort was required to pick the fruits and berries growing at the doorstep than to course endlessly after antelope. Gathering was a task suitable for the womenfolk, who could also help in the snaring of small animals. In spite of the ravages of past generations of Indians and Spaniards, not to mention those of modern times, a wealth of edible plants still offers evidence that Early Man disposed of a succulent and varied diet. Nonetheless, adaptation to the tropics was not simple; among visitors from northern climes, a tropical paradise may nowadays foster illusions of an easy way of living, but after a slow move from the Arctic, Ancient Man would have found it hard to adapt to such unfamiliar conditions.

Moreover, plant gathering offered one big drawback: much of the available food was seasonal. While winters elsewhere are cold, in most of the tropics they are dry and an all-the-year-round diet could not therefore be based on gathering without moving long distances from place to place. Partly to overcome this circumstance, Man took the momentous step of sowing deliberately some of the seeds that had been collected.

'Neolithic Revolution' is an expression that has long been favoured among scholars (in general terms the Neolithic is associated with the inception of agriculture). The term may well be suited to the Near East, but in America the switch from gathering to cultivation was so gradual and the beginnings so tentative that the process barely deserves to be called a revolution. But, however slow, the development was nonetheless decisive, for without this preliminary step cities and civilizations could not emerge.

Earlier generations of archaeologists were convinced that plant cultivation had been discovered only once, and had obviously spread from the Old World to the New. Until quite recently, therefore, scientists thought that agriculture had been introduced into America from China. The achievement of Richard MacNeish in establishing much earlier dates for the first Mexican cultivated species than any available from China was itself revolutionary. MacNeish's ample publications on his finds in Mexico and Peru are commensurate with the scope of his work.

During the early 1960s, MacNeish, assisted by a formidable team of experts, investigated the Valley of Tehuacán, lying some one hundred and twenty miles south-east of Mexico City. The intention was to study human remains, particularly in caves, and to probe the origins of agriculture. In all, 454 pre-Hispanic sites or dwelling-places were examined, and 104 samples were taken for radiocarbon dating.

The town of Tehuacán is now a spa, the main source of mineral water in Mexico. Surrounded by an arid region with sparse vegetation, the place is blessed with much sunshine and little rain. Nowadays, however, the tawny landscape is quilted with patches of vivid green, wherever sugar cane and other crops can be grown with the help of irrigation. Ten thousand years ago the Tehuacán Valley was inhabited by very small groups of humans, varying from a few persons to several families, who banded together for only certain parts of the year. These people divided their time between the pursuit of smaller animals, including rats and moles, and the gathering of wild grains in the spring and of fruit in summer, when the rains came; in the autumn the land dried up and they were obliged to move on.

By about 6000 B.C. the situation began to change; by then the last horse and antelope had disappeared, though the deer remained, and hares were replaced by rabbits. The human population was growing, and some sites indicate that individual groups had grown larger; they continued to lead a nomad life, but depended increasingly on gathering for their sustenance.

Then suddenly some forgotten genius became aware that by dropping back into the soil some of the seeds he had gathered, he could make a plant grow – a new age began. Probably the avocado pear and a kind of squash were first cultivated, while other staples, such as maize, chile and cotton still existed only in wild form. In retrospect the sowing of seeds to produce plants may seem an obvious step to take. However, Man had existed for millions of years without hitting upon this invention, which was made only two or three times in the world's history and totally escaped certain peoples, such as the Australian Aborigines. Ancient Man paid scant attention to the scientific process of cause and effect; as late as the time of the European discovery of Polynesia, people in many islands did not realize that the sexual act led to the begetting of children.

The planting of an avocado pip to make a tree grow was such a simple act that it could have happened almost simultaneously in many a village in the Tehuacán Valley and elsewhere. But one prefers to believe that the idea first came to one man only, and the news of his feat then spread like wildfire, as others eagerly copied his unpatented invention.

At this early date, marginally later than the first agriculture in the Near East, there were few domesticated plants. However, in the succeeding phase in Tehuacán, running from 5000 to 3500 B.C., their number greatly increased. To the avocado and the earliest squash were now added maize and the common bean, which still form the basic diet of the Mexican peasant. Any visitor to Mexico soon becomes aware that the typical dishes are fiercely spiced with chile, a tradition which dates from this remote era, when this species was also first cultivated.

These early cultivated plants formed only about 10 per cent of the total human diet. During the summer rainy season, wild foods abounded, but seeds could be artificially sown in such a way that their fruits ripened later, after the dry period set in, and it became possible to stay longer in the same place before reverting to the nomad existence of the winter months. Early agriculture in the New World was basically an elaboration of the gathering process; not confined to one valley, it spread slowly but surely to wider regions. Year-round cultivation, with

53

people settled permanently in one place, depended on the next logical step forward – the beginnings of irrigation.

By the painstaking probings of modern archaeology, the way of life of these first American cultivators has been brought to light with vivid precision. The daily diet, for instance, can be reconstructed by the meticulous study of fossilized excreta. The paraphernalia which the occupants left behind in caves shows how they made their tools and even how they cooked their food. The conclusion might be reached that these people were not so different from ourselves, rising each morning at a fixed time and eating three square meals a day at predetermined hours. But the cavemen's attitude to life was more carefree: he would normally sleep when he felt tired and eat when he was hungry.

But if the average day in the life of the first cultivators of Tehuacán was not governed by the clock, it certainly began early. Sometimes the men of the little human group went hunting; not unlike the modern African Bushmen, they could easily spend a whole week away from their families, pursuing a wounded animal until it finally collapsed from exhaustion. Before the hunters departed, they would have checked traps set the previous night for smaller animals, such as rabbits and mice. Remains have been found of quite complex snares; very likely the children were often sent to inspect them, as still happens in the region. When the men went out hunting, they left behind the women, who were not expected to walk long distances. Many other activities, however, involved the joint efforts of man, woman and child, who, unencumbered by school lessons, was a major addition to the labour force.

Very often the men also stayed at home, since other urgent tasks such as toolmaking, very time-consuming except for the simplest types, claimed their attention. In caves which were periodically lived in, the archaeologist can pinpoint the area used for fashioning tools and for cooking. Patches where the ground is more flattened indicate where the occupants slept. Cooking was obviously on the plain side, despite the early use of chile as spicing: very primitive ovens have been found, and also stone mortars which could be used to hold water. Remnants of mice, somewhat charred but complete with bones and fur, indicate that people were not averse to swallowing them whole, fur and all. There is even evidence of stomach infirmities caused by bacteria, under sanitary conditions that were far from ideal.

As agriculture progressed, a fully sedentary life developed and the first vestiges of permanent villages date from 3000 B.C. By this time cotton was being artificially grown and used for the weaving of fairly elaborate textiles. However, 70 per cent of the human diet was still derived from wild plants and smaller animals. The landscape differed greatly from that of the present time, when every hillside is covered with green maize during the wet season.

The life of these early Mexicans has been described in some detail because their achievements are basic. The archaeological record shows beyond any doubt that the first cultivators were able to 'go it alone', regardless of whether any refinements of civilization were later introduced from outside into the New World. Nor was the Mexicans' feat unique. After his work in Mexico, MacNeish in 1969 turned his attentions to Peru, where he found that early developments ran parallel, even if many of the plants and animals were different. An expedition of this kind, supported by an impressive range of experts from related fields, had never before been undertaken in Peru; to guarantee success, the choice of the right region was crucial. After an exhaustive search of promising areas, the Valley of Ayacucho, in the High Andes to the south-east of Lima, was selected. All the major requirements were present: not only were there many dry caves, but the valley was a likely candidate for incipient agriculture because of its astonishingly varied climate, with flora ranging from desert plants through spiny scrub to wet forest and finally to tundra in the highest altitudes. *

MacNeish's work, when recounted in terms of plants and animals discovered, together with their dates, may sound simple. But far from being a rule-of-thumb procedure, the task of unravelling such a remote past is skilled and exacting; in particular, a vast experience is needed to distinguish accurately between the various layers of human occupation that can so easily become confused. Moreover, in dry caves the dust is usually suffocating and the sun, when it enters, scorching.

In Ayacucho extremes of both heat and cold had to be endured. The archaeologists were living at a height of 2700 metres, but had to work at different altitudes, climbing as high as 4200 metres to reach certain sites. Often they would start off in their shirtsleeves, only to spend the day in the freezing climate of the higher levels. In the High Andes members of an archaeological expedition tend to be adopted by the local Indians and become to a remarkable extent part and parcel of their life. The visitors often end up with several godchildren; as adopted members of the family, they find that a portion of their time is claimed by colourful but long-drawn-out ceremonies, conducted by the hierarchy of village notables. As a revival from the past, sessions of ritual drinking may be involved, when all present are expected to swallow gargantuan quantities of liquor.

MacNeish also discovered in these caves the earliest known remains of Man in South America, over twenty thousand years old and dating from long before the dawn of agriculture. As in Mexico, Man's livelihood in Ayacucho had depended on the hunting of the larger surviving mammals, such as deer and llama. By about 5000 B.C., signs of the domestication of the guinea pig and llama appear, as well as uncertain hints of the practice of agriculture. Soon after this, indications of gourd and squash cultivation become more positive, followed by the growing of cotton, which was actually grown earlier than maize in Mexico.*

Coastal Peru, where early traces of cultivation are also visible, has an ecology totally different from that of the highlands. Sandy desert now dominates the scene, interspersed with fertile river valleys that recall in miniature the vegetation and colouring of the Nile Valley. It is no wonder that irrigation was quick to develop in such arid surroundings. Cotton appeared in coastal Peru at about the same moment as in the interior; however, before irrigation began, the inhabitants depended more for their living on collecting the bounteous supplies of shellfish, supplemented by gathering wild potato roots and hunting small animals. But as the climate changed, conditions deteriorated; large tracts of the Peruvian coastal plain had formerly been covered by fog meadows fed by sea mist and these provided pasture for animal grazing and moisture for plant life; as the climate grew even drier, plants and animals began to vanish.*

Throughout America, technical advances went hand in hand with more complex forms of religion. In Tehuacán fairly elaborate burials with bodies wrapped in nets and accompanied by fine basketware date from the very dawn of plant cultivation. Intricate ceremonies and beliefs were clearly involved, not always of a savoury nature. Skeletons of children have been located, one of which had been ritually burned; the head of another had been separated from the body and toasted, after the brain had been extracted. A third burial included a man, a woman and a child; the man had been intentionally burned, while the heads of the woman and child had been flattened, possibly also deliberately. Such finds suggest early forms of human sacrifice and may mark the beginnings of those rather savage rituals of ancient Mexico that still shock our susceptibilities, though their perpetrators would have been just as appalled by many of our modern actions and attitudes. Popular fable singles out the Aztecs as the main culprits, but their sway endured for a bare century before the Spanish Conquest, while the practice of human offerings is older than civilization itself.

The nature of the beliefs that underlay such burial practices defies speculation. Technical progress and social stratification were soon to lead to higher civilization, complete with priests and temple cults far removed from the mere magic of primitive peoples. In coastal Peru, the earliest temples appeared before 2000 B.C. when pottery was still in its infancy, although weaving was already a well-established craft. In this region, religious beliefs found their earliest artistic expression in textiles, and many of the skills for making embroidery and multi-coloured patterns are present in the pre-ceramic era.

Thor Heyerdahl's two *Ra* expeditions next deserve mention. Incongruous as such a statement may appear at first sight, they have bearing on this stage in the development of America. Heyerdahl's declared objective was to demonstrate that the Western Hemisphere could have been reached by a papyrus boat, such as he supposes the Egyptians used in pre-dynastic times. He is far from explicit as to *when* such a journey could have taken place, the mere feasibility of which he was intent to prove. In contrast to the case of the *Kon-Tiki*, Heyerdahl shuns in the case of *Ra* the adoption of a hard-and-fast theory and denies that he set out to prove that the Egyptians were responsible for bringing civilization to America.

Nevertheless, the book entitled *Ra* clearly implies that the Egyptians or other Near Eastern people *might* have reached America towards the end of the early agricultural period, say, 3000 B.C. Heyerdahl stresses that by 2700 B.C., if not before, the Egyptians were already building fine wooden boats, though he is the first to recognize that such vessels were made for cruising on the placid Nile, or at best for Mediterranean coastal commerce, never for ocean crossings.

Heyerdahl attaches great importance to the widespread use, not only in Ancient Egypt but also in modern Bolivia and Peru, of boats made of reeds – and thereby illustrates the pitfalls of drawing conclusions on the basis of a single trait shared by separate peoples. Whether on the Nile or on Lake Titicaca, reeds were the only available material for boat-building before wood was imported; people either had to make their boats in this way or do without. Necessity, therefore, simply became the mother of invention in different places, without any interchange of ideas. The author also mentions the use of reed boats in Mexico; but there also reeds were a key raw material in pre-Columbian times, and the Plumed Serpent god, of whose legend Heyerdahl makes great play, significantly possessed the calendric name of One Reed.

I shall later treat the possibility of links between Egypt and America in a broader context. Egyptians of later dynastic times may conceivably be dragged onto the American scene, but contacts between pre-dynastic or early dynastic Egypt and the contemporary American Indians remain a most doubtful proposition. Chronologies are now well established in both regions and they simply do not fit. Mexico and Peru achieved an early start in agriculture, but advanced thereafter at a slower pace. In contrast, at the beginning of the third millennium B.C., the Egyptians had already mounted the higher rungs of the ladder of civilization. The building of the Great Pyramids involved huge engineering works at a time when hardly a simple mound had yet been constructed in America. Before the Mexicans and Peruvians had produced their most primitive pottery, Egyptian craftsmen fashioned the superb furniture of Queen Hetepheres, the mother of Cheops, the Pyramid-building Pharaoh. The treasures on view in the Cairo Museum include the Queen's jewel chest, carrying chair, bed, headrest, armchairs, all with gold overlays and ebony inlays; each item was so made that it could be enclosed within a goldsheathed portable canopy.* Impressive as had been the rate of human progress in America, cave-dwellers who still devoured mice whole would have confronted the fastidious Egyptian visitor, coming from a land where furniture of a refinement unsurpassed in latter-day Egypt and indeed in the whole history of mankind was already being produced. Fifteen centuries were to pass before the Americans moulded their own higher civilizations, and such a time interval would have erased any cultural message that Egyptian visitors might have attempted to convey.

Towards the end of *Ra*, Heyerdahl writes of discussions that took place aboard his vessel; in rather disjointed form, the most familiar diffusionist arguments are put forward as to how civilization might or, indeed, 'must' have reached the New World from outside. The book does not deal directly with the birth of agriculture, but the author refers to the gourd and insists that it could not have floated independently across the Atlantic from its native Africa without being devoured by sharks or shipworms. Again problems of dating are involved. MacNeish has found gourds in America that are about nine thousand years old, and if Man was the carrier, he logically brought them before this date. Such a notion presupposes that human beings ploughed across the ocean four millennia before the first Egyptian pyramids were built. But agriculture in Egypt has only been traced back to about 5000 B.C., and it is hard to believe that people were busy transporting gourd seeds to America at a time when they had not yet learned to grow them on their own soil.

Cotton is also mentioned by Heyerdahl and is described as having been first used in the New World after the Indians of Mexico and Peru had 'crossed two useless types' to produce a cultivable strain. The statement pays little heed to discoveries already made by MacNeish of usable strains of wild cotton; these 'useless types', in whose evolution Man played no part, were almost certainly employed in the making of textiles; when Columbus reached the Island of Hispaniola, the natives were still spinning wild cotton.

The adaptability of America's flora differs greatly from that of its fauna, and is rather complicated. The animals could move on their own feet, and many were fitted to withstand the rigours of Beringia. The reverse is true of the plants: relatively few were resistant to extremes of cold and therefore those that were not native to America must have been brought thither over the ocean. If Man can be shown to have been the carrier, conclusive proof is offered of transoceanic links.

Plant migration has been the subject of much controversy, which still continues. Such discussions, however, usually proceed on a more dispassionate level than those involving lost tribes and buried cities, which arouse deep emotions. Because of a lack of archaeological data in certain regions, clear answers to simple questions are often lacking. The subject, moreover, is highly technical; competent experts are few and they often disagree. Nevertheless, though they arise from such diverse views, a few basic points stand out and may be summarized in concise form.

The Spaniards took great trouble to describe in detail the plant life which they found in America. The first discoverers were struck by the wide range of species quite unknown to them; at the same time, however, they encountered others that seemed familiar. The question therefore arises: how did Old World plants reach the New World and was Man responsible for their arrival in pre-Hispanic times?

It is easy to forget that the conquerors lacked their customary fruits, such as oranges, apples, bananas and even grapes, the absence of which prevented them from celebrating Mass, once supplies of Spanish wine were exhausted. But as a consolation, tomatoes, pineapples, peanuts, avocado pears, potatoes and tobacco would have been found in different parts of America, together with many other less known but excellent fruits, such as the native zapote. The Mexican painter Diego de Rivera was unmindful of this when, in his huge fresco in Cortés' palace in Cuernavaca, he depicted pitiful Indians groaning under the weight of loads of mangoes and goaded on by fearsome Spanish overseers; the mango is native to India, not Mexico. The staple peasant diet of the Old and New Worlds consisted of quite different items: in the New, maize, manioc (whose starchy and tuberous roots form the basic diet of many peoples of South America) and beans prevailed, as well as potatoes, which were confined to South America; in the Old, the people relied mainly upon rice and wheat. Any notion that maize existed in Asia in pre-Columbian times is on present evidence erroneous.

The oceans of the world form a fairly effective barrier to plant movement. Those whose reproduction depends upon tubers rather than seeds, such as potatoes, present special difficulties; birds can transport seeds in their crops but they can survive only a limited amount of moisture, drought or salinity. Before one considers the movement of individual plants, certain general aspects of the question need to be stressed. A given species can originate only once, but after its wild form has been created the seeds will spread far and wide; a number of different wild varieties of the same plant may then develop, some of which may later be domesticated by Man and engender not one but many cultivated forms, to be found in different places. These forms will all have derived indirectly from the original wild species, native to one place only;

equally, each different cultivated subspecies can have only one place of origin.

To translate the question into concrete terms: suppose that in Mexico a specific variety of cultivated maize is found. If this *same* domesticated variety is then found in Peru, but dated two thousand years later than in Mexico, this subspecies was presumably brought by Man to Peru. Cultivated maize, as we know it, cannot propagate itself by means of seeds transported by birds or other carrying agents.

Equally, supposing for argument's sake that the same subspecies of maize appears in China and is shown to have been grown there earlier than in Mexico, and not later as in the case of Peru; such evidence would suggest that it had been first brought (by Man) from China to Mexico and afterwards taken to Peru. Hence the significance of plant migrations becomes obvious. If the place of origin of specific varieties or subspecies can only be pinned down, then not mere suppositions but solid signs suggest that Man was the carrier. Unfortunately, with few exceptions, such clear-cut solutions are not yet available to the scientist.

The principles can be tested first and foremost with maize, which offers good evidence of continued contacts between North and South America. Like most of the plants in question, maize cannot be considered capable of surviving the frozen wastes of Siberia and Alaska; the plant is relatively easy to study, since archaeological sites have yielded vast quantities of corncobs, usually better preserved than other vegetables. It exists in a rich variety of forms, one of which, regarded as sacred by its cultivators, grew in Bolivia at an altitude of 12,700 feet, while many others are adapted to the steamy tropics.

Cultivated maize was first raised in Mexico about a thousand years earlier than in Peru, a shortish interval in those slow-moving times to allow for its transportation by human agency. However, a distinct subspecies appears much later in Peru, hybridized with an older Mexican variety known as Teosintle or 'Corn of the Gods'. The general presence of maize in Peru may be less significant, but the existence in that country of a cultivated subspecies, hybridized with the specifically Mexican 'Corn of the Gods' subspecies, is highly suggestive of Man's intervention in bringing this particular form of maize from North to South America. Admittedly, absolute proof is not forthcoming, as we cannot yet be fully sure that early cultivated varieties could not reproduce themselves without human assistance.*

These latest discoveries indicate continued contact between the Americas, but offer no support to traditional beliefs that maize came to Mexico from China or Indonesia through some form of maritime link. John Crawfurd, for instance, British Resident at the court of the Sultan of Java in 1808, convinced himself that maize had been cultivated there long before the discovery of America and concluded that its birthplace was Indonesia. The Reverend Leibbrandt claimed in 1882 that the plant was native to Amboyna, one of the Molucca Islands lying farther to the east. Other writers have maintained that maize, though native to America, was introduced into China in pre-Columbian times by the Arabs; large colonies of Persians and Arabs were founded in Canton in the mid-eighth century and persisted for a long time. The most common name for maize in India was *makhai*, meaning 'Mecca corn'.

The possibility that the plant spread westwards and was taken to China in pre-Columbian times has provoked long and complicated discussions. Magellan found what he termed in Italian *miglio* in the Philippines in 1521, but no one knows whether by this he really meant 'maize'. However, no cobs – so durable and easy to recognize – have been found among plant remains of early agriculturalists in China or elsewhere in Asia. Accordingly, if corn *was* introduced into China before Columbus, the transfer could not have occurred in prehistoric times but during a later period. However, when I deal with the possibility of ocean voyages during the apogee of America's higher civilizations, I shall quote Chinese records showing that maize was introduced not before but after the Spaniards discovered America, and then spread very quickly from province to province. The speed with which New World plants were adopted in the Old World after the Conquest and vice versa suggests that, if they had arrived earlier, the effect would have been dramatic enough to be amply recorded in Chinese and other writings.

At times the view has been advanced that cotton was brought from India to America by a sea route skirting Japan and the Aleutian Islands, but the known antiquity of the plant in America invalidates this theory, which also overlooks the marked differences between New World and Old World varieties. Equally, suggestions that coconuts were brought across the Pacific by Man, or that he transported gourds from their native

Africa, lead to negative conclusions. The notion is far-fetched that in Africa in 7000 B.C. boats were available of a kind that could have made transatlantic crossings. Moreover, if the gourd *was* imported, why was no other plant included in the package, such as coffee, which was later to thrive in the New World to such an extent that Brazil and Colombia came to be the world's largest exporters?

Cotton is of crucial significance and presents in reverse the problems of maize, since it was probably first domesticated in Peru rather than Mexico. Cultivated cotton is found in Peru dated at 3600 B.C. and in Mexico some four hundred years later; in both places textiles had been made from wild varieties before this time. The Peruvian and Mexican forms differ one from the other, but are nonetheless related, both possessing twenty-six chromosomes while Old World cottons have only thirteen. Sauer, a leading American botanist of his time who specialized in problems relating to this plant, suggested that an Asiatic thirteen-chromosome cotton had reached America, where it had combined with an original thirteen-chromosome American variety to produce a twenty-six-chromosome wild species, the ancestor of all future New World cultivated varieties.* Finally, the American rather than the Asian species was dispersed over most of the Pacific islands, where twenty-six-chromosome cottons prevail.

Sauer proposed that Asian cotton was brought to America by Man, but his views to that effect no longer command acceptance, and recent research suggests that Man did not intervene in the process.* Cotton, unlike maize or the sweet potato, can be introduced with relative ease by birds, since the seeds are small, hard, and extremely long-lived.* The presence of this plant in the New World cannot, therefore, conceivably be cited as proof of contact between America and Eurasia; birds offered an alternative means of transport for any ancestors of New World varieties, before Man had taken to the sea.

The stories of certain other plants relate to the problem of maritime links. The bottle gourd, already mentioned, is comparable to cotton since it also existed in somewhat different form in the Old World and is also not incapable of making the journey to America without human help. In the New World the gourd is ubiquitous in early archaeological sites, for it proved an admirable container before the invention of pottery. Until about 1962, the provenance of the plant was not surely known, but recent studies have shown that it is native to Africa and occurs there in virtually wild form.* Other studies have demonstrated that the gourd would be capable of floating from Africa to the Brazilian bulge, and still retain viable seeds, assuming that ocean currents were as they are today. And the possibilities of human contact with Africa in the era of the first known American gourds are so remote that it seems probable a few *did* float across (and somehow eluded Thor Heyerdahl's sharks). The only snag in this theory is that the gourd is not a strand plant. However, the act of one beachcomber who picked up a single specimen and cast it upon his rubbish heap would have sufficed for a debut to have been made in new surroundings. The gourd definitely could not have withstood the latitude of the Bering Strait and did not, therefore, accompany Man by this route. The same is true of another potential floater, the coconut, which grows in profusion on the seashore and is well suited to conveyance by water.

The avocado pear suggests links between North and South America, but not between America and Asia, where it did not exist in pre-Columbian times. Specimens have been found among the early cultivated plants of Mexico (the name derives from the Mexican Nahuatl language) but do not appear on the Peruvian coast till about 800 B.C. More probably, therefore, the avocado pear was brought from North to South America, possibly via the Caribbean Islands; no wild variety has been discovered in Peru. Moreover, even wild avocado pits would be rather large to be carried by any bird, or to adhere to an animal's fur. Man remains the more likely carrier.

The common bean (Spanish, *frijol*), a basic ingredient in the Mexican peasant diet, has lately become a candidate for transportation in the reverse direction from South America to North. L. Kaplan, the world's leading expert on this type of bean, reports that in the latest finds in Peru the *frijol* can be dated to nearly eight thousand years ago – or a thousand years before its first appearance in Mexico. The pineapple is another plant which apparently travelled from South to North America, and the peanut was also believed to belong to the same category. Recently, however, this New World plant has been reported occurring in China in a very ancient context. If this information were to be confirmed, its significance would be very considerable.

Leaving aside for the moment the case of the sweet potato – so intimately linked with the problem of later contacts between South America and Polynesia – the biological evidence of transoceanic contacts is mostly negative: in some cases American plants did not exist in the Old World; and, in others, species common to both hemispheres could have floated or been carried by birds. The study of plants does, however, suggest that some form of contact between North and South America was maintained in early agricultural times and led to the transfer of maize, the common bean and the avocado pear.

In general terms, plants native to Eurasia or Africa but also present in America appear in the New World at such an early date that human intervention in the process is almost precluded, since at that time Man's only vessel was a primitive dugout canoe. Furthermore, MacNeish has now proved that the first agriculture in the New World is earlier than anything so far known in China. Radiocarbon dates for early Chinese agriculture do not abound, but Ho Ping-Ti suggests that fully fledged plant cultivation started in the Honan Province of central China only between 4000 and 5000 B.C. Efforts were based originally on millet, not rice, and events moved more rapidly than in Mexico since the first Chinese cultivation was quickly followed by the domestication of the pig, the establishment of settled village life and the production of quite sophisticated pottery.*

A third agricultural revolution may have taken place in South-East Asia, quite apart from those of America and the Near East. South-East Asia is one of the regions of the world least known to the archaeologist, but fairly recent work in Thailand, near the Burmese border, has unearthed signs of plant cultivation as long ago as 13,000 B.C. and, in other Thai sites, of pottery dating from 9000 B.C., though this information is not yet fully confirmed.* However, in the absence of any proof that such inventions reached China at an early date, they hardly affect America. According to present evidence, agriculture came earlier in Mexico than in China, though no scientist has yet been bold enough to suggest that the Chinese learned the art of cultivation from the New World.

During the period of early agriculture, beginning in about 6000 B.C., concrete signs of long-distance contact are lacking, but clearcut evidence of links between America and Asia of a more localized nature exist. In a sense the Bering bridge never closed, and from about 5000 B.C. onwards the territories facing each other across the Strait were again in touch with each other. By that time the climate had become a little warmer than today and the ice-caps farther inland had receded. But the people who now crossed over the narrow stretch of water dividing the two continents were not southerners who had edged northwards in pursuit of game, but people who were already fully adapted to the rigours of arctic life, and who preferred to remain in those bleak expanses rather than to push onwards into temperate and tropical America.

Caucasian or European traits are more in evidence in the bones of these new immigrants than among the earlier settlers. Some of those Palaeo-Siberians who had been pushed by later Mongoloid arrivals into the north-eastern extremities of Asia had moved on across the Bering Strait. A few may have filtered down to more clement regions, and their presence would help to account for the aquiline features typical of certain North American tribes; the Haida Indians even possess a legend telling of ancestors who had come from the Aleutian Islands. The Eskimos, who came across the Strait later still, also have Caucasian blood. Though their appearance hardly suggests that of the average European, they are comparatively hirsute: many have walrus moustaches and a few wear beards. The rotund features may be an example of quick mutation, to adapt to an extreme climate for which round faces and bodies are more suitable than lank ones.

In marked contrast to yet remoter times, human remains of this post-glacial period abound in the lands where America and Asia almost touch. In the Chukchi Peninsula itself, traces exist of a population skilled in stone cutting; in that climate no plants were cultivated and people lived by hunting.* Seven thousand years ago tribes on both sides of the Strait had similar cultures, and specific traits flowed from west to east. Tiny blades and tools (microliths) were in common use in both continents. Implements of this kind had already spread far and wide throughout Eurasia in the pre-agricultural era; the fashion never caught on in America as a whole, only among these pre-Eskimos of the north-west, whose tools were, therefore, typical products of Asian rather than American technology.

Such artefacts were the outcome of a new influx across the Bering Strait, and the culture to which they belong is known in the New World as Dorset; early antecedents are found in the Aleutian Islands in about 5000 B.C. Eventually Dorset spread across the whole extent of northern Canada. About two thousand years later, the Denbigh culture appeared in Alaska; its small flint instruments, also recalling those of

Eurasia, abound on the earliest levels in many sites later occupied by Eskimos.

Recently in the Aleutians finds have also been made that throw light on post-Ice Age migrations from Asia to America. In the summer of 1974 a joint Soviet–U.S. expedition directed by A. P. Okhladnikov of Novosibirsk University and William S. Laughlin of the University of Connecticut worked in the Aleutian Islands. The preliminary report of this undertaking tells of remains of human occupation on the Island of Umnak dating from 6700 B.C., where blades were found that predate the microlithic period and greatly resemble those located by Soviet members of the team in Siberia and the Gobi Desert, while other stone tools recall those of Araya in Japan. These discoveries support the view that the Aleuts, the Eskimos and the inhabitants of the Kamchatka Peninsula in eastern Siberia all belong to the family of 'Bering Sea Mongoloids' that is in many ways distinct from the American Indian. Of those who crossed the Bering Sea, some became the ancestors of the Aleuts, and those who pushed even farther north were the pre-Eskimos.

The Eskimos themselves did not cross from Siberia until the beginning of the Christian era. Their direct relationship with Asia is indicated by their fairly frequent possession of blood group B, so rare among American Indians. Eskimo roots stretch deeply into the Old World, and among their earliest American remains such possessions as earth-covered houses with an entrance passage, skin boats and toboggans bear witness to Asian links hitherto unknown in the New World. Incidentally, the famous igloo dwellings do not exist in Alaska, and occur only in north-western Canada.

Every schoolboy knows of the Eskimos; with their fuzzy fur garments, their round igloos and round bodies, they have come to symbolize winter and all it stands for. In world history they stand out as the first people who, without firewood, could adapt themselves to such extremes of climate and even appear to enjoy them. Forests lie close to the shore in Siberia, but in Alaska the treeline runs far inland, and the Eskimos had to boil their food over stone or pottery lamps, using blubber as fuel. In Alaska such shortcomings belong to the past, and Eskimo life has changed notably. Even so, in Kotzebue, a village of two thousand five hundred inhabitants lying above the Arctic Circle, the people still live in wooden houses that are little more than shacks, though they may have a colour television set.

As a concrete case of contact between the two hemispheres, the Eskimos are important; to this day we have before our eyes a living example of a people with one foot in Eurasia and the other in America, since a few Eskimos still live in Siberia although the majority are fairly evenly divided among Alaska, Canada and Greenland, which has the largest population.

Connections with Asia persisted throughout the centuries, and Eskimo pottery of the fourteenth century A.D. follows in New World site traditions also present on the Siberian side. Eskimo origins are hard to trace, but affinities exist with older cultures of the Lake Baikal region, investigated decades ago by Soviet archaeologists. The remains of their immediate ancestors may one day be discovered somewhere in the vast area between Baikalia and Beringia, where they lived in the last centuries before the Christian era, dwelling amidst the rivers and lakes of this forest zone, whence they gradually moved to the shores of the Arctic and Bering Seas. The migrants' way of life remained primitive, but in the Bering Strait region their culture probably took new shape, once they encountered better conditions and more abundant food, including walrus, seals, caribou, birds and fish; now ideally adapted to life in the Arctic, they spread over the Strait and at the time of the Vikings reached as far as Greenland.

The first part of this chapter focused on the beginnings of New World agriculture and the possibility that the Old World lent a hand in the achievement was discounted. But another phenomenon still requires mention – the emergence of pottery in America after a much longer time-lag than occurred between the invention of agriculture and the appearance of ceramics in the Near East. The importance of clay vessels in the life of Man is appreciated when one imagines the problems of a kitchen provided with no kind of container except for gourds and an occasional skull. Pottery, like agriculture, is a precondition of civilization, and ceramic design is an art as well as a craft. However rudimentary the efforts of the first American potters, they were the forerunners of the splendid painted wares of coastal Peru, or the Cholula plates from which the Emperor Moctezuma ate fastidiously.

Writers on prehistoric ocean travel often begin their story at an intermediate stage on the road to artistic perfection. Spurning the study of unprepossessing potsherds, they prefer to compare later and more glamorous trophies such as the carved jade of Mexico and China. But one serious effort has been made to start at the beginning and to prove that the potter's art was not invented in the New World but introduced from Japan; this attempt has provoked keen controversy among professional anthropologists of many nations.

In 1956, at Valdivia, a coastal site in south-western Ecuador, a new type of pottery was discovered by Emilio Estrada, an Ecuadorian businessman turned archaeologist, who during the later years of his life made a great contribution to our knowledge of his country's ancient past. Together with two outstanding anthropologists, Betty J. Meggers and Clifford Evans, Estrada evolved a theory as to the origins of this Valdivia ware, which had proved to be of great antiquity since the oldest radiocarbon date gave a figure of from 2800 to 3200 B.C. — many centuries before the time of any other ceramics then known in America.

Its discoverers were excited not only by Valdivia's age but by its stylistic resemblance to the Middle Jomon period of Japan, which is approximately contemporary. Concise arguments were advanced to link the two cultures, ranging from general similarities of design to specific traits present only in Ecuador and Japan, such as a unique form of vessel rim and a peculiar kind of stone neck rest. Illustrations were also published of similar clay model houses deriving from the two centres. In fact the neck rests and model houses belong to a much later period than the first pottery, but resemblances to Japanese work are still in evidence.

Backed by this data, Betty Meggers made a rather ambitious historical reconstruction: she suggested that, in about 3000 B.C., a boatload of Japanese fishermen were swept out to sea from the shelter of a bay in the Island of Kyushu and eventually reached the coast of Ecuador, after skirting north-eastern Siberia and the Aleutian Islands, but leaving Hawaii well to their south. As Heyerdahl has often stressed, this great circle route is the shortest way from Asia to Ecuador and Peru; most maps merely create the illusion that such a journey is longer than a voyage cutting straight across the mid-Pacific.

In Ecuador, according to Betty Meggers, these involuntary mariners met small groups living by fishing and shellfish gathering, supplemented by a little plant cultivation: in other words people not unlike themselves, possessing comparable technical skills. The Ecuadorians differed from their Japanese visitors in one respect, however: they still lacked pottery. The newcomers supposedly taught them this craft, which then spread by land and sea northwards to Colombia and southwards to Peru.

So far so good; but this theory bristles with snags. Jomon pottery may indeed look very like Valdivia, but the latter is also closely related to a number of other American wares. French archaeologist Antoinette Nelken, who has worked closely with MacNeish, saw sherds from the Brazilian jungle that recall Valdivia more vividly than do the Jomon designs, while MacNeish himself sees striking parallels between Valdivia and the earliest pottery of the United States, which comes from Georgia.

Marked differences as well as similarities may be noted between these Ecuadorian and Japanese specimens.* In fact certain Valdivia objects do not fit into the Jomon pattern at all: what, for instance, is the resemblance between the Valdivia figurines in the Quito Museum and those of Asia? And to judge by available photographs, similarities between Ecuadorian and Japanese house models are far from convincing. To stylistic objections, others yet more emphatic may be added: Valdivia is no longer the oldest known Ecuadorian pottery; on the same site another type has been found, called San Pedro, that is even older and bears no relationship whatsoever to Japanese Jomon. Moreover, the dating of Valdivia has been questioned: the German archaeologist, Henning Bischof, doubts whether the single radiocarbon date of 3200 B.C. is correct and suggests that the Valdivia style really originated as much as a thousand years later. And even if the early figure of 3200 B.C. were right, another South American pottery, from Puerto Hormiga in Colombia, has now been dated to a further five hundred years before this. Accordingly, since the oldest wares now known in Colombia and Ecuador have no Jomon affinities, it becomes hard to maintain that the art of pottery-making was imported from Japan.*

Studied from the purely Japanese angle – too seldom taken into account – the theory becomes even less tenable. The original Middle Jomon dates, coinciding with Valdivia, were taken from sites on Honshu, not from the more south-westerly Island of Kyushu, the supposed point of departure for those fishermen who ended up in Ecuador. Furthermore, the Japanese have now revised their dating system and reduced the estimated age of Middle Jomon by about five hundred years. All but one of the Kyushu sites in question are situated on the west side of the island, from whence any boat swept out to sea would normally be borne not south-eastwards, but westwards towards Korea. At all events, signs of deep-sea fishing at this early date are not in evidence, and fishing gear is conspicuous by its absence in Kyushu sites; seafood was probably collected in sheltered bays and shallow waters.* Admittedly oars have been found, which demonstrate the use of some kind of dugout canoe – hardly the ideal vessel for a transpacific voyage.

If a single canoe, as suggested, *had* skirted along the arctic shores of the North Pacific, why on earth did it end up in Ecuador? During the coast-hugging journey through those forbidding latitudes, land would inevitably be sighted and the involuntary mariners would have ended their ordeal at the first opportunity on the western seaboard of the United States, if not before, instead of prolonging their agonies by drifting onwards for no obvious reason to distant Ecuador; between North and South America winds and currents are much more treacherous than in the North Pacific.

Many examples can indeed be cited of modern oceanic crossings in tiny craft. Among these, the nearest approach to a canoe seems to be a sailless propelled craft, 17 feet in length, which crossed from New York to the Scilly Isles in 55 days, manned only by two men. Another solo voyage was made in a converted Indian dugout canoe, 30 feet long, from Vancouver to Cook Island, covering some 5500 miles in 56 days.* Eric de Bisshop, the well-known navigator, travelled from Hawaii to Cannes in 264 days in a double canoe (unlikely to have existed in early Japan). Among the boldest of marine adventurers was Dr Alain Bombard, who, to prove the premise of his doctoral thesis that it is possible to remain alive on the products of the sea alone, rode an inflatable rubber liferaft from Casablanca to Barbados; however, he did use some kind of sail. Last but not least, the Eskimo kayak preserved in the Museum of Aberdeen deserves mention, since it beached on the Scottish shore in the seventeenth century, having apparently been paddled across from Greenland.

To be sure, the ocean held fewer terrors for these modern voyagers, for they were guided by instruments, knew where they were going and what they must do to stay alive. If a Japanese canoe *had* arrived in Ecuador its crews' experiences would have been much more harrowing. Moreover, a tiny fishing boat is most unlikely to carry skilled potters, let alone pottery of different designs that can be copied. The reactions of primitive Man to complete strangers were usually ferocious, and the

Japanese crew would have been very lucky indeed to have survived their landing at all.

A few exhausted fishermen are improbable candidates for the distinction of launching a technical revolution in a new continent. More probably the castaways would have gone native and adapted themselves, if they survived, to local customs in their new surroundings. This occurred in the documented case of the Spaniards Gonzalo Guerrero and Jerónimo de Aguilar, who were marooned on the Mexican coast and found by Cortés when he first arrived there. In contrast to these shipwrecked Spaniards, a group of 17 Negroes who were stranded upon the Esmeraldas coast of Ecuador in the seventeenth century came to dominate the local population for a generation. But this case is hardly parallel, for their number far exceeded the capacity of a primitive Japanese canoe, and superior arms would have helped them to become masters of the situation.

In short, the problem differed where prehistoric travel across the ocean, as opposed to mere local contacts, was concerned. And new chapters of history cannot be written on the sole basis of parallels between potsherds; these do not prove the point since startling similarities may arise when two totally unrelated peoples hit upon like elements of design; the example has already been cited of the near-identical stirrup-spout jars from ancient Peru and contemporary Africa.

The Valdivia controversy merits attention because it posits early links across the oceans achieved by people who had not yet become city-dwellers. Moreover, the theory has been backed by noted anthropologists, who present their case soberly and seriously; the arguments, therefore, fulfil certain prerequisites without which such propositions become meaningless. Not merely one trait, but a whole complex is listed as common to the two cultures: Jomon and Valdivia at least belong to the same millennium and had attained a comparable degree of technical skill. And yet the whole idea is beset with uncertainty, unless its sponsors can show more convincingly just how Japanese fishermen could have reached Ecuador. And another doubt lingers in this and many other instances. Even supposing this tiny band had landed, could their arrival have brought about the results that Meggers envisages? One persists in doubting that her canoe could have reached Ecuador at all, much less changed the course of history.

*

On the basis of available evidence, New World pottery, like its agriculture, developed independently. And alongside the art of making ceramics, other techniques that formed part and parcel of the gradual metamorphosis of the nomad hunter into the urban dweller were evolved. Textiles came relatively early in the New World's inventive sequence, and primitive examples of this art predate the period when Man abandoned his caves and established the first villages. Simple forms of cotton clothing were worn in Peru before the plant was domesticated, and some of the more complex techniques for making embroidery were elaborated before the invention of pottery; these early textile designs are basic to the development of art in Peru.

In Mexico basketware long preceded the production of textiles. In this field North America followed close on the heels of its southern neighbour, and baskets contemporary with early Mexican specimens were being produced in the south-west of the United States. The first signs of the so-called Desert Tradition appear as the big mammals became extinct. This culture can be traced in south-eastern Arizona to before 6000 B.C. The early remains belonged to the precursors of the great desert cultures that flourished in the region over the centuries, of which the ultimate successor, the Pueblo, built those imposing ruins that can still be seen today. Agriculture had also spread quickly from Mexico to the United States: cultivated corncobs in Bat Cave, New Mexico, date from *circa* 4000 B.C. The early southerners left behind them a rich variety of baskets, sandals, mats and netting; although no permanent houses have been found, pits were dug and lined with stones for use as hearths.*

Metalworking began in North America much earlier than anywhere else in the New World. The Old Copper Culture, centred upon Minnesota and Wisconsin, is a remarkable phenomenon: here the oldest metal artefacts of the New World have been found, dated to about 4000 B.C. The range of copper implements includes knives, chisels, axes and harpoon-heads derived from prototypes made of stone. For those ancient coppersmiths, their material differed from flint mainly because it did not require to be chipped or ground but had merely to be beaten, and their skills do not, therefore, relate directly to the development of more complex metallurgy in South America. The 'native' copper which was used occurs in nature as a relatively pure metal and did not have to be extracted from the ore by smelting.* These pioneers of metalworking continued to exercise their craft for about two millennia, or until the time when the scene shifted to Georgia, where as noted the earliest North American pottery is found.

This chapter has been devoted to the possibilities of transoceanic links during the key period that opens with the first American agriculture and closes with the introduction of pottery, prior to the rise of the great civilizations. It was a time marked by continued human contacts across the Bering Strait and the establishment of the proto-Eskimo cultures. The patterns of earlier times persisted and the ties that bound the north-west tip of America to Asia survived long after the disappearance of the great ice-caps. Certain of these Asiatic influences seeped southwards, and localized moves across the Strait are reflected in North American pottery, typified by cordmarking, found both near Lake Baikal in Siberia and in the American Woodland culture. But although Siberian and North American pottery designs reveal parallels, those between the crafts of quite separate regions of the two Americas are far more striking, even if they cannot always be traced directly from one area to the next. The early or formative cultures of North and South America have so much that is similar that they appear to rest on common foundations.

Therefore between 6000 and 3000 B.C., during the period when first agriculture and then pottery was developed, it can be assumed that the peoples of North and South America were not entirely separated, although there was a time when all links with Asia were severed apart from the incursions of proto-Eskimos. Certain ceramics of south-eastern Mexico are virtually identical to pottery from Tumaco on the Caribbean coast of Colombia, where figurines are also found that so resemble those of a Mexican deity known as the 'Old God' that they seem to have been imported. And yet no signs of this particular style have been identified in the intermediate lands, though their absence may be due to the yawning gaps in the available data. People often imagine that archaeologists have explored America from tip to toe and that scarcely an ancient stone remains to be upturned. It is too seldom understood that most of the work has been confined to Mexico and Peru; notwithstanding rare but notable exceptions, the intervening territories in Central and South America are virgin soil. The goldwork seen in the museums and private collections of Colombia and Costa Rica mostly derives, not from official digs, but from the efforts of grave-robbers, who tear these treasures out of their context and destroy for ever the archaeological evidence in the process. In many cases the cultures that produced the gold cannot be properly dated for lack of scientific information.

The question remains open as to whether agriculture was invented twice in the New World or simply spread from the northern continent to the south, where it appears very slightly later and then develops on parallel lines. The suggestion has been made that South America was typically a 'non-centre' with regard to the emergence of plant cultivation − in contrast to Mexico, the Near East, and probably Thailand.*

Much of what has been written on transoceanic contact really hinges on the relationship between the Americas. If the two continents were indeed separate entities, then Asiatic connections with, say, Peru would have nothing at all to do with ties between Asia and Mexico. Any interconnection between the two halves of the New World is, therefore, basic to the relationship between the Americas and other ancient civilizations beyond the seas.

In treating this problem, the same key question must never be overlooked: if North and South America continued to enjoy certain links, just how did people travel from the one landmass to the other and return? The matter has been overcomplicated by comparing the problems facing the voyager between North and South America with those of moving from Eurasia to America via the Bering Strait. At first sight it may seem simpler to paddle across a narrow stretch of the Bering Sea than to make for South America, either by braving the ocean or by struggling through the dense Darien jungle, over whose marshy expanse a motor road is only now being built, to fill the last gap in the Pan-American Highway. But this analogy is false. Eurasia is not mainly divided from the New World − as I have insisted − by a stretch of water scarcely wider than the English Channel; the real barrier is the endless expanse of chilling tundra on either side of the Bering Strait, and any alternative route involves crossing the boundless ocean.

Where the Americas are concerned, Man could proceed from one half to the other without entering a boat. The Darien region may not be the ideal gateway to a new territory, but its limited expanse is today passable under certain conditions and is, moreover, still inhabited by the Cuna and Choco Indians; drawing fish from its rivers, wild pig and monkey from its jungle, and sugar cane from small clearings, they have changed little since Balboa first stood upon a peak in Darien.

Very recently a British team of explorers thrust from north to south through the endless tangle of marsh, morass and jungle; they describe the forbidding terrain they encountered:

> Buckled by the massive roots of even more massive trees, eroded by torrential rains, folded and creased by a million years of wear and tear, cluttered with vines and thorn trees, guarded by hornets and ants, it offered no easy access even to horses; to anything larger it looked like nature's version of barbed wire entanglements, a tank-trap and blitzed Berlin combined.*

The author, Russell Braddon, significantly stresses the hazards that face horses and 'anything larger', i.e. motor vehicles. But his account amply demonstrates that many obstacles vanish if the crossing is made on foot, especially in the annual dry season which lasts for about one hundred days. During these months people from Panama City, members of the 'Four Wheel Club', drive out on weekends and make a routine trip that covers about a third of the distance between Panama City and Baranquillita, at the Colombian end of the gap. Beyond this point, in areas inaccessible to weekenders, the going gets tougher. But provided the traveller is not burdened by a heavy jeep, much of the remaining trek can be made by canoe. The Choco Indians still hollow out their piraguas from tree trunks felled on the hillside and bring them down to the abundant streams; when necessary these light craft can easily be dragged from one rivulet to the next. The last part of the Darien Gap is different, consisting of the watery Arato Swamp, beyond the border dividing Panama from Colombia; but this stretch of the journey can be negotiated by boat.

At the very beginning of their undertaking, the British expedition met another party composed of two New Zealanders and one Englishman. The three pioneers had just crossed the Isthmus, equipped solely with a bag of sugar, a bag of rice, some machete knives, a compass and – rather oddly – bicycles. Such conditions, so hard on the motor vehicle, were no insuperable obstacle to Ancient Man, who could quite well have used this route had he wanted to. After all, some of his descendants still live there happily today.

*

Besides, feasible alternatives to the jungle route exist. The issue is often confused by the notion that Man had *either* to face the inland journey *or* travel by the open sea, instead of following the coast. A direct voyage from, say, Ecuador to Guatemala is not entirely out of the question, but it would have been highly hazardous as well as unnecessary. Anthropologists have been at pains to explain that early pioneers could sail from La Victoria in Guatemala in December, and then take advantage of trade winds and currents running in a south-easterly direction. But all agree that the Gulf of Panama, on which Panama City now stands, presented special dangers to primitive craft and that navigators could not, therefore, have hugged the Panamanian shore at this point, but would have braved the open sea between the Azuero Peninsula (in the northern part of the Panamanian Republic) and the tip of Ecuador. Return travellers from Ecuador would equally have tended to make straight for the Peninsula, impelled by westerly winds that prevail across the Gulf of Panama in September. But then comes the most difficult part of the journey since beyond the Peninsula flows the Mexican Current, which could simply drive a boat back southwards to its point of departure. Alternatively, mariners could have hugged the shore between Azuero and Guatemala, taking advantage by day of the westerly breezes that blow in November and making for safe harbours at night.*

Gene Savoy, President of the American Explorers Club and an intrepid adventurer on land and sea, actually set out on a raft of a type used in pre-Columbian Peru in an attempt to prove that the northward journey to Mexico was feasible. But Savoy's efforts to cross these treacherous waters and negotiate such changeable winds and currents ended in failure, and his account of the journey underscores the perils of this voyage. The raft, like the *Ra*, was built of reeds and based on vessels often illustrated in Peruvian pottery dating from the early centuries of our era. Savoy decided to stay near the shore to avoid another hazard – the danger of being swept westwards towards Asia. He set forth from a point on the coast of Peru some distance to the north of Lima, but soon fell into the clutches of the cold Peruvian current. The raft began to fall apart and was towed into the harbour of Chicáma, not so far from the place of departure. Savoy took to the water again and continued to steer near to the shore, to avoid being carried off by the same current towards the Galapagos Islands. From south Ecuador onwards the voyage was

77

more or less plain sailing until a heavy storm blew up off the coast of Colombia and the sail was lost. For seven days Savoy and his crew drifted, pounded by the relentless elements, ignorant of their whereabouts; by this time the raft had been reduced to a shambles. Eventually land was sighted; Savoy thought he had already crossed the Gulf of Panama, but in reality he had merely made an enormous loop out into the Pacific and back again, and he reached Colombia more or less at the point he had attained when the storm hit him. Another tempest now put an abrupt end to their struggles on the rocks and reefs off Cabo Marzo, near the Panamanian border.

Like all modern navigators, Savoy was well provided with instruments: he lists his equipment, which included sextant, magnetic compass, barometer, chronometer, anemometer, together with patent log, charts, light list, tidal and current tables.* But the insuperable obstacles encountered – notwithstanding such modern aids to navigation – show that at the best of times such an expedition is fraught with hazards, probably greater even than those of a drift from Peru across the Pacific, propelled by currents usually running from east to west. But while regular sea travel between Mexico and Ecuador, therefore, becomes a most doubtful proposition, an *occasional* voyage from Ecuador to Guatemala or Mexico remains a possibility: the London *Times* of 9 July 1973 carries a report of a British couple, Mr and Mrs Bailey, who passed through the Panama Canal in a nine-ton yacht, heading for the Galapagos Islands. Near its destination, the yacht was hit by a whale and the mast was lost. The couple then drifted in an open liferaft for 117 days, until finally picked up off the coast of Guatemala. During the voyage, safety pins were used to catch fish, including six sharks (presumably baby ones). On being rescued, the Baileys could at first only swallow eggs and milk and were too weak to climb out of their liferaft. If such an ordeal proves that the voyage is physically possible, it also serves to illustrate its dangers and shows that people who make unintentional ocean crossings are not always fighting fit when when they arrive at the other side.

Ancient Man surely had no need to face a voyage governed by such unpredictable winds and currents; unlike ourselves, he was seldom in a hurry. The feasibility of proceeding from North to South America, or vice versa, not by struggling against giant waves in a tiny craft, but by merely plodding along the shore is often overlooked. Southbound travellers can perfectly well step along the beach most of the way from Mexico down through Guatemala, Nicaragua, Costa Rica and Panama and on to South America. Any modern map will show the existence of a coastal plain on the Pacific side, quite broad in most places. In exceptional cases, short stretches of the way might be barred by mountains reaching down to the shore; at such points a way can usually be found over rocky headlands or promontories, if it is not possible to walk round them by wading through the water. As an alternative to a continuous plod along the coastline, short cuts could be effected by canoe; such daytime sea trips, followed by a night on shore, hold no terrors remotely comparable to the ordeal of embarking on a journey straight across the ocean. Weather permitting, fishermen or even tourists daily set out from certain beaches; on stormy days they naturally stay at home.

The maze of inland waterways and interconnecting lagoons offers a third method of north–south travel; rather farther to the north, for instance, a stretch of 160 miles from Mazatlan to San Blaz on the Mexican Pacific coast can be negotiated during the rainy season by canoe, taking advantage of the innumerable rivulets that join one lagoon to another. Equally, Indians today proceed by canoe northwards up the coast of Colombia; they too make use of the waterways that intersect the mangrove swamps along that shore, travelling only by day. From Panama onwards, the journey to Guatemala and Mexico, whether inland or along the shore, presents no insuperable problems.

There is no need, therefore, to risk an open sea route between North and South America, since less adventurous if slower alternatives exist. This viewpoint may be questioned on the grounds that few signs of occupation suggesting the passage of ancient Man have been found along the coast between Ecuador and Guatemala. But attention has already been drawn to the tendency for a given style to crop up in two places that are remote from one another, while the archaeologist can find no evidence of similar patterns in intermediate areas. In this instance, the appearance of certain traits in Guatemala and Mexico that also occur in Ecuador, but not in the intervening territory, has inspired belief in direct sea travel between the two regions. The argument is not valid because the trait most often cited is the presence in western Guatemala and Mexico of shaft tombs, very similar to those found in Ecuador and Peru; for a few shaft tombs have also been found on the

Pacific side of Honduras and Panama, and therefore this characteristic *can* be traced through the land route leading from north to south.

Moreover, the archaeological record of the Pacific coastline is very incomplete, particularly where mangrove swamps occur. The whole shore is one of the most unstable regions of the world and would have been rocked by countless volcanic upheavals in the course of several millennia; the sea is apt to change its level and would have blotted out many traces of human occupation if they had not already been swept away by hurricanes. A beachcombing route would not be viable unless the travellers could also find food, but in these tropical latitudes ample scope exists for plant and fruit gathering all the year round; the coast abounds in shellfish, and to this day certain less frequented parts of Mexico's Pacific coast offer excellent oysters and clams to be gathered up by the casual visitor.

CHAPTER FOUR

AMERICA'S FIRST CAPITALISTS

HERNÁN CORTÉS entered Tenochtitlán, the capital of Aztec Mexico, in A.D. 1519. The small band of conquerors was overcome by the grandeur of the imperial city, without equal in mediaeval Europe. Long afterwards, as an old man, Bernal Díaz del Castillo recalled the scene that the Spaniards beheld as they reached Tenochtitlán, ringed by its constellation of lakeside cities:

> When we saw so many cities and villages built both on the water and on dry land, and this straight, level causeway, we could not restrain our admiration. It was like the enchantments in the book of Amadis, because of the high towers, *cués* [temples] and other buildings, all of masonry, which rose from the water. Some of our soldiers asked if what we saw was not a dream.*

Both Cortés and Díaz describe in detail the imposing architecture of the city and its teeming markets and dwell on the Sardanapalian splendour of Moctezuma II's court. Needless to say, the Inca emperor in Cuzco lived in comparable style, and the bounds of his realm were even wider. These great empires witnessed the sunset of Indian rule and the closing of a chapter in world history. But we must now look to the dawn of American civilization, when the first cities and palaces were built, and ask how it came into being. Was the first flame kindled by a torch borne across the sea, or was it fired by native genius alone?

The 'dawn of civilization' – like the 'Neolithic Revolution' – is an overworked expression. But the metaphor of the rising sun is apt; for both in the Old World and later in the New, the prehistorian detects the same prolonged burst of activity. The birth of the great civilizations can be compared to the way in which the Sun's round red disk rises from the tropical sea or the Egyptian desert to dispel the surrounding obscurity. In Mexico the east, the land of Quetzalcóatl, inventor of human culture, was known as the 'Land of the Black and the Red', symbolizing the contrasting colours of the dawn.

As already noted, earlier writers insisted that the rise of civilization was too momentous an event to be repeated more than once in human history. But whether in the Old World or the New, the marvel was not achieved in a flash; in places where the first great American cultures flourished, Olmec and Chavín, traces appear of previous human settlement and progress. Certain antecedents therefore exist, though the life of former dwellers in those chosen regions was more bucolic and had changed only slowly.

Four thousand years before the Olmecs, Man began to cultivate crops. Then he emerged from his caves and began to live in villages, subject to certain laws and taboos; he gradually learned to cultivate his land, weave his textiles, mould his pottery and domesticate such animals as were suitable. A comparable way of living continues to this day in the remoter parts of America; whether in the jungles of Brazil or the highlands of Bolivia, people can still be found who elect their elders and obey their dictates, barely aware that they are citizens of a modern state. Such communities weave their own cloth, make their own pots and pans, and might be living in pre-Columbian times, save for the occasional reminder of the outside world in the form of a Coca-Cola bottle or a petrol can.

But such a level of existence, whether today or long ago, cannot remotely be termed 'higher civilization' – an expression requiring some definition. For the Greeks, civilization was equated with city-dwelling and the people who had no cities were therefore barbarians. Among the Aztecs the same distinction happened to be drawn between the man of culture and the barbarian. (I say this at the risk of being taken as pretending that the Aztecs came from Athens!) Fray Bernardino de Sahagún's native Mexican informers described certain peoples who were formerly barbarians, but who had since become civilized: 'These three [tribes] were peaceful; the way of life which corresponded to them, civilized. They had rulers, they had noblemen; and they were city dwellers, they were clothed, they were clever.'*

Sahagún associates civilized life in Mexico not only with residence in a city, but also with the possession of kings and nobles. Many surviving examples of Olmec and Chavín sculpture portray the earliest members of this ruling hierarchy; whether priests or rulers, their proud bearing and exotic finery make them tower above their companions. So things were at the beginning, and so they remained till the end; Moctezuma II, when he greeted Cortés from beneath a canopy of rich green feathers, worked with gold and silver, pearls and precious stones, was the ultimate heir of these early kings. Whatever cultural values Ancient America had imported from across the ocean, democracy was not included.

For thousands of years after the birth of agriculture, people continued to live in scattered villages where the head man was little more than a big fish in a tiny pond, corresponding perhaps to the mayor of a small modern community; in dress and manner he differed little from his fellow beings. Society was comparatively egalitarian and continues to be so in those surviving Indian villages where older patterns of life prevail and pre-Columbian beliefs still permeate the practice of religion.

In the early part of the second millennium B.C., from the midst of such rustic settlements arose the first ceremonial centres, where pyramids and palaces dominated broad plazas tiled with mosaics. Where formerly village chiefs ruled, kings and courtiers now hold sway; in place of cottage crafts delicate sculpture abounds. Such creativity could scarcely draw its inspiration from simple nature worship, served by shamans; instead of mere animism, a gaudy pantheon of gods emerges and elaborate rites are conducted by scores of priests, who become Man's first intelligentsia, learn to observe the stars, study the mysteries of time and space, and declare themselves sole guardians of the esoteric knowledge needed to interpret the deities' commands.

The social fabric of human existence had been altered beyond recognition, even if the new rulers were in some respects tribal chiefs writ large and dressed expensively. The rise of higher civilization must be viewed in a worldwide context and, wherever it appeared, whether on the banks of the Indus or the shores of Peru, common features are present. Gordon Childe, father of modern studies in the growth of civilizations, saw these changes as produced mainly by material forces, culminating in what he termed the 'Urban Revolution'. But 'urban' is a rather modern concept, not always applicable to the ancient world. The early Mesopotamians built cities, but in America, and even in Egypt, archaeology first reveals royal or ceremonial centres rather than towns.

Childe regards as a prelude to progress the increased food supply that resulted from the adoption of farming. As a consequence, the average family was able to grow more than it consumed and for the first time Man achieved a production surplus, essential to the amassing of wealth. In those days no one gave a thought to redistributing such newfound riches, and they inevitably ended up in the hands of the dominant class. The Marxists may be right in viewing this change as the beginning of human exploitation, for the simpler villages of former times lacked any surplus value worth exploiting. Accordingly, by implication, the Olmecs and the people of Chavín were America's first capitalists. Historians may disagree as to whether civilization could have been founded on any other basis, and whether a more egalitarian society could have bequeathed such a rich artistic legacy. For the creation of surplus production begat not only a ruling hierarchy, but also a specialist class of craftsmen and artists dedicated to the satisfaction of their foibles.

Certain basic tenets of Childe may nowadays enjoy fairly general acceptance. However, Jacquetta Hawkes, among others, denies that the miracle of civilization owes its sole origin to a build-up of economic forces, which would favour the growth of mere market towns rather than glittering cities. She objects to Childe's notion of the 'inevitability' of this materialist view of early human history. Such developments were surely not 'inevitable', and civilization, when taken as nothing but a sum of material factors, is like a suit of armour without its knight; if economically inevitable, it would not have been confined to a few centres, and might also have arisen in the temperate and well-watered plains of the eastern United States. On the contrary, this region lagged behind others such as the arid south-west.

Efforts at surplus accumulation were devoted not to humdrum necessities but, in the words of Jacquetta Hawkes, to the 'wildest fantasies', such as the moving of millions of tons of stone by the Egyptians, or equivalent quantities of earth by the Olmecs. Overemphasis on economic factors ignores the spiritual urges latent within the human psyche. Creative forces surged up from the unconscious and invaded the conscious mind: 'Emotions of fear, love and hate, of wonder at the tremendous features of the outer world, could release the archetypal invaders. Their expression then became a matter of compulsion rather than of purpose.'*

So the beginning of civilization presents two faces, the material and the psychic; in the beginning was the word, as well as the food surplus. Both art and economics are involved and, notwithstanding a thriving commerce, spiritual motives probably prevailed over the temporal in the early cultures of America. The first of these, Olmec and Chavín, display a deep dedication to the same jaguar or feline deity that had sprung from the surrounding jungle.

If visitors from across the sea had played a major part in the process, the results should be evident in this first flowering of Ancient American genius – if not before; had the Old World only intervened when New World cultures were already in full bloom, the effects would have been merely marginal. In the search for outside influences, therefore, the precise manner in which Olmec and Chavin made their debut is of the utmost significance and needs to be examined more closely.

Many centuries before the appearance of the Chavín culture, a settled pattern of life prevailed in certain areas of Peru. By 2000 B.C. the earliest temples appear on the coast. Unlike many later Peruvian cultures, Chavín spread its tentacles far and wide, and Chavinoid influences are detectable throughout the coastal region. However, the finest remains, from which the name derives, are located in Chavín de Huántar, lying inland about two hundred and fifty miles north-east of Lima. In this place, the principal monument is called the Castillo, or Castle; it is built of stone masonry and the interior is intersected by many passages. The whole structure is so complex as to be unique in its time in the New World.

In Chavin de Huántar many low-relief figures were carved on stelae or slabs forming part of the main buildings; strange human heads, cut in the round, are inserted into the walls of the Castillo. Sculpture was the principal but not the only artistic medium. Mexico was to remain in the Stone Age for a further two millennia, but the people of Chavín developed the goldsmiths' art to a high degree of perfection; the techniques of annealing and soldering were mastered, and examples survive of the finest jewellery. Their pottery was notable for its variety and beauty, and norms were established that the potters of later Peruvian cultures still respected.

When Chavín was first discovered, nobody believed that it was the oldest civilization of Peru, so advanced were its art forms. But the earliest radiocarbon dates now go back to 1600 B.C.; the initial period, before Chavín reached its full efflorescence, lasted for nearly eight hundred years, refuting the widely-held assumption that higher civilization the world over was a flower that blossomed overnight; the developmen may have been spectacular, but not always rapid.

Indisputably the Chavín style was the embodiment of a great religious cult, and its presence throughout Peru shows that such new beliefs were widespread. Graven on slabs and stelae ferocious animals abound: jaguars, serpents, hawks and condors. As in the ancient art of many lands, the human and animal elements are confused, and men as well as beasts display serpent or jaguar fangs. Composite forms are frequent, combining feline head with bird's bill and condor wings. The style verges on the surrealist, and the meaning is often hard to interpret; a central face appears, together with a number of secondary ones, surrounded by peculiar volutes recalling snakes or tongues. The feline is omnipresent, and the whole civilization polarizes round this great deity which never appears alone, as in Olmec art, but always accompanied by other motifs, such as the condor and the serpent. The Chavín feline, often called jaguar, is really a puma, whereas that of the Olmecs is an ocelot, or true jaguar. The Chavín style is also distinctive in other respects, and no matter how often it is likened to the Mexican Olmec, or to later Peruvian civilizations, its pieces are readily distinguishable from those of any other culture.

American archaeology poses a special problem because in many respects so little is known. About the Shang Dynasty of China information is also rather patchy, notwithstanding primitive writing, found mainly on oracle bones, and other brief inscriptions on bronzes. However, of the Chou Dynasty, which succeeded Shang in about 1000 B.C., detailed and colourful records survive. It is easy to forget that Confucius was born in 551 B.C., at a time when the Olmec and Chavín civilizations were not yet extinguished. In Chou Dynasty China armed conflict was endemic, but during this turbulent era scholars and sages were held in such esteem that they were often called upon, not merely to guide, but to govern.

Some warrior poems, telling how the Chinese went to battle, date from as far back as 700 B.C. These epics recall descriptions of those other contemporaries of Chou and Chavín, the Mycenaean Greeks – the Palace of Agamemnon in Mycenae was destroyed about 1200 B.C. and therefore belongs to approximately the same period as the Castillo of Chavín. But the magic of Homer's verse breathes individual life into these Greek heroes. In Greece as in China, noblemen rode in chariots while the commoners fought on foot. The chroniclers tell of the foibles of the favourite concubine of Emperor Woo 'the Gloomy', and even of the dishes prepared for the King's table, such as roast turtle and minced carp.* But, for lack of a readable script, the American record remains inscrutable; no human details of the past survive until the final period of Spanish contact. Copious data have been compiled, but the silent stones leave many questions unanswered. The archaeologists may analyse what kind of food the Chavín people ate, but they cannot provide us with the palace menus or tell who the Olmec rulers were or how they satisfied their mistresses' whims.

The classic civilizations of Mexico were studied in the nineteenth century. But the Olmecs, the precursors of them all, first came fully into view a bare generation ago – though their first discovery was less recent, since one of the famous stone heads was described in 1869.

The true significance of the Olmecs was only revealed in the 1940s by the Danish Frans Blom and the American Oliver le Farge; the German anthropologist, Hermann Beyer, was also among the the first to use the term *Olmec*, which derives from Nahuatl, the language of the Aztecs, though no one has ever suggested that the Olmecs spoke that tongue. The name means 'People of Rubber', from their place of origin in the rubber-growing region of south east Mexico where La Venta is situated, then a marshy island but now a shabby if growing oil town. In Mexico agriculture and irrigation probably began in the more arid highlands; but civilization came to full fruition in these torrid lowlands, amidst a tangle of swamp and jungle interspersed with sluggish rivers.

Originally, as with Chavín, the age of the Olmec culture was underestimated and it was thought to have followed after the Maya. Mexican archaeologists, however, always insisted on Olmec antiquity and were proved right when radiocarbon provided more precise dating. The civilization is now known to have flourished between about 1200 and 400 B.C., though its beginnings can be traced back several centuries farther. Like Chavín, the Olmec style burst its bounds and spread extensively; related cultures appeared in many different parts of Mexico, whether on the Gulf or Pacific coasts, around Mexico City, or farther to the south.

In La Venta are found the great stone heads that are typical of the Olmec civilization. There the remains of an imposing ceremonial centre were revealed, dominated by an earth mound over thirty metres high, known as the Great Pyramid. Its orientation is not due north–south, but deviates eight degrees westward from that axis – precisely as occurs with many later Mexican pyramids. La Venta constitutes a prototype of the typical Maya ceremonial centre, where the priests and rulers resided in the temple area, while the majority of the inhabitants lived in the surrounding country; stone stelae depict these priest-rulers, and in some cases these may be true portraits. Opinions differ as to whether the Olmec metropolitan area was ruled from one place or comprised a number of city-states, after the Greek pattern. Many other Olmec sites exist, but Ignacio Bernal believes that La Venta was a true capital; apart from other factors, graves that might be justly called 'royal tombs' are found only in this centre.*

The Olmecs pose a familiar problem for students of ancient civilizations: how did they transport from their place of origin the great blocks of volcanic basalt from which their stone heads were hewn and which can only have come from the Tuxtla Mountains, 65 miles west of La Venta? As Michael Coe, who has written much on the Olmecs, both for the specialist and for the general reader, points out, part of the journey could have been made with the help of enormous rafts, but the blocks still had to be dragged an appreciable distance across land. The largest heads weigh eighteen tons.

The Olmecs certainly possessed organizing ability as well as artistic talent. In San Lorenzo, one of the most important sites, traces survive of an elaborate system of water control – that hallmark of a complex society. The imposing ruins lead Coe to suggest that San Lorenzo was also the centre of a coercive state of considerable extent.* Moreover, finds made as far afield as the Central American Republic of El Salvador bear witness to the existence of a widespread trade network, and even the earliest Olmecs made knives and weapons out of obsidian brought from places over a thousand miles distant. However, they were by no means the pioneers of long-distance trade since absolute proof exists of commercial contacts nearly two thousand years earlier between the Queretaro region, 120 miles north-west of Mexico City, and the Gulf coast of Mexico. The trap of supposing that Olmec civilization, any more than Chavín, lacked antecedents should be avoided.

An elaborate pantheon of gods is much in evidence. Some of the later Mexican deities, such as the sinister flayed god, dressed in a human skin, are discernible at this early stage. Olmec art is expressed first and foremost in monumental architecture and site-planning. Second to this comes sculpture, outstanding for its 'classic' quality; great figures stand in space, free and unadorned. At the opposite end of the scale, an infinite range of small objects has been found, exquisitely carved in jade.

The feline figure is central to the Olmec as well as to the Chavín religious upsurge, but unique to Olmec art is the 'were-jaguar', half-child and half-feline, with a deformed mouth and sometimes a cleft in the middle of the head. This infantile 'jaguarism' has no Chavín counterpart and displays facial features ranging all the way from snubbed and cat-like noses, accompanied by drooping downturned mouths, to sharp-fanged and snarling animal countenances.*

In marked contrast to the were-jaguar, other reliefs depict an elderly man with aquiline nose and full beard, sometimes carved with portrait-like realism. At first sight such very different profiles suggest the presence of two distinct races; but this simple solution hardly fits since elements of both forms, the bearded man and the feline child, are sometimes found in combination – as in the case of the famous 'wrestler' statue which has the beard of the sharp-nosed old man and the Negroid lips of the were-jaguar. Another figurine of a typical Negroid child also displays the little goatee beard of the aquiline warrior.

Thick lips and snub noses are characteristic of both the huge heads and the tiny jade figures, only some of which are part-jaguar, and these traits have led to endless speculation as to Olmec origins, on the grounds that they are not typical of the American Indian. Suggestions have been made that an influx from Africa took place at a relatively early date, and the two distinct types have been held to represent bearded Phoenicians and their Negro slaves. However, no one has ever explained why the slaves are universally portrayed, while their aquiline-nosed masters appear much less frequently in large statues and never in the small jade figurines.

The stone heads are really only part-Negroid, and the lips may best be described as sensuous rather than African. In many cases, moreover, Olmec art combines Negroid characteristics with slit eyes, and Mongoloid traits figure prominently. People can still be found with the precise features of the monoliths in the very region of Tabasco where they were located. The heads are more like certain native Tabascans than like Africans, and similar types can even be found in South-East Asia to this day, particularly among the aboriginal non-Mongoloid population of such places as Pleken in South Vietnam. Olmec features find ancient parallels in Khmer heads and to an even greater extent in the earlier Cham sculptures of Cambodia, of which many were located in the Phnom Penh Museum. Equally, certain Chinese busts of the Guardians of the World, or the Divine Protectors of the Faithful, dating from the tenth century A.D., display Negroid features, with huge mouths and flat noses. Such traits are at times so exaggerated in Olmec figurines as to appear pathological and could have arisen, not from the presence of African migrants, but through a process of inbreeding caused by the isolation of a small ruling class over many generations.

Dr Alexander von Wuthenau, who lives in Mexico, has made a vast collection of small pre-Columbian heads, admirably illustrating the medley of profiles – including Negroid – portrayed in the art forms of the various regions and peoples of the country. Such a living testimony to the variegated American scene is most instructive, and one may only regret that the picture is not completed by more specimens from South America.

The diversity of this collection, to which Dr von Wuthenau has devoted tireless energy and enthusiasm, may remind us that America was an ethnic melting pot; and scientific data now available can account for such diversity without implying that people of different races came paddling across the Seven Seas in prehistoric times, whether from Africa, Asia or Europe. Von Wuthenau seems to favour such notions, however, and is fond of referring to long-nosed figurines – not all of which have a wholly human look – as 'Semites'. He tends to forget that 'Semite' is basically a linguistic not an ethnic definition, embracing ancient Akkadians, as well as modern Israelis and Arabs. Moreover, visitors to an Israeli kibbutz can see for themselves that modern Semites do not all have long noses, and von Wuthenau gives no added force to his arguments by insisting on the presence in a Maya relief of part of a 'star of David'. The proverbial swallow does not always make a summer, particularly in the case of such an elemental design as a star, which any infant might chance to draw. The star of David, mainly a latter-day Jewish emblem, was also used by the Arabs, who were among the great navigators of the first millennium of our era and therefore better equipped than the Children of Israel to visit the Maya.

Negro usually implies African origin, whereas *Negroid* is a more generalized term, applicable to people who did not necessarily come from Africa. (Africans, incidentally, have mouths that are structurally different from other Negroid peoples, having an unusually strong muscle known as Klein's muscle.) But von Wuthenau and others write of 'Negroes' as though they really came from Africa. Curiously, however, they seldom mention the more intriguing documentary evidence attesting to the presence of people of this type in prehistoric America long *before* the Spaniards brought their African slaves. Spanish eye-witness accounts offer a more reliable proof of Negroids in America than 'portrait' heads, many of which are more like caricatures. On his third voyage Columbus noted the presence in the Caribbean of black men, who also appeared in the interior of the Isthmus of Panama; in one instance they are referred to as 'slaves' of a certain local chieftain and were assumed to have come from Ethiopia; Balboa himself saw them on one occasion. The reference to 'slaves' was obviously an anachronism resulting from their subsequent introduction into Spanish America. Bishop Las Casas, the intrepid defender of the Indians against Spanish excesses, writes of a Negro 'king' in the same part of Panama.

Such reports are worth mentioning, since I am far from denying that Negroid types existed in pre-Columbian America, but believe that simple logic can explain their presence better than flights of fancy. Immediate origins need not be sought in Africa, since such people abounded in Asia, and some of them naturally tended to join the various migrant bands who came across Beringia. Small men of Negroid features were the most ancient inhabitants of lands facing the Indian Ocean, not only the Malaya Peninsula and the Philippines but also the Andaman Islands.

These people are often called 'Negritos', especially in the Philippines. One does not have to travel farther than the Manila airport to find proof of their existence. Nearby stands the Museum of Philippine Traditional Cultures. Facing the entrance to the Museum is a wall covered with photographs entitled 'unfamiliar faces'. Among them are peoples of the Ayta, Agta, Alta and Abyan indigenous tribes, known as Negritos, who came before the Mongoloid peoples and now live scattered on the east side of the main island of Luzon; all are very Negroid in appearance and differ little from the typical African. A map in the same museum shows a small island at the south-west tip of the Visayan group called Negros, so named after the physique of its present-day inhabitants.*

The Melanesians, with their black skins and woolly hair, are taller than the surviving dark-skinned peoples of Asia and are most probably not of African origin but represent a parallel evolution. Negroids still exist today in India, and in former times the Greeks used to refer to some of the inhabitants of Baluchistan as 'Ethiopians'; another black group are the Weddas of Ceylon.*

It would, therefore, be almost surprising if Negroid elements were not found among the earlier migrants over Beringia before the land bridge closed. Probably later, as the population became more mobile, the Negroids merged with other peoples; over an infinitely shorter time span the mass of African slaves brought by the Spaniards to Mexico intermarried with Indians to a point where they are seldom recognizable. In South America the situation is rather different and some regions contain elements of obviously African descent. Moreover, at the time of the Conquest, notwithstanding Spanish reports of people with dark skins, nothing approaching a full-blooded Negro can have been present in Mexico or Peru, since in both places the few black Africans whom the Conquistadors brought with them terrified the inhabitants, who had never before seen anything like them.

Even if one accepts the uncertain premise that Olmec art more often portrays Negroids than were-jaguars, no logical conclusions can be drawn as to African origins. The colossal heads may be more reminiscent of modern Tabascans or even of Vietnamese hill-dwellers, but many of the small figurines clearly depict creatures that are not solely human, but in varying degrees part-human and part-jaguar. The concept is expressed in an interesting Olmec statue of a jaguar copulating with a woman.

The peculiar mouth of these hybrid figurines has serpent fangs and some have jaguar paws, which are also found in a few of the larger statues. The combination of human and animal elements is evident in other rather striking pieces that portray a human Negroid who holds in his arms another smaller being, a were-jaguar child. A fine example is known as the Man of Limas; in this carving, so full of pathos, a man holds an apparently dead child, who may well be a sacrificial victim – the predecessor of all those later immolated to appease the Rain God, so fond of infant offerings. In similar works the smaller figure, held by the larger, does not have a human face at all; either he has jaguar features or wears a jaguar mask. A striking characteristic of these composite groups, well illustrated by a fine piece in the Brooklyn Museum, is the mouth: both beings have similar noses, but the human mouth of the adult differs from the animal mouth of the child, though the contours of the two faces run parallel. In other words, Olmec features of this peculiar kind do not derive from Africans but principally from jaguars, or at times from Negroids present in America.

The other Olmec 'race', represented by the bearded and aquiline figure, is sometimes described as 'Uncle Sam'. The presence in one culture of two peoples of different descent is not uncommon in Ancient Mexico and is confirmed in written reports of the last century before the Conquest. The Olmec Uncle Sam has no monopoly of beards, and the question of whether American Indians had facial hair and whether this trait derived from Semitic Phoenicians or from alien gods belongs to a later chapter. Certainly these hirsute reliefs do not represent a race of supermen, since in some instances the bearded men are shown as captives of the Negroid-Jaguar people.

The possibility remains that the Olmec and Chavín feline might derive from Asia since the tiger motif is an integral part of Chinese art, particularly in the first and second millennia B.C. Nonetheless many pumas and jaguars prowled the American jungles, and they were natural candidates for local deification in view of their strength and swiftness. Moreover, Indian worship of the jaguar is no more hypothesis, drawn from the study of ancient art, since in remote regions the feline cult is still demonstrably alive; American anthropologist Peter Furst has made this point cogently.*

Among certain South American peoples the animal is cast in the role of tribal ancestor; for instance, the Chibchan Cogi of Colombia are the 'people of the jaguar' and their ancestors were wild jaguars. The presence of the child-ocelot among the Olmecs and the idea of the hybrid feline are reflected in the story of shamanic initiation among the Bolivian Tacana Indians by the Great Jaguar Shaman, recorded in 1961 by German anthropologists Karin Hissink and Albert Hain:

The tradition concerns a 12-year-old boy who walked into the forest to collect the fruits of the saual palm. While he climbed about in the crown of the tree, Iba Banu, the giant-winged jaguar, who is also a great yanacana [shaman], sat down by the tree to wait for the boy. The boy stepped on to Iba Banu's back and flew off with him to another world.*

Certain tribes of the Amazon region of Brazil use the same basic word for shaman and jaguar; when they grow old their shamans are transmuted into jaguars simply by donning the animal's skin — an apparent carry-over from the ancient custom of wearing feline masks. Men who escape unharmed from a tiger in the forest are thought by the Majo of Bolivia to be the god's elect and are initiated into a guild of the jaguar deity, to whom the Majo still devote a temple cult.

Father Martin Dobrizhoffer, a German priest who served in the mid-1700s among the Abipon, a Paraguayan tribe, gives one of the earliest accounts of shamans changing into jaguars. Such conjurers were thought to have the power to inflict disease and death, to make known the future, to cause rain and tempest, and to call up shades of the dead, whom they consulted on hidden matters; significantly, wizards could put on the form of a tiger and handle every kind of serpent without danger. Dobrizhoffer describes his efforts to convince these people that the transformation of a shaman into a feline was impossible.*

Among remote tribes the feline is therefore still linked with the shaman; the tendency is now more pronounced in South than in North America, though it was formerly in evidence in Maya writings, such as the Chilam Balam (Chilam Balam means 'jaguar prophet'). When the Olmec and Chavín civilizations arose, they not unnaturally adopted a deity paramount among the early shamans, who were the ministers of religion before the creation of a priestly hierarchy and who, in outlying jungles and sierras, long outlived those great temple cults. The jaguar god was not invented by the first civilizations, but was promoted from the role of a village headman's *alter ego* to the apex of an elaborate cult. Early native roots of the feline worship are therefore not hard to find; whether inspiration was also drawn from the Chinese dragon is a point which still awaits an answer.

Apart from the common catlike images, Olmec and Chavín styles present further parallels. Among the most striking is the similarity between the monoliths of Serro Sechin on the coast of Peru, north of Chavín de Huántar itself, and the famous 'dancers' of Monte Albán in southern Mexico, which coincide with the culminating phase of Olmec civilization. Even closer likenesses between the Cupisnique culture (contemporary with Chavín) and Tlatilco, situated on the outskirts of Mexico City, emerge. In Tlatilco graves yielded a vast amount of pottery with Olmec affinities but also reminiscent of Chavinoid styles.

Chavín and Olmec are the first civilizations of their kind. Starting before 1500 B.C., the one in North and the other in South America, both spread far and wide; and each established artistic and technical norms that prevailed until the Spanish Conquest. In this they compare with the early Egyptian dynasties whose achievements were modified but scarcely surpassed during the eighteen centuries that followed.

The possibility of physical contacts between the Olmecs and the people of Chavín has been hotly debated. Some anthropologists have laid stress on like motifs in the two cultures, and have pointed to specifically Olmec traits present in Chavín pieces; others describe the marked differences underlying any superficial resemblance and insist that objects from the two cultures could seldom be confused. Chavín lacks the Olmec baby-face, and the serpent plays a bigger role in Peru, where the feline deity invariably goes accompanied not only by serpents but by condors, not found among the Olmecs.

The divergent forms of the two regions may well have sprung from a common basis in a remoter past, though I do not feel that they constitute a single culture, created in one place and transported to the other. If styles differ, Olmec and Chavín do seem to share some ancient undercurrent of belief that inspired their art. They presumably ignored each other's existence, but represent the same stage in man's progress in the two halves of America.*

The strength of earlier contacts between North and South America and the lack of any impassable barrier to movement from one to the other have already been stressed; their peoples shared the same origins and their cultures rested on common foundations, since all had come across the Bering Strait. Contacts evidently did not cease altogether, and certain near-identical styles emerged in the two continents, a pre-Olmec example of which has been given. At the risk of repetition, a few more instances are worth citing, relating to the Olmec–Chavín period and the centuries that followed.

Betty Meggers, who makes such play of early links between Japan and Ecuador, describes the discovery of close resemblances between

Ecuadorian and Mexican art as an unsuspected by-product of her work. In Ecuador and in certain parts of Mexico a rather strange three-pronged incense burner appears, so unusual that duplicate evolution of the object is unlikely. A marked likeness exists between pottery of about 1500 B.C. from coastal Ecuador and from Ocos, in Guatemala.* Cuspidors have been found in both places that are amazingly alike; their identity of form goes beyond any comparisons made between Chinese and Chavín tigers.

To quote another example: close parallels occur between the ceramics of Ancon in Peru and Playa de los Muertos in the Central American Republic of Honduras. In the American Museum of Natural History, these sherds from Honduras and Peru would be indistinguishable, were it not for their catalogue numbers. Extraordinary similarities of this kind are apt to crop up in unconnected places, rather as a stream of water may run underground and only spring to the surface at a few separate points on its long subterranean journey.

Arising from an early common base, later developments follow a parallel course in Mexico and Peru to an uncanny degree. The two regions form an axis, along a line that runs from Mexico through Central America and onwards along the Northern Andes; around this nucleus all the main aboriginal civilizations of the New World seem to crystallize, and this cultural core has come to be known as 'Nuclear America'. Comparisons have even been made between the civilizing Mexico–Peru axis and the Near Eastern Oikumene of the Old World, two focal centres from which culture flowed outwards to other regions like ripples in a pond. And at each end of the American axis, by accident or design, historical developments often coincided. The Olmec and Chavín cultures were both followed by others of a more localized nature, notable for their artistic genius, of which the Maya are typical. In the two areas these great regional cultures then subsided, and the lead was taken by people whose gifts were more martial than artistic.

Thereafter, at precisely the same moment, barely a century before the Spanish Conquest, an oecumenical empire arose in each continent, bent upon universal dominion. The Aztecs and Incas ignored each other's existence, but despite differences they had much in common. According to legend, both used forceful and cunning means to establish a power base in the region which they had penetrated as unwanted and supplicant intruders. Thereafter, each fought bitter campaigns to crush local rivals; then, using these neighbouring territories as a springboard, Incas and Aztecs quickly subjugated vast domains, embracing the traditional peoples of Middle America and the Northern Andes respectively. Finally both empires collapsed like a house of cards under the assault of a handful of Spaniards.

The notion dies hard that North and South America were two separate entities, divided by the impassable Darien Gap. The Gold Museums of Bogotá, Colombia, and San José, Costa Rica, show a number of pieces that have so much in common that only an expert could tell them apart, though the two countries are separated by the Isthmus of Panama. Typical of both regions are the strange and varied bird motifs, and in particular the ubiquitous double tailed bird. But Costa Rica's northern neighbour, Nicaragua, produces nothing of this type and unquestionably belongs to Middle America, conforming to Central Mexican and even Mayan traditions; migrations from Mexico to Nicaragua are mentioned in Mexican historical documents.

Language follows the same pattern: Costa Rican tongues generally belong to the Macro-Chibchan group, centred upon Colombia, while some Nicaraguans spoke languages akin to those of Mexico, whence they had come. If *any* dividing line existed between the ancient cultures of north and south, it more or less followed the present-day border between Costa Rica and Nicaragua and was therefore easily crossed in either direction by human migrants. This relative unity of the two Americas must always be borne in mind in contemplating the barriers that divided America as a whole from the continents of the Old World.

The pace of progress at this time in Mexico and Peru makes it easy to lose sight of events farther north, where a civilization was formed that showed rather more signs of Old World influences. Approximately during the late Olmec era, the Early Woodland Culture flourished in the Great Lakes area; it produced pottery that bears a likeness to that of Siberia and used cord-marked patterns that also occur throughout the northern forest zones of Europe and Asia.

The Woodland people were among the first Burial Mound builders and gave birth to a long tradition in North America that had no early equivalent in Asia. These mounds aroused keen interest as early as 1827, when a book was published in Heidelberg entitled *Accounts of the Early Inhabitants of North America and Their Monuments*, written by Friedrich

Wilhelm Assall. The author had come to the United States as a miner in 1818 and after also serving as a soldier, became head mining officer of the State of Pennsylvania. In 1823 Assall revisited Germany and talked about the great Indian ruins of Ohio with Professor Franz Joseph Mone of Heidelberg, who strongly urged him to write about his discoveries, saying that the University of Göttingen had recently offered a prize for a critical comparison of American and Asian monuments. Assall then gathered all the available writings on the subject and compared their findings with his own; the work was the first to call the attention of German and other European scholars to the archaeology of North America, but it was soon forgotten, and C. W. Ceram thought himself lucky to secure a battered copy.

The Hopewell culture came into being in about 600 B.C. It was named after Captain Hopewell, on whose property more than thirty mounds were found. In his eagerness to offer evidence of American antiquity at the Chicago World's Fair of 1893, Warren K. Moorhead dug at the Captain's farm and brought the pick of his findings to the Fair. Pottery styles related to Hopewell appear as far east as New York and extend southwards to Kansas; a wide trade network was established; raw materials such as mica, shells, pearls, grizzly-bear teeth and obsidian were brought to Ohio from places as remote as the Rocky Mountains and the Gulf of Mexico.

The Hopewell people were highly skilled in copper-working, an ancient craft that had already begun in North America in 4000 B.C. Metallurgy was then still unknown in Mexico though well-established in South America; the technique may have been transmitted directly across the Caribbean, whose islands provided a useful stepping stone. Also characteristic of Hopewell are very original clay pipes, delicately carved, often in the shape of animals such as bears, dogs, opossums and otters, and displaying a refinement comparable to that of Olmec art.

The burial mounds are not pyramids in the strict sense of the word but gigantic heaps of earth; some have a base area greater than the Pyramid of Cheops. Effigy mounds were also built in the shape of animals. These monuments exceed the Nile Valley pyramids in number, and the total expenditure of labour on them went far beyond the Egyptian achievement. Not unnaturally the Egyptians, as well as the Phoenicians, Welsh and even the Lost Tribes of Israel at different times have been held to have built them. Because of their size, Frederick Larkin suggested in

1880 that the Hopewell mounds were constructed by people who had domesticated the mammoth and used him as a living bulldozer.*

In this chapter possible human contacts within America at the time when New World civilization was emerging from its chrysalis have been discussed but little has been said about Asia. The Olmecs were unknown until fairly recently, and therefore ignored in discussions about early links with Eurasia. The fashion may now prevail in some circles of crediting them with African origins because of the Negroid features evident in certain pieces, but comparisons between Olmec and the Chinese Chou Dynasty are more to the point, though hard to prove. For instance, Olmec pyrite mirrors recall bronze versions that the Chinese used to kindle sacred fires. Suggestions have been made that the Olmecs could not possibly have invented mirrors on their own; but the idea of the reflected image would surely tempt members of any sophisticated society, and people dressed in the sumptuous attire visible in Olmec reliefs might be curious to know how they looked. Like their Chinese contemporaries, Olmec and Chavín were distinguished for their working of jade or green stone, which in both regions enjoyed a peculiar sanctity.

However, a mere penchant for mirrors or jade offers fragile evidence on which to base a case for contact. Writing, like agriculture, is a unique achievement and arguments have been advanced that the art was invented in one place only and conveyed thence to the Olmecs. But when civilization develops — with its concomitant bureaucracy and priesthood — the need for keeping records is no longer a luxury but a necessity; the sequence starts with simple pictures of objects stored in temples or paid in tribute and eventually leads to a fully fledged script. Experts are not sure if writing was invented more than once in the Near East and are even less certain whether Chinese writing later drew inspiration from that region.

Anthropologists who point to similarities between Chavín and China can offer more concrete examples. The typical Chavín-type felines recall East Asia in general and, according to the distinguished Orientalist Dr Robert Heine-Geldern, are almost identical with those of the mid-Chou style of the tenth to eighth centuries B.C. Chavín ceremonial centres can be seen from the air to resemble in outline a jaguar or a Chinese dragon. Nevertheless the latest dating shows that Chavín beginnings long predate this mid-Chou period, so that the likelihood of the Peruvian feline deity being an imported product is correspondingly diminished.

Undoubted similarities occur between the art forms of the two sides of the Pacific. A leading American archaeologist, Gordon Willey, who has pondered deeply on transpacific contacts and who till recently remained sceptical, now confesses to an 'uncanny feeling' when looking at some Shang Dynasty items that display 'disturbing similarities' to Chavín, relating not only to content but to style.* Though Shang used bronze and Chavín stone, Willey stresses that their dates more or less coincide; he asks that the question be at least left open — a plea that is surely not unreasonable. Even if proofs of contact are lacking, the two peoples produced forms in some respects so alike as to remind us of their remote common past.

In addition to these parallels, others of a religious nature might be cited as common to early China, Mexico and Peru. In Shang times there were many gods, but the supreme deity, Shang Ti, was a god of vegetation; in Mexico the Olmec jaguar is clearly also linked with rain or fertility. Human sacrifices existed in China at that time, and slaughtered slaves or servants in rulers' graves bear witness to a practice that was to assume giant proportions in parts of America. The Shang people, moreover, built their temples on platforms of earth, not unlike the Olmecs.

In the Chou period China was divided among a number of warring petty states. Religion had altered by this time since there were no priests and heads of families performed religious rites; heaven worship predominated and the ruler was already known as the 'Son of Heaven'. Such practices are hard to relate to anything that appears on stones and stelae in America; however, on a practical level, the constant conflicts between small Chou states might find parallels among the Olmecs, whose chieftains are often shown clad for war.

Finally the argument remains that the 'sudden' emergence of Olmec and Chavín civilizations demonstrates their Old World origin. Thor· Heyerdahl, for instance, asks how it is possible that New World cultures arose so rapidly unless they were imported from another continent. But his assertion that Olmec or Chavín arose suddenly is inaccurate. We now know that the growth of Chavín was a long-drawn-out process. Indeed the Old World civilizations seem to have arisen more quickly than the New. The Shang Dynasty, for instance, is conspicuous for its meteoric rise to prominence, according to the rather inadequate available data.

But in this context Heyerdahl had in mind Olmec links with Egypt rather than with China. To label all those who doubt such contacts as 'isolationists' does not contribute much to useful discussion; nor are matters clarified by an insistence that the Olmecs had acquired all the astronomical knowledge later possessed by the Maya – a statement that cannot be substantiated. In Egypt itself, the phenomenon of speedy development is more in evidence, and Jacquetta Hawkes writes:

> Only a few centuries before [3200 B.C.], the Nile Valley had been a land of tribal villages and rustic craftsmen. Now it was a civilized kingdom with one authority recognized from Aswan to the Mediterranean. The dramatic speed of this transformation had encouraged Egyptologists to look for something in the nature of a magic wand.*

The growth of American civilizations is sluggish by comparison and offers no possible grounds for believing that they derived from Egypt or elsewhere. The hypothesis of the 'cradle of civilization' has led to endless discussion, but attempts to locate this common fountainhead have produced negative results. If civilization was a tender flower, it seems to have bloomed profusely in several different places when the right preconditions prevailed.

Enough has been said to show that this writer rejects the probability that these early cultures were borrowed lock, stock and barrel from the Old World. But in succeeding chapters a closer look will be taken at the evidence to see if any meaningful cross-fertilization occurred between the two hemispheres, whether at this early stage or during the high noon of the American classic cultures. Possible contacts between the New World and East Asia in the early centuries of our era will be treated in the next chapter and thereafter we shall go back to the first millennium B.C. and consider the countless works linking Egyptians, Phoenicians and other Mediterranean peoples with the Olmecs and succeeding cultures such as the Maya. East Asia must be considered first because the case for contact has been presented with greater expertise and because the problem of American links with the eastern Mediterranean is complicated by the fact that leading theories were formulated before the true antiquity of Olmec and Chavín was known to science.

CHAPTER FIVE

THE EASTERN OCEAN

'THE ambassador of the Han, Chang Chien, won through across the Western Seas to reach Ta-Chin [the Roman Empire] . . . but the Eastern Ocean is yet more vast, and we know of no one who has crossed it.' So wrote the Chinese naturalist, Chang Hua, in A.D. 285. The eminent Sinologist Joseph Needham cites this passage in his great work, *Science and Civilization in China*, and comments that Chang Hua's words might also be taken to mean that no one had ever *returned* from the Eastern Ocean's farther shore.* Herein lies a difference. Needham accepts that voyagers to America in primitive craft stood little chance of getting back to China. But the question remains: did any subjects of the Celestial Empire make the journey? Needham, with certain reservations, believes that they did.

Long before this time, the rulers of China were persuaded that drug plants granting longevity or even immortality grew in the islands of the Eastern Ocean. In the third century B.C. many sea captains were sent out to find them, but met with no success. Of these explorers, only the name of Hsü Fu has survived, although several reports of like expeditions are included in the Shih Chi, the earliest of the dynastic histories, finished in the first century B.C.*

The Shih Chi mentions three blessed isles, situated in the Eastern Ocean, though not too far distant from China itself. But would-be visitors knew that their boats were likely to be snatched away by the wind at the moment when they neared their destination. According to certain accounts, many immortals inhabited the islands, where the drug that would prevent death was freely available. All living creatures, both birds and beasts, were perfectly white; palaces and gate-towers were made of gold and silver. In another version of the story, the islands looked like clouds, but when ships approached, they sank beneath the water.

The Emperor Chin Shih Huang Ti came to the shores of the Eastern Ocean, but, fearing failure, would take no personal part in the illusive search. Instead, an expedition was commissioned which, as usual, returned empty-handed. A little later, in 219 B.C., Hsü Fu and his friends approached the Emperor, repeating the familiar tale of the three isles, inhabited by beings immune from the pangs of death, and begged to be permitted to put to sea. Hsü Fu's prayer was granted, and after due purification he set forth in quest of the immortals of the Eastern Ocean, accompanied by three thousand young men and maidens. Certainly no expense was spared, for the Emperor complained bitterly of the cost. But alas! The nature of the vessels used is unknown. Needham suggests that the fleet consisted of sailing rafts and observes that a little over two hundred years earlier, a naval force had been dispatched by the State of Wu to attack its northern neighbours; in that instance numerous paddled canoes were probably employed, large enough to carry deck-castles for archers, but made strictly for coastal voyages.*

The Shih Chi includes an alternative account of the same expedition:

Chin Shih Huang Ti also sent out Hsü Fu by sea to search for magical beings and strange things. When he returned he invented excuses, saying: 'In the midst of the ocean I met [on an island] a great mage who said to me, "Are you the envoy of the Emperor of the West?" to which I replied that I was. "What have you come for?" said he, and I answered that I sought for those drugs which lengthen life and promote longevity. "The offerings of your Chin king," he said, "are but poor; you may see these drugs but you may not take them away." Then, going south-east, we came to Pheng-Lai, and I saw the gates of the Chih-Cheng Palace, in the front whereof there was a guardian of brazen hue and dragon form, lighting the skies with his radiance. In this place I did obeisance to the Sea Mage twice, and asked him what offerings we should present to him. "Bring me your young men," he said, "of good birth and breeding, together with apt virgins, and workmen of all trades; then you will get your drugs."'

Chin Shih Huang Ti, very pleased, set three thousand young men and girls at Hsü Fu's disposal, gave him [ample supplies] of the seeds of five grains, and artisans of every sort, after which [his fleet again] set sail. Hsü Fu [must have] found some calm and fertile plain, with broad forests and rice marshes, where he made himself king – at any rate, he never came back to China.*

The narrator suggests that Hsü Fu already knew of good and vacant lands in the east. Later generations of historians believed that he had settled in Japan. But a faint possibility remains that beneath the mystical veneer of Taoist concepts, a report lies hidden of the first voyage to the American continent.

Chinese documents of rather later date refer to lands lying to the east as Fu-Sang. Like the magic isles, Fu-Sang first appears in a magical context, but later came to be regarded as a real place. The most vivid report was written in A.D. 629 and tells of a monk named Hui-Shen, who had given an account of what he saw in A.D. 499 in Fu-Sang, a country lying to the east of China. The curious trees from which the land took its name are described. The ten suns were supposed to perch on their branches before taking off on their journeys of the ten-day week; these trees provided food and bark-cloth, and a kind of writing paper was also made from them. The people lived in unfortified wooden houses and were unwarlike; they possessed oxen and drank the milk of deer. Gold and silver were not esteemed in Fu-Sang and copper existed, but no iron. The monk's account of the new lands includes details such as the ruler's robes and adds the story of a country inhabited by Amazons, which lay even farther to the east, beyond Fu-Sang. The text concludes with a statement that in A.D. 507 a Fukienese ship was blown far out into the Pacific by a tempest and reached another island where the men had faces like dogs and lived on small beans.

Certain features of this tale, such as the eating of beans and the making of paper from bark, tantalizingly recall pre-Columbian America. Moreover, a seventh-century astronomer states clearly that Fu-Sang lay to the east of Japan, just as Japan lay east of China. Nonetheless, like Hsü Fu's mysterious destination, Fu-Sang was later identified with Japan, and in Chinese literary usage the name often came to be employed as a poetical term for that country.

Before indulging in further speculation on the whereabouts of Fu-Sang, the known situation in East Asia and America at the time of the accession of the Han Dynasty must be considered. In China the third century B.C. marked the dissolution of the warring states and the unification of the country under one ruler. The feat was first accomplished by the short-lived Chi'in Dynasty, and the process was completed by the Han, who ruled from 206 B.C. to A.D. 220. In theory the emperor now held supreme power, but under his tutelage the state was administered by a hierarchy of officials who formed the nucleus of a highly centralized government and were chosen by competitive examination. The great Han legal code, consisting of 960 volumes and 17 million words, bears witness to the complexity of the system.

The copious reports of Chi'in and Han times contain features oddly more reminiscent of the end of American Indian civilization than of its beginning and in particular recall the Aztec period preceding the Conquest. The monuments of the first Chi'in emperor outrival the courts of Moctezuma as described by the Spaniards. The Ch'in ruler is said to have constructed two hundred and seventy royal palaces, all replete with gorgeous furniture, skilful musicians, obedient slaves, dancing girls and other ministers of delight.*

Further details call to mind the Aztecs and Incas. The Chi'in 'rewrote' Chinese history to produce a suitably edifying version and, like one Aztec ruler, indulged in a burning of books. The same veneration for precious materials prevailed: on the Chinese side, pearls, jade, gold and silver: among the Mexicans, turquoise, jade, gold and feathers; in each land, their use was rigorously confined to the emperor and nobility. Sumptuary laws checked the presumptions of rich merchants: the founder of the Han Dynasty forbade tradespeople to wear silk or to ride in carts; the Aztec emperor gave his merchants capes of plaited paper, bordered with butterflies, and others made of rabbit fur, but proscribed the use of the feathered garments that were reserved for the rulers. The founders of both empires were great conquerors, even if the Aztecs never thought to protect their domains with a great wall; moreover, both faced like problems, including rebellious subjects, famines and floods.

But if we turn from China to the opposite shores of the Pacific, at a time no longer corresponding to the Aztecs and to the English Wars of the Roses but to Julius Caesar and to the Han Dynasty, a hazier pattern emerges. From Spanish reports much is known of Mexico and Peru in the reigns of Moctezuma and Atahualpa; but of events in the year o the details remain obscure. Lacking eye-witness accounts, only the lamps of archaeology can light our way and the assumption is not valid that in the first century A.D. things were much the same as in the fifteenth.

The Christian era marks the upsurge of great regional civilizations, the heirs of the more universalized Olmec and Chavín described in the previous chapter. In Mexico the scene was now dominated by

Teotihuacán, a centre that outshone all rivals. The solemn rows of pyramids, known as the Street of the Dead, are seen by every visitor to Mexico and to this day bear witness to the past glories of a city whose circumference exceeded the bounds of Rome. Teotihuacán culture spread to lands never conquered by the latter-day Aztecs, reaching northwards to the present border of the United States and southwards to the modern Guatemala City, whose suburbs now engulf Kaminaljuyú, a site closely inspired by the great metropolis. Vestiges of delicate frescoes and monumental sculpture still give a notion of Teotihuacán's genius and, because its buildings are of stone, the architectural legacy surpasses that of contemporary East Asia. But though the palaces remain, the documents are lacking and obscure glyphs offer scant compensation for the outpourings of the Chinese scribes. Teotihuacán, like Han China, was a complex state, though we ignore how far the sacred city gained physical control over its vast sphere of influence.

Fractionally later than Teotihuacán, the Maya civilization rose in the jungles of south-east Mexico and Guatemala. Because of the exuberance of their art and the inscrutability of their script, the Maya have surpassed all pre-Columbian peoples in firing the imagination of posterity.

Comparable developments occurred in Peru: on the north coast flourished the Mochica civilization, with its mountainous pyramids built of adobe blocks and its copious output of the most striking ceramics of all the Americas. The rich realism of the Mochica potter portrays every detail of daily life: the houses and boats they built; the dress they wore; the illnesses that afflicted them and even the operations they performed. In the south of Peru, the Nazca culture has bequeathed a varied artistic legacy, outstanding for its fantastic textiles, used as shrouds for rulers and nobles and preserved intact in the dry desert climate. The Mochica portrait heads and the Nazca shrouds are the outward and visible signs of an intricate society, probably as hierarchized as any in the Old World. However, unlike China, no signs are present in Peru of a land united under the aegis of a single ruler.

In Asia, not only China but India was then making great strides towards unification, though progress in that respect was to prove more ephemeral. The Emperor Asoka, who reigned from 273 to 232 B.C., controlled virtually the whole sub-continent. India at this time tended to be more outward-looking than China; an extensive trade network was established and such luxuries as gold, silverware, spices, cosmetics and pearls were imported from different lands. Asoka was converted to Buddhism and sent missionaries to the ends of the known world.

Such was the general situation in the early centuries of our era in the kingdoms of Asia and America that faced each other across the Pacific; in some respects they are comparable, in others utterly disparate. Overall similarities, including the possession of markets, city walls, clan organization and a class of craft specialists, have inspired suggestions of Chinese influences in America. But a convincing case cannot rest on mere generalities and requires stricter parallels of a kind that certain scholars have proposed.

Possibilities of contact were first mooted by leading authorities on China in an age when the study of Ancient America was in its infancy. In 1761 the eminent French Sinologist, de Guignes, said that Fu-Sang must have been Mexico. Klaproth, an equally famous Prussian scholar, refuted de Guignes' theory in 1831, and an argument ensued that has never ended. In 1875, more than a century after de Guignes' time, the controversy provoked the furore in the first Congress of Americanists already mentioned. In more recent times connections between America and Asia (not solely confined to China) again became a matter of hot debate, largely arising from the work of the American archaeologist Gordon Ekholm and the Austrian Orientalist, the late Robert Heine-Geldern.

The case has been propounded by experts and mainly printed in professional journals; as might be expected, scholars of this category approach their subject with caution. The arguments are not hard to follow; they concentrate upon possible contacts between Asia and Mexico. Although comparisons with Peru have also been made, artistic parallels between Mexico and East Asia are the more striking in this period — and also the more feasible since, to reach America, Chinese ships would follow the easterly current across the Pacific, which carries the voyager to the northern half of the New World.

Early Chinese awareness of the existence of a west—east current is not in doubt; already before Han Dynasty times it was known as the Wei-lü and by its direction and force gave rise to the singular notion that the Eastern Ocean sloped downward from a starting point in Java.

Ekholm, Heine-Geldern and their followers believe that the period of contact was prolonged, beginning with the feline motif shared by Chou and Chavín-Olmec and ending with parallels between China and the Late Maya of Chichén Itzá. Accordingly Mexico is seen as permeated by Asian influences from the beginning of the first millennium B.C. until the end of the first millennium A.D. Such theories are all-embracing in terms of space as well as time and affect a vast region of Asia; among donors to American culture, not only China but India, Cambodia and Indonesia are included.

In defence of his views Ekholm refers to the isolationist trend that formerly prevailed among thoughtful students of New World origins and held the field during the growth period of American anthropology, beginning with John Lloyd Stevens or even with Thomas Jefferson. Insistence upon the independence of New World civilization may not, according to Ekholm, be solely the product of dispassionate judgment, but may also result from a reaction against the wilder theories about sunken continents and lost tribes. The teaching of the *Kulturkreis* school, fervent in its belief that all human culture had sprung from a single creative centre, was important at this time. Professor Wigberto Jimenez Moreno, the leading historian of Ancient Mexico, has described these earlier tendencies as an archaeological Monroe Doctrine on the part of United States scholars. As he rightly remarks, with the extension of American interests to other continents in recent decades, attitudes favouring the cultural isolation of the first Americans have been relaxed.

Ekholm tells how he became convinced that the go-it-alone approach had been overdone when in 1945 he unearthed wheeled toys on the Gulf Coast of Mexico and began to speculate on their wider implications. In vain he searched for other instances where a given people had devised a miniature object that involved a mechanical principle of which they then made no practical use. Nonetheless, Ekholm continued to assume that these toys had been evolved by the American Indian, even if the wheel was neglected as an aid to locomotion; only after further study did he envisage Asia as their logical source of inspiration.

So Ekholm came to accept the likely introduction of elements from the Old World; but he carefully went out of his way to disavow extremist views on the subject; he insists on the local invention of New World traits such as the use of rubber and tobacco, and even the beginnings of plant cultivation.* He stresses that at its apogee the Han

Empire spanned the Pacific coast from Korea to Indochina, while towards the interior it reached up to the deserts of Central Asia. Han culture penetrated still farther, from Indonesia as far as Mongolia and Siberia; its emissaries made contact with the Roman World of the Mediterranean. Heine-Geldern introduces into the equation the sub-continent of India, which was also expanding into South-East Asia at the time. Archaeologists find evidence of Han Chinese trade in the great Indian colonial city of Oceo in the Mekong Delta, south of the modern Saigon, as well as in Java, Sumatra and Borneo. Accordingly Indian merchants must have come into contact with those of China in South-East Asia and been inspired by Chinese tales of fabulous lands beyond the Eastern Ocean and of sweeping currents that wafted vessels over its vast expanse. Viewing them in their wider historical context, Heine-Geldern regards any Indian voyages to America as a mere continuation of that eastward surge that had already brought their fleets to the shores of Indochina and beyond. Later, according to the same theory, the initial impetus of the movement from India faltered, but the challenge of the Pacific was taken up by other peoples of South-East Asia, by now thoroughly Hinduized. Prominent among these were the Khmer of Cambodia and their predecessors, the Cham.*

The impact of Indian culture upon Indonesia and Cambodia was deep and gave birth to that magic blend of Hindu and Buddhist genius still visible in the graceful sculpture of Borabudur in Java and Angkor in Cambodia. This vast stone metropolis of the Khmer Empire, set deep in the tropical forest, more than any other Asian site recalls Tikal and other Maya cities of whose mysterious rise and fall so much is written. In Angkor and Tikal, meticulously restored pyramids and palaces, rich in baroque carving, stretch for many miles; in both places other structures, untouched by the restorer, are still held firm in the embrace of the jungle.

The reasoning of Heine-Geldern and Ekholm transcends generalities: these serve as a point of departure from which stems the naming of specific motifs common to East Asia and Mexico, so numerous that only the more striking may be cited. Prominent on their list is the lotus, so universal in Indian and Chinese Buddhist art; a comparison is made between the lotus friezes of the second century A.D. at Amaravati on the east coast of India and those of the Late Maya Temple of the Jaguars at Chichén Itzá. The alleged portrayal of elephants in Mexico (which are more usually regarded as stylized macaws) offers another instance of Asiatic penetration.

Chinese influences are seen in the cylindrical tripod vessels with conical lids that originally appeared in central Mexico at Teotihuacán and then spread to other regions. Remarkably similar jars, some made of bronze, are typical of the Han period; the lids of certain tripod vessels from the Maya area have rings at the top and are highly reminiscent of the ringed lids used in Chinese bronze or pottery. In both Han China and Teotihuacán lids were sometimes also surmounted with birds. Other Teotihuacán pottery forms also recall those of Chinese bronzes, as can be verified from the varied Han specimens displayed in the Taipeh Museum. In addition, Heine-Geldern and Ekholm compare the stone interlace patterns – a common feature of the Tajin style of Gulf Coast Mexico – and near-identical designs in the Late Chou period in China.

Parallels are plentiful between the art of America and that of India. South-East Asia was already influenced by Indian civilization in the first and second centuries B.C., when the earliest Hindu–Buddhist kingdoms were established in the Malay Peninsula, Indochina and Indonesia. As examples of this Hindu–Buddhist penetration into Mexico, Heine-Geldern cites the rows of colonettes decorating the panels of Puuc-style Maya buildings, so similar to those used as window gratings in the Khmer temples from the ninth century onwards. In Cambodia these stone colonettes were copied from wooden gratings still used in the windows of religious buildings in Laos.

The stepped pyramids of Mexico have repeatedly been likened to those of Cambodia, but Heine-Geldern agrees that pyramids appear too early in Mexico to be of Cambodian derivation. He gives, however, a closer parallel with that country: trees in the reliefs of the Maya Temple of the Cross at Palenque resemble the cosmic tree represented in the Javanese shadow-play figures that in turn derive from older art forms.* The Makara, a legendary sea-monster combining traits of the crocodile, fish, elephant and Hellenistic dolphin, is another Indian image present in Mexico, and such hybrids, often called serpents, also appear in the Maya land. In India, moreover, a human figure frequently emerges from the Makara's mouth, as occurs in parallel Maya designs; in both continents the monster sometimes lacks the lower jaw.

Problems of chronology are inseparable from such comparisons. In that respect the appearance of Han-type conical jars in Mexico makes sense. Late Han (A.D. 24–220) corresponds with early Teotihuacán. But, however striking the similarities may be between Tajin scroll patterns and Late Chou Chinese designs, the Chou Dynasty ended in 256 B.C. while Tajin is unknown until nearly five hundred years later. Heine-Geldern proposes that the Tajin motifs, carved in stone, might have been previously used for several centuries in wood-carving and mural-painting of which no trace survives. But not a shred of proof supports this theory and I know of no parallel case in the New World; Maya date glyphs inscribed on wooden lintels correspond closely in time to those carved on stone stelae in the same style.

Moreover, even if Heine-Geldern's explanations of the delayed spread of Chou styles to the Gulf Coast of Mexico were accepted, they would not fit the other instances he cites. The same drawback arises in comparisons between East Asia and the Late Mayan Chichén Itzá, which fell in about A.D. 1200. Almost a millennium divides the Indian Amaravati lotus friezes and the water-lily friezes of the Temple of the Jaguars at Chichén. The uncertain premise is again advanced that lotus designs of this type were still used in Asia to adorn woodcarvings (which have since perished) for many more centuries before they were transferred to America.

The means by which artistic designs were conveyed from one place to the other presents another problem. To meet this objection, the two scholars briefly state that large boats existed in East Asia in the period A.D. 200–400 and that several centuries earlier maritime contact had been established between India and Roman ports. In addition, the Indians of the Han period had large four-masted ships. Heine-Geldern and Ekholm do not propose a large-scale colonization of America, or envisage any conquest; they think in terms of occasional voyages that account for Asiatic influences; boatloads bringing small groups of travellers could have landed from time to time on the coast of America and moved inland to some important cultural centre. Such journeys are not seen as accidental, effected merely by ships driven off course by storms or currents. Heine-Geldern points out that artists and astrologers (without whom such voyages would have borne no result) are averse to sailing off into the blue and would only contemplate journeys to known destinations, where their services would be appreciated. A return trip had to be feasible since Chinese intellectuals might have been slow to embark without the prospect of returning to their home comforts.

*

To aesthetic comparisons between China and Mexico, suggestions of religious proselytism have been added; taking advantage of the two-way traffic across the Pacific, Buddhist and Brahman missionaries were surely eager to convert the new lands. No trace of such efforts remains, but Heine-Geldern offers the comparison of Sumatra, which was duly converted but later lapsed into cannibalism.

Other authors have pointed to parallels in ritual and belief between America and Asia. For instance, both Chinese and Mexicans associated the cardinal points with certain colours: both placed pieces of jade or green stone in the mouth of a dead person (however, the notion is mistaken that Mexican jade — or rather jadeite — came from China).

Dr Paul Kirchhoff, who died in Mexico in 1972, was outstanding among students of Ancient Mexico in his time. He devoted much of his energies in later years to comparisons between the religious calendars of India, China, Java and Mexico. Kirchhoff's principal findings were based on similarities between the respective pantheons of these countries, in the study of which he was aided by the research of other German scholars who had demonstrated that the Indian and Javanese deities did not reach their present form before the second or third century of our era — or precisely the moment when Indian influences, both Hindu and Buddhist, transformed South-East Asia and, according to Heine-Geldern and Ekholm, reached Mexico.*

Prompted by the German anthropologist Fritz Graebner's previous discovery of parallels between the names of the days in the Chinese and Mexican calendars, in both of which many days are called after animals, for example, the Day of the Rat or the Day of the Leopard, Kirchhoff drew up an intriguing table of comparisons. He first placed side by side the twenty-eight animals of the Chinese lunar mansions and the twenty-seven names of the Indian lunar mansions; then, by bracketing two or three names together, each list was reduced to twelve groups. To this table Kirchhoff added two more columns: in the first he put a shorter Chinese list of twelve animal day-names (used also to designate the years) and the second column consisted of the twelve central day-names of the sacred Mexican calendar (containing twenty day-names in all); the usual order of both the Mexican and of the shorter Chinese god-list was reversed. The German scholar was then able to point to some extraordinary parallels between these four lists of names or groups of names, emanating from China, India and Mexico; for instance, tiger or jaguar appears as item 3 in each list, and the dog as item 7.

When I studied with Paul Kirchhoff, he invariably encouraged independent thinking on my part, in preference to a blind acceptance of his own ideas. I know, therefore, that had he lived longer he would have respected my view that these coincidences lack conviction, because of the rather involved and arbitrary methods of arrangement such as taking only part of one list and then reversing its order. Kirchhoff also provided other comparisons among Mexican, Indian and Javanese god-lists that are simpler but offer fewer noteworthy parallels.

And yet even people who do not accept the implications of Kirchhoff's calculations must sense a hint of some latent link, however remote, connecting the imagery of American and Indian religions (the early disappearance of polytheism in China limits comparison with that country). For instance, Shiva's and Ganesha's necklace, the rope that Ganesha statues carry in one hand and the god's single elephant tusk reappear in the day-names 'skull', 'malinalli-rope' and 'tooth' that occupy corresponding places in the Mexican calendar list.

Kirchhoff's work is too penetrating to be lightly dismissed, although he described it as merely a promising set of data for future studies of Chinese–Indian–Mexican relationships. One day a combined effort on the part of scholars may prove Kirchhoff's point by reconstructing an original god-list, from which the later versions of America and Asia derived. Unfortunately the instigator of this research was not spared to continue his absorbing task.

Finally, comparisons between Asia and America remain incomplete without mention of the odd likenesses between the Hindu game of Pachesi and the Mexican Patolli, still played when the Spaniards arrived. Sir Edward Taylor, in 1879, was among the first to draw attention to this phenomenon: in both games the counters were moved along tracks that were cruciform in shape, drawn on mats or boards; in each case their movement was determined by throwing lots, consisting of six cowrie shells in the Hindu version and in the Aztec game of five black beans with white dots on one side; although the scoring was arbitrary, there was a common tendency to give greater weight to the more difficult throws.

Since the early Spanish chroniclers gave only fragmentary

information on the rules of Patolli, Taylor studied equivalent games played in other parts of Mexico and in the south-western United States; their similarity to Pachesi led him to conclude that the American lot-games had somehow been brought from Asia before Columbus. While Taylor assumed that Patolli itself had been the original New World version, later writers thought that the more basic and simpler versions of the south-western United States had inspired the Mexican game. Needham, incidentally, though he writes little on the subject, provides an interesting chart of possible relationships between New and Old World games and divination techniques.*

Whole volumes could be written on the perplexities of this conundrum. However, as C. J. Erasmus has pointed out, the alleged similarities between Pachesi and Patolli are less convincing when examined singly and in detail. For example, both boards are cruciform but the cross is a basic human motif, predominant in the Old World but also present in Mexican codices. Dice-throwing could easily be invented twice, and distinct New World variations could have sprung from a common notion of gambling with lots. Alternatively, American dice could have originated in very simple games of chance such as that played by the Eskimos, who simply tossed figurines into the air, winning those that landed upright.*

So far arguments favouring Asian contacts have been advanced, with brief mention of obvious flaws. Before enlarging on my own views, I prefer to cite Doctor Alfonso Caso, certainly the greatest Mexican archaeologist of his generation if not of all time. Probably nothing served more to stimulate my interest in Ancient Mexico than the privilege of accompanying Caso on a visit to Monte Albán, the scene of his greatest triumphs, and to the Oaxaca Museum where the famous jewels that he found are housed.

Caso categorically rejected diffusionist theories on American origins. At the 35th Congress of Americanists in Mexico City he produced illustrations of near-identical art forms just as striking as those arising between Mexico and China; but Caso's photographs concerned styles and civilizations between which any notion of contact was ludicrous. For instance, virtually indistinguishable pitchers from Bronze Age Palestine and from Monte Albán, Mexico, were shown; the unbridge-able time-gap between the two excludes borrowing. Also cited were peculiar patterns of braid, enclosed between parallel lines, which were almost identical although deriving from Mycenae, Pompeii and Monte Albán. In a second series of matching patterns, two came from Mexico and the third from a Louis XVI table in the Louvre! Caso demonstrated that a central Mexican method of drawing the rattles of a rattlesnake was also used on a Louis XVI commode; and he added an illustration of a strange criss-cross decorative design found in such disparate contexts as Peru, Mexico, Africa and Norway.*

Caso does not exclude all possibility of Old and New World contacts; he simply stresses the danger of leaping to conclusions on the basis of stylistic comparisons unbacked by other data. He also warns against hasty judgment on the origins of the New World calendric and writing systems. Elementary glyphs occur in Mexico around 600 B.C., when the basic forms of the sacred 260-day calendar also appear; logically, therefore, if the Chinese introduced the concept of writing, they did so before that date. The Shang Dynasty, ending in about 1000 B.C., admittedly possessed a form of recording, found on the famous oracle bones, but it has nothing in common with Olmec glyphs or with later Chinese ideograms (Shang writing is indeed unlike the modern Chinese script, although it contains the same six principal sign varieties). Caso also poses the key question: cultural traits can only be transferred when a means of transportation exists, and transoceanic voyages in this early period are unlikely. The Shang and their Chou successors were a land, not a sea power; at best they made coastal voyages or crossed short stretches of open sea, such as the strait dividing mainland China from Formosa. The Mexican scholar even rejects the likelihood of visits from Polynesia to South America and regards navigation by the sun and stars as impractical. On this point I tend to differ, as will later be explained in more detail.

Unquestionably striking parallels, mainly related to art forms, arise between Asia and America. However, when Heine-Geldern writes about proselytizing by Buddhist missionaries, the sceptics are entitled to raise their heads. The most cursory study of Mexican religion suffices to show that its pitiless pantheon stood for opposing values to those of the gentle Buddha. Both creeds may prefer penance to pleasure; however, the true Buddhist goal is the extinction of self as a release from suffering, while the Mexican religions appease the gods with human blood, precisely to preserve the self and its surrounding world; the Buddha condemned war and violence while the Mexican gods demanded them. When the Emperor Asoka was converted to Buddhism, he tried desperately to prevent his people from killing animals; his missionaries would have faced an uphill task in America, where human beings were the gods' favourite food.

Certain of Caso's arguments are hard to refute; in particular the *absence* of certain traits in the New World is important. Chinese records significantly state that when an expedition was sent out into the Eastern Ocean in search of the longevity drugs, the seeds of five grains were taken, as well as artisans, implying that this was routine procedure for explorers. The Chinese are therefore unlikely to have made contact with the New World without carrying seeds thither, if not on the first trip, at least on later journeys; the staple Chinese crops of rice and millet were *not*, however, found by the Spaniards when they arrived. And if the Chinese made a practice of carrying seeds on voyages of discovery, they are even less likely to have returned (as Heine-Geldern postulates) without also bringing back New World plant specimens, such as tobacco and maize. The effort would have paid sure dividends since, when introduced into China after Columbus, maize was most popular and its cultivation spread like wildfire.*

The same principle applies to the animal kingdom and provides some compelling arguments. If human beings reached America from Asia in the first millennium of our era, the rat and the pig were oddly reluctant to accompany them. The pig had spread gradually from Asia all over Polynesia long before European discovery; but these fabled Chinese voyagers apparently gave no thought for the gastronomic needs of their hosts and went out of their way to deny this benefit to the poor Mexicans, whose supplies of domestic animal protein were so sadly deficient, being limited to a monotonous diet of dog and turkey. The two kinds of rat that mainly prey on Man, as opposed to some five hundred other known varieties, spread from Java to China at an early date, and from there arrived in Europe. But archaeologists have shown that this same rat is a post-Columbian migrant into America. American-bound Chinese or Indian vessels miraculously purged themselves of rats, those expert stowaways that managed to make repeated voyages on Polynesian outrigger canoes, where far fewer hiding places existed. On some Oceanic islands Europeans later found the rats in sole possession, while the humans who unwittingly brought them had disappeared; in Oceania the rat at least served a useful purpose, and rat-hunts used to be undertaken, partly in sport but also to supplement scarce supplies of protein.

At the opposite end of the cultural spectrum the same reasoning applies: not only were the common rat and the domestic pig absent, but many of the finest manifestations of Han Dynasty art are also lacking in America. Certain parallel forms may indeed be found, but the great pottery tower houses, the bronze vessels and the delicate lacquer, so typical of contemporary China, are conspicuous by their absence.

In dealing with Asian–American contacts, transport problems are paramount. Generalized assertions by eminent Sinologists that early Chinese or Indians could have crossed the Pacific are not sufficient, and such vagueness is out of keeping with their more pointed observations on art and culture. Boats designed for plying up and down the coast would stand a poor chance against the giant ocean rollers, and Caso is surely right in depicting Shang and Chou China as a land, not a sea power. These dynasties occupied a limited coastline and the centre of gravity of their realm was landward. The Chinese of that time were not born sailors – a point well illustrated by the fate of one Chou ruler, King Chao (1052–1002 B.C.), of whom the encyclopaedic dictionary Tzuhai relates: 'The king was making a tour of inspection in the south. When he reached the river Han, the people of Ching [proposed to] ferry him across in a boat held together with glue. When it reached the middle of the stream, the glue dissolved and the boat came apart. Both the king and the Duke of Chi were drowned.' A Fu Chien story tells of an emperor who was such a bad sailor that he was seasick whenever he was rowed on a canal.

The Phoenicians built vessels theoretically capable of cutting direct across the high seas as early as 700 B.C. But in Asia the first known oceanic voyages took place between the first and third centuries A.D.; the ships that made them were Roman in name, but in fact belonged to Graeco-Egyptians, who discovered in about A.D. 50 that with the help of the monsoon winds a rapid direct crossing was possible from the opening of the Red Sea to Indian ports situated at the extreme tip of the sub-continent and previously attainable only by hugging the coast. Probably towards the end of the third century B.C. , a few India-bound vessels went on to Indochina.

However, these were Mediterranean ships and Needham in his detailed study concludes that only *after* the third century A.D. did the Chinese themselves develop long-distance navigation. Their ships sailed to Malaysia in about A.D. 350, visited Ceylon a few decades later and by the fifth century probably voyaged as far as the mouth of the Euphrates. The situation was then partly reversed, and Islamic shipmasters began to visit China and established factories in Hangchow and Canton in the ninth century, as did the English a thousand years later; the Arabs also reached Korea and Japan. Later, however, the Chinese once more gained the upper hand and their maritime skills reached their peak just before the arrival of the Portuguese in the early sixteenth century.

Until fairly recently information on Han Dynasty craft was patchy, since no model boats had been found in tombs. But excavations in Canton in 1954 yielded an excellent example of a river craft propelled by oars, together with several ships for use in estuaries and on the sea, dating from about A.D. 100. One of these clay models represents a boat with a typical Chinese flat-bottomed hull; for two-thirds of its length the vessel is covered by a barrel-vaulted roof, perhaps made of matting, out of which rise three deckhouses, of which the aftermost is clearly the steersman's cabin; the siting of the mast remains a mystery.*

In 1974 Kuno Knöbl had a full-sized replica of this clay model junk constructed in Hong Kong. Manned by a crew of five, and captained by Danish Carl Frederik Grage, the junk set out across the Pacific, intending to take advantage of the Kuroshio current that flows from Japan towards California, following approximately the 40th parallel. The boat, named *Tai-Ki*, meaning 'The Great All', was 20.10 metres long. No metal was used in the construction, which was held together by 3,000 wooden nails and 1,000 wooden bolts. Influenced by the obvious similarities between Mexican and Chinese art forms, Knöbl had set out to prove that the Chinese of the first century A.D. were capable of crossing the Pacific.

The expedition sailed on 16 June and its progress is described in Knöbl's book *Tai-Ki*. Because of a damaged rudder, the voyage was first interrupted at Kaoshing in Formosa. When they set forth again, a violent hurricane tore the sail in half, though it was eventually repaired. A complete calm followed this storm, and for three weeks the boat proceeded at a snail's pace, reaching the vicinity of Japan on 11 August. Having survived a typhoon, the junk finally fell victim to the action of teredo worms that bored into the hull until it became riddled with holes and sank in mid-Pacific on 9 October after a voyage of nearly four months.

This abortive attempt offers no conclusive proof either way. The ancient Chinese presumably knew more about protecting their ships from the ravages of the teredo. But apart from this deciding factor Knöbl's account leaves the reader with the impression that the junk was ill-suited to the task in hand; and Needham's statement that real seagoing ships were introduced about two centuries later, a date too late to coincide with Early Teotihuacán in Mexico, is probably right. If they were to exercise a major influence on that civilization, travellers from China had to arrive when it was still in its infancy, not at its zenith.

Yet harder to explain is the absence of Han Dynasty contacts with Japan. In 10 B.C., at the very .time when links with America were supposedly forged, the Chinese had invaded Korea, but did not proceed to nearby Japan. Four centuries later even Korea was abandoned. The Japanese are known to have visited China once during the interval, but not until the sixth century did Japan really come under the influence of the Chinese, after they had introduced Buddhism into the country in A.D. 552. A great reform of government was then undertaken in Japan, which became a united empire administered by a Chinese-style bureaucracy.

If the Chinese shrank from braving the short crossing from Korea to southern Japan, the mere contemplation of a vast journey to America in ill-suited craft would have been whimsical. Between America and China lay 6,000 miles of ocean, whereas by a process of island-hopping the widest stretch of open sea between Korea and Japan amounted to a bare 40 miles. Since the Chinese did in fact stay away from Japan, avoiding a crossing that might be achieved without losing sight of land, I remain unconvinced that *deliberate* trips to America were made.

And even if the Chinese did reach America, they tell us absolutely nothing of their adventures. References from historical sources have already been cited, insisting that no expedition had crossed the Eastern Ocean and returned thence. The Chinese were the most painstaking keepers of records, so copious that modern scholars rely partly on their writing for news of happenings in neighbouring countries such as India, whose recording of events was more spasmodic.

Chinese chronicles start at an early date. The great Shih Chi was written by Ssuma Chi'en, who was born in 135 B.C. and has been called the first historian of the modern type. The work consists of annals, including tables on the occupants of official posts and fiefs, together with biographies of important personalities and of the hereditary ducal families. But no Chinese Columbus earned a place in the record. The same historian also provides chronological tables, as well as many monographs on specialized fields of knowledge such as astronomy, calendrics, music, economics and even official court dress. In addition to the Shih Chi, a number of encyclopaedias were compiled. But nowhere in this voluminous documentation, richer than its equivalent in fifteenth-century Spain, is one syllable to be found relating to journeys to the New World.

Heine-Geldern and Ekholm may be on rather firmer ground when dealing with India and South-East Asia. From Chinese Han Dynasty records of the third century A.D., we learn of 'foreign' boats, perhaps Indian, that carried between six and seven hundred persons and had four sails. In the great temple of Borabudur in Java, eighth-century reliefs depict five large sailing ships. The Indians probably reached Java in the second or third century, and in the fourth century an Indian kingdom was established in the western part of the island, though no traces survive. If Indian ships had indeed reached America, they would presumably have made the voyage under the sway of the Gupta Empire, whose conquest of northern India dates from A.D. 320 and heralded an age of material expansion and artistic creativity. But the same problem again arises: to reach Java from Malaysia involves crossing something like ten miles of open sea, as compared with the six thousand that separate the opposite shores of the Pacific! Again, not one mention is to be found about such adventures in any record, although the Indians had possessed an efficient alphabet for a thousand years and many Gupta writings survive.

In the final analysis, what, if anything, unites China and Mexico? Of common language no trace exists; of plants introduced by Man no knowledge survives; religious comparisons are confined to ritual details; and political institutions present few parallels. Only similar art forms remain, such as the lotus motifs, the elephant trunks, the ceramic scroll designs and the human heads emerging from animal bodies.

The lack of fresh evidence is another discouraging aspect of the problem. The intrusion of the elephant and the lotus into Maya art has been debated for over a century and even the wheeled toys of Mexico were found a generation ago. New and spectacular finds may one day transform the scene, though as far as I know not one Asian object has yet been found in a truly pre-Columbian context. The nearest approach was perhaps the Chinese 'soapstone lamp' that was unearthed in the Maya region but so near to the surface that it could easily have been introduced into its pre-Columbian mound after the Conquest, when Chinese wares were being shipped to Mexico via Manila.

Navigational limitations, the lack of reports by Chinese sages and scholars, the absence of common fauna and flora make deliberate travel between China and America hard to credit. Accidental journeys remain a possibility since junks are known to have been blown off course and reached the coast of the United States at the rate of about one every five years during the nineteenth century. However, in the varied list of modern ocean crossings by small craft given in *Man across the Sea*, not one example occurs of a voyage from East Asia to America. People have tended to cross the Pacific in the opposite direction; and significantly they invariably landed in Australia or Polynesia, whither the east–west currents propelled them, never in China. Obviously Chinese visitors to the New World who tried to return home would have been more likely to end up as lifelong guests of the Australian Aborigines.

Once Asians possessed ships that were not reduced to matchwood by the first ocean rollers, they could have survived a voyage to America if they had luck on their side. The record of accidental Chinese transpacific voyages in the nineteenth century suggests that crossings could conceivably have occurred in much earlier times after a boat had totally lost its bearings in one of the many typhoons that visit the seas of China and Japan. The casualty rate would have been high, and the early Chinese discovery of the compass does not affect the issue; the instrument first appeared in China in A.D. 1080 – for use in divinatory practices and games of chess, not for sea travel!

A faint possibility exists that earlier sailing rafts, such as Hsü Fu used in the third century B.C., were occasionally blown across the Pacific and survived – completing a *Kon-Tiki* voyage in reverse. But I persist in doubting that the arrival of involuntary passengers on rafts or junks would have had revolutionary effects in the place where they landed. The expedition of Alvar Núñez Cabeza de Vaca reached Florida in 1528, but when the peninsula was finally occupied by the Spaniards in the 1560s no trace of the previous visit was to be found among the local Indians. The Vikings remained in Greenland for five hundred years but their presence made no impact upon the Eskimos.

If a Chinese junk had been wafted over the ocean and landed upon the shores of pre-Columbian Mexico, the crew might have been welcomed not as distinguished guests but as very special sacrificial victims; the offering of a Chinese mandarin to the Rain God would alone have sufficed to ensure a bumper harvest. Recent evidence suggests that human sacrifice was more frequently practised in Teotihuacán times than had previously been considered likely. Such Chinese visitors would have then been ritually eaten, but not in their own pots, which were perhaps carried off to Teotihuacán or some important centre where the designs were copied. The Spanish parallel may again be cited. The first gifts of Cortés to Moctezuma were treated with veneration, piously preserved in jewelled casks and taken to the holy city of Tula. But despite their respect for the relics the Aztecs had no scruples about sacrificing Cortés' men when they had the chance, though their complaints about the bitter taste of Spanish flesh were loud.

If similarities between Teotihuacán and Han styles were anything more than coincidental, they could more realistically be explained in this way. And supposing the people of Teotihuacán had copied a few Asian designs, the effect on their civilization of this interchange would have been exiguous. This metropolis, the imprint of whose genius is found throughout the length and breadth of Middle America, acquired an intellectual momentum of its own, regardless of whether it chose to borrow a few foreign forms; the same may be said of the Maya. Large-scale importation of Chinese wares in the eighteenth century inspired the Europeans to make Chinoiserie objects; but the fashion had no impact upon the march of events.

CHAPTER SIX

WHITE GODS WITH BLACK FACES

FOR several centuries the Toltecs of Tula had dominated central Mexico. But in about A.D. 1180 the city lay at its last gasp, rent with internal dissension. The supreme ruler was then Topiltzin Quetzalcóatl, named after the Plumed Serpent god, the presiding deity of the Toltec realm. Believing that Tula was doomed, the king prepared to depart, having been tricked into this faint-hearted decision by supporters of rival gods; they employed the simple device of showing the king in a mirror his own face, which was by then so wrinkled and ugly that he shrank from appearing ever again before his subjects.

Quetzalcóatl, therefore, sent for his chief feather-worker, who would prepare him for the journey and who proceeded as follows:

> He first made him the plumed headdress of Quetzalcóatl. Then he made his green mask; he took red colouring with which he made his lips crimson; he took yellow colouring, to make the facial stripes; then he made snakes' fangs, finally he made his beard of feathers, of the red spoonbill and the blue cotinga, which he then folded backwards.

Quetzalcóatl again took the mirror, and at the sight of his own form arrayed in all the traditional finery he once more felt contented.

Amid the lamentations of his people, Quetzalcóatl thereafter set out on his long journey to the place in the east where he was destined to meet his end, known as the 'Red and Black Land':

> In this year I Reed, having arrived at the heavenly edge of the diving water [the sea-coast], he [Quetzalcóatl] stopped, wept, drew up his vestments, arranged his feather headdress and his green mask. Then he arrayed himself, and by his own hand set fire to his body and was consumed. For this reason the place was called the place of burning. They say that when he was burned, and as his ashes ascended, all the birds of paradise came out to see them, as

they rose to heaven: the red spoonbill, the blue cotinga, the trogan, the parrots and many other beautiful birds. . . . As far as is known, he rose to heaven and entered therein. The old men say that he was transformed into the star which appears in the morning.

The account then describes how he remained four days in the land of the dead and, on the eighth day, reappeared as the Morning Star.*

This moving passage, providing the most authentic Indian account of the final destiny of the Plumed Serpent, is taken from the Annals of Cuauhtitlan, a year-by-year record of pre-Conquest history and legend recorded in the Nahuatl language. Such sagas were faithfully committed to memory and handed down from one generation to the next, both in the schools for the common people and in those set aside for the Aztec nobility.

The tale is rich in symbolism, and every detail of the departing ruler's attire has its religious significance. Quetzalcóatl is depicted both as demi-god and as human being in a story in which fact and myth are inextricably woven; the Plumed Serpent deity is also the bearded hero (his 'beard' being an artificial one of blue and red feathers), who departed to the east, was consumed by fire, and became the Planet Venus. A rather different version of the tale, also derived from strictly *native* informants, simply describes Quetzalcóatl as departing on a serpent raft:

And when he [Quetzalcóatl] had done these things, he went to reach the sea-coast. Thereupon he fashioned a raft of serpents. When he had arranged the raft, there he placed himself, as if it were his boat. Then he set off across the sea.*

Other variants of the story of Quetzalcóatl, however, introduce new and different elements. To the basic narrative was added the detail that he had a white skin and a flowing natural beard, and that he was traditionally expected to return, not at set intervals as the Planet Venus, but once only, in human form.

Many writers have made such great play of these added refinements that it becomes necessary to consider how far they form part of the truly Indian legend, and how far they are mere Spanish embellishments. The same question also applies to parallel tales in Peru, where a leading deity,

Viracocha, also departed across the sea. According to certain accounts, this god too had a white beard, and was destined to return.

The American historian William H. Prescott, writing in 1843, preferred the modified version of the Mexican story and tells how Quetzalcóatl of Tula, who was tall in stature, with white skin, long dark hair and flowing beard, was expected one day to return to his people; this tradition, deeply cherished in the Mexicans' hearts, paved the way for the Spanish advance. Prescott, who never visited Mexico or Peru, wrote in stately prose a history of the conquest of both countries. His story leans towards the Spanish rather than the Indian point of view, but the work has never been surpassed as a classic account of the triumphs and tragedies of ancient America.

From the time of Prescott onwards, in the countless books about the Conquest, this legend of the expected return of the white bearded god has been blindly accepted; the tale has been put to a variety of uses, and nowadays no book on Indian origins is complete without a section devoted to the activities of this itinerant pale-faced deity, appearing in human form. His alleged existence has been cited as positive proof of the arrival in America of an infinite range of peoples, including Etruscans, Greeks, Phoenicians, Egyptians and even Irish. The legend has even served to support the notion of a reverse migration from South America to the Polynesian Islands. And, more incredibly, the presence of white gods has been offered as evidence that the American Indians received visitors not merely from other continents of this planet, but from outer space.

Scholars who cautiously seek Chinese and Indian influences in America have steered clear of this line of reasoning. In any case white skins and flowing beards add nothing to their arguments, and these writers realize that parts of the saga rest on flimsy foundations and might only weaken their case. In contrast to this more conservative approach, nearly every non-specialist who enters the field is determined to extract the maximum mileage from the alleged presence in America of white gods.

The surviving records certainly make ample mention of humanized versions of the gods Quetzalcóatl and Viracocha. So the deities themselves and the heroes who personified them were no mere latter-day invention. Moreover, both Quetzalcóatl and Viracocha are often, but not always, depicted as wearing beards. And yet the key questions remain: were these gods really conceived as having white skins, and were they expected to return in human guise? Are such additions to the saga of their departure from Earth part of the truly Indian myth, or were they a clever fabrication of the Spaniards, designed to reinforce beliefs that they personified returning gods and were therefore invincible?

A richer store of early records of American Indian history has survived than is generally realized, notwithstanding deliberate destruction by the Spaniards. But few people read those accounts; their perusal is left to specialists, historians more often than archaeologists, who (with notable exceptions) pay too little heed to documents relating to the sites where they dig.

Pictorial codices are confined to Mexico and none is known for South America. In central Mexico, most codices are post-Hispanic copies the originals of which were burned in great quantities by the Spaniards as representing works of the devil. But in addition, abundant accounts of Indian history and civilization survive, written by the early friars who came to America. In Mexico much pre-Conquest history was also recorded in the native Nahuatl language by Indian pupils of the friars, including several princes of former reigning houses.

The main records now exist in printed editions and can be studied without poring over moth-eaten manuscripts; the principal Nahuatl documents have been translated into European languages with varying degrees of accuracy. However, the non-specialist usually finds such material long-winded, confused, repetitious, contradictory and, therefore, unreadable. Historical narrative is often interspersed with long dissertations on Christian virtues and native vices, in which the author is quick to dissociate himself from any praise of Indian idolatry. As a result modern writers are more often content to accept second-hand accounts of what the original sources relate, and one single interpretation – frequently erroneous – is then passed from book to book without its accuracy ever being called in question.

Moreover, without some experience of the problems, direct study is of limited value. Mexican and Peruvian ancient histories are not always strictly factual, since they were designed to edify as much as to inform. An early Aztec emperor actually burned many of the existing records, keeping only those which supported his 'orthodox' version of tribal origins. These expurgated versions consisted of part myth and part fact, and the task of separating one from the other is baffling. The work is further complicated because the original accounts mostly reach us through the medium of Spaniards or Hispanized Indians, who put their own gloss on native documents and on the reports of native informants.

Even nowadays people of mainly Indian origin usually tell their listener what they think he *wants* to hear, in preference to an unvarnished and less palatable version of the facts. Accordingly, after native history and legend had been bowdlerized by the native rulers themselves, it was again refurbished to conform to Spanish susceptibilities. Students of ancient American history are therefore nowadays increasingly cautious in their interpretations. This attitude is not altogether new; certain nineteenth-century writers were already over-sceptical and treated Indian records as pure myth.

The non-specialist writer, however, prefers straightforward conclusions and all too often will pick on an uncertain tale and record it as a historical fact. Current versions of the Plumed Serpent story accordingly tend to derive, not from what Fray Sahagún was directly told by *native* informers, themselves former worshippers of that deity, but from what Prescott or other less notable figures had later gleaned from *Spanish* chroniclers.

Certain errors concerning Quetzalcóatl arise because people take for granted that all American Indians were facially hairless; therefore, if any bearded figure is portrayed in ancient art, *ipso facto* he is not an Indian but an immigrant from another continent, if not from another world. But if assertions that the American Indian was beardless turn out to be exaggerated, this line of reasoning collapses. The *average* Indian is indeed comparatively hairless. Moreover, any search for exceptions to this generalization defies scientific proof, for if bearded men nowadays appear in Indian villages, this trait can be attributed to traces of Spanish blood, introduced into their community perhaps centuries ago. Alternatively, if evidence is sought from the past, Mexican codices can also mislead, since they often portray gods who were bearded by tradition and whose beards were false.

But clearly *some* Indians possessed *some* facial hair, even if it was relatively sparse. The presence of long-headed Caucasoids among early American Man has already been stressed, even if the Mongoloids were predominant. The Ainus of Japan and other Caucasoids of eastern

Siberia have fairly abundant facial hair. Part at least of the Indian population of America could have inherited this trait, even if the situation varied from one tribe to another, and among individuals of a given group.

Supposing, moreover, that some or all Indians were indeed hairless: such a quality should presumably be attributed to Mongoloid blood, rather than to Caucasoid or Negroid. But this argument is self-defeating because the Chinese are typically Mongoloid, yet in China since time immemorial old men and sages have been commonly depicted as wearing beards, though usually of a rather straggly kind. Some Chinese were more hirsute; of the founder of the ruling house of Han, it was written: 'He was a man with a prominent nose and a dragon forehead. He had a beautiful beard on his chin and cheeks.'* This point can be demonstrated just as well without recourse to ancient texts and paintings. Any modern visitor to Hong Kong, or to any other city inhabited by Chinese, can see for himself that they can and do grow beards in old age. The same is even truer of Japan; I was struck by the number of typically Japanese men with moustaches to be seen nowadays in Tokyo, and a wrestler who sported a bushy beard even appeared on television.

Therefore the three principal elements from which American Man sprang, not only the Caucasoids and Negroids but also the Mongoloids, in varying degrees possessed facial hair. In addition, the Eskimos are much more hairy than the average American Indian, and many of those whom I saw in the Arctic had walrus moustaches. Every anthropologist agrees that the Eskimos came from Asia, even if they arrived later than the original American Indians. But, once an Asian origin for the hirsute Eskimo is accepted, no earthly reason remains for insisting that other inhabitants of America who have beards and moustaches must be Phoenicians or Greeks who arrived from Europe.

Unfortunately the written records offer fragmentary data on facial appearance since in pre-Hispanic times people were not much given to portraiture or to personal descriptions. However, the eyewitness report by Bernal Díaz del Castillo of the first meeting between Cortés and Moctezuma says that the Emperor's beard was light, well-arranged and thinnish. Of the appearance of earlier Aztec rulers, no accounts survive.

In Peru other evidence is available: fair quantities of pincers specifically designed for the removal of facial hair have been unearthed (some of these instruments have also been found in north-western Mexico). Peruvian specimens are often made of gold, suggesting that beards – or their absence – had some sacred or religious significance. In the Museum of Archaeology in Lima a Mochica 'portrait' head illustrating a man busy removing hair from his cheeks with pincers can be seen.

So much for the notion that all Indians have hairless faces. Probably most of them, like Moctezuma, could grow only light beards; but to this rule exceptions surely existed since in any given group certain individuals are invariably more hairy than the average. American Indian art is highly stylized and imbued with religious symbolism. Therefore, if beards were portrayed at all, they would naturally be drawn rather larger than life. It seems that, as in China, they became a symbol of old age since the oldest Mexican gods are usually depicted as wearing beards; the fire god is an example, as well as another deity simply known as the 'Old God'. Furthermore, in certain cases such gods are shown as having *white* beards; this trait is nothing but an outward sign of old age, among black people as well as Europeans, and has nothing whatsoever to do with the possession of a white skin. In the Codex Borgia another older god is several times portrayed with a white beard but with coffee-coloured face and body. The depiction of bearded figures in Indian Art from many regions is based on religious ritual rather than exact portraiture. Nor is this a purely American phenomenon; Quetzalcóatl donned a beard of feathers before he was to die; but the death mask of Tutankhamen also displays a false beard.

Volumes have been written about Quetzalcóatl, whose name means 'Plumed' or 'Precious Serpent'. Stone images of the Plumed Serpent do not appear at a very early date and are seldom found among the Olmecs or the classic Mayas. The full cult of Quetzalcóatl, represented either as a stone serpent or as a god in human form, only reached its climax in the era dominated by the Toltecs of Tula (from A.D. 900 to 1200). This humanized Quetzalcóatl, usually equipped with beard, first appeared in carvings and codices in about A.D. 700. From then onwards he was worshipped as a creator god who brought culture to the human race; in this creative role a beard was the unfailing symbol of his antiquity.

For the Toltecs, Quetzalcóatl is both the god and the legendary king who abandons Tula at its fall. But in addition to being bearded, was

Quetzalcóatl also a white man, and did his people expect him one day to return? The two suppositions were used to further Spanish aims and have become imprinted on the minds of contemporary authors who seek Indian origins. Speculation on the peculiar relationship between Cortés and Moctezuma never ceases, and most writers attribute the spineless attitude of the Aztec ruler to a conviction that his adversary was the great white god, returned from across the Eastern Ocean to claim his heritage.

Moctezuma himself seems to have evolved this theory, in the absence of any deep-rooted Indian tradition that Quetzalcóatl was destined to return. The Emperor, driven to frenzy by reports of rare happenings and prompted more by magic than by reason, became persuaded that because these bearded strangers approached his kingdom from the east, and in the year known as I Reed in the fifty-two-year Mexican calendar cycle, they *had* to be Quetzalcóatl and his followers. The conclusion seemed logical to Moctezuma because, according to a perfectly authentic legend, the bearded and divine hero of that name had left Tula and departed eastwards in the same year I Reed.

To people who thought mainly in magico-religious terms, the Spaniards inevitably appeared as divine beings. The invaders came in weird houses floating on the sea; their terrifying weapons belched fire and sounded like thunder; they were mounted upon horrendous beasts, and at first horse and rider were even believed to be one. Nevertheless Moctezuma remained uncertain as to whether Cortés represented Quetzalcóatl or another god. When the Conqueror was still on the coast approaching Vera Cruz, the Emperor sent magnificent gifts which included the traditional attire not only of Quetzalcóatl, but also of the Rain God and of another deity known as 'Smoking Mirror'.

Cortés himself, quick to take advantage of any situation and well-briefed by his Indian mentor, Doña María, about the Quetzalcóatl legend, chose to don the accoutrements of that particular deity, and the Spanish hidalgo was momentarily transformed into a plumed serpent. The new god then caused his cannon to be fired, upon which Moctezuma's envoys fell to the ground as if dead – such was the initial effect of this display of divine powers. The Spaniards tried to revive the natives' shattered spirits with wine, but the unfamiliar potion merely made them drunk.

Moctezuma may have drawn his own deductions from the

direction of Cortés' coming and the date. But the notion that Quetzalcóatl was generally regarded as a white god, in the sense of possessing a white skin, is plainly a fabrication of the Spaniards, designed to further their own ends. The story that the Indians expected the Plumed Serpent god to return also rests upon flimsy foundations.

The assertion that Quetzalcóatl was white and that he was destined one day to reappear can be traced not to native sources but to Hispanized chroniclers, whose references to the subject are vague. Fray Motolinia, writing between 1530 and 1546, tells of a god of the wind called Quetzalcóatl, who came from Tula and would one day return.* Fray Mendieta, towards the end of the sixteenth century, repeats the same tale, but improves upon the original by adding the detail that he was white as well as bearded.* Alva Ixtlilxóchitl, writing even later, repeats this but with the added refinement that Quetzalcóatl was expected to come back in the year I Reed.* However, the *native* sources, written in Nahuatl, say nothing about Quetzalcóatl returning — except as the Morning Star.

Writers continue to harp on the Spanish accounts of the white god who was destined to come back one day. People unaware of the deep vein of symbolism permeating ancient Mexican thought may be impressed by such a story. But both Alfonso Caso and Hermann Beyer, foremost among scholars versed in Mexican religion, ridiculed the notion.* They both rightly insisted that more often than not Quetzalcóatl is depicted as wearing a strange duckbill mask, an integral part of his attire as god of the wind. When, however, the deity appears in codices without this adornment, then invariably his face is totally black (the symbolic colour of priests), or else it is black with vertical yellow stripes. So much for the 'white' god.

A further point needs to be explained: the Spaniards, eager to foster the notion of their invincibility as the incarnation of the white god and his followers, naturally turned to their advantage any kernel of truth that might add substance to such reports. Now a certain link between Quetzalcóatl and the colour white indeed existed, but of quite a different kind. As I have said, Quetzalcóatl was the personification of Venus as Morning Star, but he was equally identified with Venus as Evening Star, and hence with old age, with nightfall, and with the west, where the sun ends its course. But in ancient Mexico, though the north was more closely associated with the colour white, the entrance of the house of the dead was situated in the west, and since white was the colour of death, attributable to corpses and skeletons, Quetzalcóatl did enjoy a connection with the colour white through his identification with old age and with the west. But this association does not mean that he was ever conceived as having a white skin.

In short Quetzalcóatl as creator god did possess a beard as a token of old age, even if it was often made of feathers; after he took on human form, he had indeed departed to the east. Equally, *symbolically* at least, he was expected to return from the east, not once but repeatedly as the Morning Star. Remoter links also connect the god with the *colour* white. But no authentic legend even implied that he was of a different race, let alone a white European. Other Mexican gods were also identified with the cardinal points and with specific colours. But to pretend that Quetzalcóatl was a white man is no more logical than to insist that the great Aztec god of war, often known as 'Lord of the Southern Sky', represented a blue man, merely because he was ritually associated with the sky at midday and hence with the colour blue. No writer has yet dared to suggest that this deity was really an ancient Briton, painted with blue woad.

In Peru the situation runs curiously parallel, though marked by certain differences. In the first place, Peruvian expectations that bearded white gods might appear out of the sea could easily have arisen not from some time-honoured myth, but merely from reports of recent happenings in lands lying farther to the north. Even before Balboa came to Panama, Columbus on his fourth voyage tried in 1503 to found a trading post at Santa María de Belén, but was driven away by hostile Indians. Santa María lies about forty miles west of the Caribbean opening of the Panama Canal and only about nine hundred miles as the crow flies from Tumbez, in the north of Peru, where Pizarro first landed in 1527, though the distance would be greater by a coastal route. Moctezuma's intelligence service reported in a matter of days that Cortés had landed at a point some five hundred miles distant from the Aztec capital. Therefore the Incas, whose northern boundary lay well beyond Tumbez in the direction of Panama, presumably were at least dimly aware, through a kind of jungle telegraph, of the appearance of miraculous white beings who travelled in houses upon the sea and who, like Jupiter, made their own thunder. Smallpox, previously unknown, had spread from Panama to South America before the Spaniards arrived in person; the same is probably true of the domestic chicken. News also travelled, perhaps in garbled form, and reports of exotic travellers would be hitched on to any existing legends concerning a god who had previously abandoned his people and gone off across the sea.

Pizarro was keenly aware of the magnificent use to which the Spaniards had put such legends in Mexico as a means of furthering their own designs. This ruthless conquistador was, therefore, on the lookout for any bearded Peruvian deity or for legends of men with fair faces that might be used as a basis for propaganda to convince the natives that the invaders were gods and, therefore, irresistible. The quest was not a hard one, for the Peruvian pantheon, like the Mexican, boasted of at least one bearded god, worshipped under a variety of names. This deity in earlier times had been known as Cons, the first creator of the world, or, alternatively, as Con or Con-Ticci (hence the name Kon-Tiki). On the coast Con later came to be called Pachamacac and, in the interior, Viracocha, first at the Bolivian site of Tihuanaco and subsequently in the Inca capital of Cuzco.

In some repects Viracocha was a sun god since his name *Pachamacac* means 'Son of the Sun', and in his original role he appears as a solar deity in the great Tihuanaco stone statues. But in later times the god, like Quetzalcóatl, was principally revered as creator and, according to Inca legend, had fashioned the different tribes of Man out of figures of stone and clay which he had made in Tihuanaco.

Like Quetzalcóatl, Viracocha eventually departed the land. The orthodox and generalized report of Ticci Viracocha's disappearance from the world relates that he first went to Cuzco and then after many vicissitudes reached the coast of Ecuador, spread his mantle and like foam rushed forth, walking across the sea (Viracocha means 'foam of the sea'). According to alternative accounts, the departing deity, after walking on the sea and on rivers, rose into the heavens and there-after lived in the sky. A third version states that (like Quetzalcóatl) Viracocha was consumed by fire on the coast. Since he is often credited with sons and other companions, it became natural to talk in the plural of 'Viracochas'; with these the Spaniards could aim to become identified.

In these legends, no expectation that Viracocha would one day return is in evidence. The tradition that he walked away over the sea simply symbolizes the motion of a solar god. The sun, as it rises and sets, itself 'walks' or glides over the water.

Spanish sources often portray Viracocha – again like Quetzalcóatl – as a benevolent figure who travelled from place to place, preaching repentance and performing miracles. This itinerant god, dressed in a long white cloak and leaning upon a staff, is inevitably bearded, but not always white-skinned. Such accounts of his career transform the blazing (and beardless) sun god into a mild-mannered missionary.

But from the different Viracocha legends three salient points emerge: first, the original deity is seldom reported as being white; secondly, no clear prediction occurs of his subsequent return; thirdly, certain embellishments to the original tale bear an indelible stamp 'made in Spain'. The white robe and the flowing beard might have been inspired by an early report of Viracocha stating simply that he was tall, dressed in white, tonsured (a custom not unknown in South America) and bore in his hand an object resembling a breviary.*

On two occasions this aged, benevolent and Europeanized version of Viracocha is compared with a Christian saint. Juan de Santa Cruz Pachacuti even suggests that the god might have been St Thomas and other versions liken him to St Bartholomew. Accounts of how Viracocha healed the sick and gave sight to the blind read exactly as if they had been taken from the New Testament. Both in Mexico and in Peru, chroniclers developed the practice of adding biblical touches to their accounts of local history and legend. For instance, the Aztec tribal god was credited with his own version of the Ark of the Covenant. Viracocha, however, displays a rather un-Christian fondness for turning his congregation to stone wherever they scorn his message.

Many notions of Viracocha's non-Indian origin arise out of a curious but oft-repeated story concerning a statue in a place called Cacha, in which he is depicted with a flowing beard and a long white robe. But only one chronicler, Cieza de León, says that the stone figure of the god was not only bearded but also white. This author, however, then goes out of his way to discredit the whole tale and tells how he personally visited the statue in question since the Spaniards were insisting that it represented a Christian saint. Having seen the figure for himself, Cieza de León states that only a blind man could believe that it bore any relationship to one of Jesus' Apostles and that this pretence was nothing but a bad joke. The same chronicler remarks that if a Christian preacher had indeed visited Peru, his efforts had been singularly ineffective since the people still held fast to their pagan beliefs. Originally the Indians did not think of the invaders as Viracochas; the Spaniards themselves, however, told certain Indians whose support they sought that they had been sent by Viracocha and were his sons. The title then stuck and continued to serve the ends of its bearers.*

Nevertheless, the magic effects of this assumed name were at times overstressed. Garcilaso de la Vega explains that, because the Spaniards did not know the Quechua language, they were unable to assess the standing of the gods; Viracocha was not really the principal Inca deity, but ranked below their newer sun god, Inti. However, the Indians, in order to flatter the Spaniards, who had gone out of their way to assume the mantle of Viracocha, affirmed that this god was the more important. Garcilaso de la Vega also makes the curious statement that the Spaniards themselves destroyed the famous bearded statue of Viracocha.

In Peru, therefore, the situation ran closely parallel to that in Mexico. In the two territories Indian legends of a bearded god-hero were current but lacked any suggestion that he had a white skin. Spanish chroniclers tell how Quetzalcóatl and Viracocha travelled through the country on a kind of preaching tour, sporting long beards and clad in flowing white tunics. But such notions of a god in human form, walking from place to place, healing the sick and preaching repentance, is a Christian–European concept, and no American Indian traditions remotely conform to this pattern.

Such embellishments to the legends of two typically callous Indian deities, the one a wind and the other a sun god, could only have benefited the Spaniards, who abhorred all Indian religions. The Aztecs and the Incas were only too ready to make one of their innumerable gods look a little more respectable, and if the Spaniards then managed to become identified with this emasculated version of the pagan deity, their battle was already half won. As part of the same process, Hispanized accounts credit Quetzalcóatl with a revulsion against human sacrifice. But other sources describe the mammoth sacrifice – reputedly of eighty thousand victims – which took place in the Aztec capital thirty years before the Conquest, and in which priests dressed as Quetzalcóatl played a leading part. To appreciate the pitiless nature of the *Indian* god before he was whitewashed (in every sense of the word), a glance at the Codex Borgia will suffice. There Quetzalcóatl is displayed in the not-very-

Christian gesture of gouging out the eye of a wretched little captive. In this drawing he wears his characteristic red and black duckbill mask and a beard of yellow ochre feathers. (When, in the same codex, he is depicted without his mask, the god normally has a black face, sometimes with a yellow nose and in one case with a red mouth.)

The views of Thor Heyerdahl deserve mention again, since the modified version of these myths lies at the very root of his thinking. Not content with one or even two white divinities, he postulates the existence of a whole clan of such non-Indian beings in both Mexico and Peru – an alien Caucasoid master-race from across the sea, who made a long sojourn in America and then went off to people Polynesia. In *American Indians in the Pacific* he devotes more than a hundred pages to explanations as to why he accepts without question the legend of the white god.*

Heyerdahl correctly draws attention to the presence of bearded statues and figurines dating from early times in both North and South America; and he adds several illustrations of a curious, rather hunched-up Peruvian figure of an old man with a long and usually white beard who invariably wears a strange and distinctive form of cap or turban. He generally attributes these figures to later Peruvian civilizations, but in fact some at least are Mochica and date from the first centuries of our era.

This little old man crops up in almost every museum and private collection in Peru. However, he appears less frequently than, say, the serpent, the jaguar, the condor, or even the bat. The small bearded statues, therefore, seem to represent an early hero or deity who, though much revered, was not a leading member of the pantheon and in some respects may be compared to the Mexican 'Old God' who was also bearded. In both regions such figures of ancient gods or heroes occur long before Quetzalcóatl or Viracocha rose to prominence and assumed the role of bearded gods in human form. These two divinities therefore adopted previous deep-rooted traditions and can by no stretch of imagination be conceived as immigrants of another race, or from another continent.

Unlike some authors, Heyerdahl has personally studied the historical sources and he quotes copiously from them. But important details are lacking from his account, such as the black and yellow face of Quetzalcóatl in the codices, or Cieza de León's scepticism over the portrayal of Viracocha as a Christian saint. Besides, Heyerdahl backs his theories regarding the presence in America of white men by quoting nineteenth-century authorities such as A. F. Bandelier or Daniel Brinton, now regarded by scholars as utterly outmoded. Hirsute as well as hairless people crossed the Bering Strait; contrary to what others may write, we have no need to look to Europe or to the Near East to explain Caucasoid traits displayed in very early American art, and only later appended to the persons of Quetzalcóatl and Viracocha.

CHAPTER SEVEN

PHARAOHS AND PHOENICIANS

ARTICLE 8, Chapter 15 of 'The Articles of Faith for the Book of Mormon' expresses the belief that the New World was peopled by the Jaredites, who came direct to America after the great dispersal caused by the collapse of the Tower of Babel that is recounted in the book of Genesis.

The Book of Mormon, according to its author Joseph Smith, derives from a text describing the history of the American Indians written in Egyptian hieroglyphs on gleaming plates of gold; this record had been compiled in the period 600 to 400 B.C. Smith related that in 1827 a 'resurrected personage', who gave his name as Moroni, revealed that he had unearthed the tablets in a hill situated between Palmyra and Manchester, N.Y., not far from his own home; he was able to translate them 'by the gift and power of god'. Eleven witnesses in all attested that they had seen the plates. Their discoverer deciphered them with the aid of Urim and Thummin (the biblical instruments by which the Ancient Hebrews interpreted divine communications) and gave the world the Book of Mormon, so named after its original compiler, who was Moroni's father and who had hidden it in the hill.

The history of the American Indian thereby became part of the doctrine of an established church. According to another Mormon version, the Jaredites had crossed the ocean in eight vessels and landed in America, where they founded great nations and cities. Their descendants, however, defied the Lord and were destroyed in 600 B.C. Undeterred by the fate of the Jaredites, a second migration then took place, consisting of Israelites who came direct from Jerusalem to North America and later pursued their journey as far as South America. The Mormons do not maintain, as is commonly believed, that the ten Lost Tribes of Israel fled to America after their captivity in Babylon.*

The story of the New World, according to this alternative version, then devolved into an armed rivalry between the Nephites, named after the prophet Nephi, and the Lamanites, whose leader was the wicked Laman and who soon lapsed into paganism. After endless struggles between the two peoples, the Nephites also fell from grace and were punished by earthquakes and fire from heaven. Jesus then appeared to the remnants of the Nephite tribe, and his apostles preached the gospel in the Americas, converting both Nephites and Lamanites. But the two tribes again fell back into their pagan ways and the Nephites finally perished in a great battle near the Hill of Cumorah, where Mormon then buried the sacred golden tablets, recovered by Joseph Smith in 1827.

The Mormons were not the first people to maintain that the American Indians derived from Israel, but they kept the notion alive and gave it a new aura of sanctity. Among its many activities, the Mormon Church directs the New World Foundation, created originally to seek archaeological proof of Mormon traditions; in practice, the original objective has proved elusive, but the Foundation makes valuable contributions to science. Archaeologists who work for the New World Foundation have told me that they are expressly forbidden to take doctrine into account when they report their finds.

In more recent times Thomas Stuart Ferguson, former president of the New World Foundation, has been prominent among writers on American origins. Not surprisingly, the author no longer insists that America was exclusively populated by migrants who came from Israel, though he denies with equal emphasis that *all* the different racial groups had come across the Bering Strait. In Ferguson's book, *One Fold, One Shepherd*, he makes a brave attempt to reconcile radiocarbon dates for the archaeological sites of Mexico with the salient events of the Jaredite era (2800–600 B.C.) and the subsequent Nephite–Lamanite age (587 B.C.–A.D. 421); maps are provided to illustrate the point. Ferguson also claims that seals with Egyptian glyphs have been found in Chiapa de Corso in southern Mexico, where for many years the New World Foundation has done outstanding work. A photograph is shown of a kind of triangle with a cleft carved in its base; the claim that this is an Egyptian sign is not very convincing.

To prove his case, Ferguson falls back on those two unfailing weapons in the armoury of all who look for connections between America and the Near East: the white god theory and the word-list game. The bearded Quetzalcóatl is really Jesus, and the Book of Revelation links our Lord with the Morning Star, which Quetzalcóatl also represented. In another passage Ferguson refers to the Mexican deity as the Good Shepherd, and Jesus of Nazareth is claimed to be the 'fair god' of the Western Hemisphere. Incidentally, Ferguson is not alone in seeking a new identity for Quetzalcóatl, whom other authors have recognized as Atlas, St Thomas, Votan, Osiris, Dionysus, Bacchus, a Buddhist or Brahman missionary, Viracocha and Mango Capac of Peru, Poseidon, and Hotu Matua of Easter Island.

Had any of these writers cared to consult the Mexican codices, they could have discovered for themselves that Quetzalcóatl is not so different from other remorseless members of the Mexican pantheon, though none of these, as far as I know, has even been associated with Osiris or Buddha. In the Codex Borgia – as we have seen – Quetzalcóatl is shown as a series of gods, each depicted in the act of plucking out the eye of a tiny human victim.

Ferguson, like other writers, points to ostensibly Christian rites practised in the New World: crosses abound in certain codices; people went on pilgrimages, performed baptismal rites, and confessed themselves before death. The gruesome sacrifice peculiar to the Mexican god of hunting, in which the human victim was tied to a cross-shaped bracket and slain with arrows, is treated as a variation upon the crucifixion.

As an extra string to his bow, Ferguson falls back upon the time-honoured practice of finding words common to Hebrew and the Mexican Nahuatl language; he explains that the Nahuatl name for Quetzalcóatl is Yohualli, which could also be written as 'Yohalli' and hence as the Jewish 'Yahweh'. But Yohualli, means 'night' and is more often connected with another god, known as 'Smoking Mirror', who was Lord of the Night Sky. Besides, Ferguson's phonetics are faulty – Yohualli cannot by any stretch of imagination be transcribed as Yohalli.

Ferguson and other Mormon writers lean heavily on passages of Alva Ixtlilxóchitl, which are interpreted as supporting their version of events. But Ixtlilxóchitl was a seventeenth-century Mexican historian, descended from the royal house of Texcoco; his work contains no hidden mysteries, although it does provide invaluable data, which on occasion can be unreliable. More than anything, Ixtlilxóchitl is the ardent apologist of his native Texcoco and his history is ordered to serve that end; moreover, he lived a century after the Conquest and is thoroughly Hispanized. Ferguson, in short, notwithstanding the excellent work of the New World Foundation, is one of the less convincing of the writers seeking connections between the Old World and the New.

Of people who suggested that the Americans were not merely Israelites, but actually constituted the Ten Lost Tribes, I have already mentioned Lord Kingsborough and Brasseur de Bourbourg, both of whom were among the first great investigators of the American past. Another prominent advocate of the Lost Tribes theory was James Adair, who traded in Indian territories for some forty years and formulated his theory as early as 1775. Adair claimed that during certain ceremonies the Indians chanted the phrase, 'yo Meshica, he Meshica, va Meshica'. Meshica is the Nahuatl name from which Mexico derived. For Adair, however, it clearly indicated 'Messiah'; and by taking the first syllable of each phrase, the word 'Yoheva' is produced – in other words Jehovah, or Yahweh.

Mormon doctrine leads inevitably to the general topic of links between the New World and the Bible Lands, though it is far from clear why Mormon preferred to record his revelation in hieroglyphs rather than in Hebrew script, of which an early form already existed in the seventh century B.C.

Where the Near East is concerned, the laymen enter the field in force. The flood of books on possible connections between America and the Mediterranean lands never ceases; most are emphatic rather than logical. Their authors have much in common. In the first place, they tend to work in isolation and lack colleagues with whom they can cross-check their data. As a result, unnecessary errors in matters of simple fact are frequent, such as mistranslated words, muddled dates and the confusion of two peoples with similar names. In addition, up-to-date evidence is missed, and antiquated sages whom the professional has long since ceased to consult are quoted. Writers on the Maya, for example, persist in using the terms 'Old Empire' and 'New Empire', definitions that were discarded by scholars a generation ago and would be greeted with derision in any serious discussion today.

For lack of newer or better arguments, firm reliance is placed upon the story of the white, bearded god and upon the word-list game.

Sometimes a single word, such as Ferguson's mispelled rendering of the Nahuatl 'Yohualli', becomes a basis on which to build a hypothesis. Charles Berlitz, author of *The Bermuda Triangle*, in a previous book entitled *Mysteries from Forgotten Worlds* detects a linguistic connection between America and Africa on the sole grounds that Nahuatl (he incorrectly calls it 'Aztec') used the same word for 'water' (*atl*) as did the Berbers. Berlitz then firmly identified the Aztecs with the Azores (and hence with Atlantis), simply because they told the Spaniards that they were the people of Az. Even if the information were correct, sweeping deductions cannot be based on a single syllable. In reality the Aztecs never told anyone that they were the people of Az – and Berlitz is also wrong in saying that their homeland, Aztlan, was 'a point in the east', since it is commonly associated with north-western Mexico.

The more adventurous theorists nurse a common grudge against the crusty professionals. Even Thor Heyerdahl, who writes in a more serious vein, spoke bitterly of the hard-headed opposition which he encountered in 'a dark office, on one of the upper floors of a big museum in New York' – obviously the Museum of Natural History.

The authors of oversimplified solutions to American problems often see themselves as victims of a diabolical design on the part of the archaeologists to quash information that confounds their pet theories. A. Ryatt Verrill, in a book written jointly with his wife and published in 1953, suggests that the existence of wheeled toys in pre-Columbian Mexico had long since been known to the experts, who deliberately hid the news from the public. As the Verrills expressed it:

> However, in certain scientific papers never seen or read by the layman, there were, from time to time, brief references to wheels having been known to the early Americans. . . . Once the truth had been revealed, it was useless to continue to maintain that wheels were unknown in ancient America. . . . Once these anti-Old-World-contact archaeologists had been forced to admit the presence of the wheels in ancient America, they began to see the light and to change their opinions in many ways.*

The very notion of such pranks strikes the archaeologist as ludicrous. But – strangest of all – the very people who, like the Verrills, do not stop at charges of fraud go out of their way to drop scholarly names and seek flimsy pretexts to quote leading experts in order to give an academic veneer to their own views. As Robert Wauchope writes:

145

One cannot help but see some regularity in these attitudes. The typical advocate of the 'wild' theories of American Indian origins begins his book with the underdog appeal; he points out that he has been personally scorned, ridiculed, or at best snubbed by the professionals. He then predicts that his writings will in turn be ill-received or ignored, and he proceeds to attack the thick-headed bigotry of the men in universities and museums. Frequently he implies that they are not only hopelessly conservative and jealous of any scholarly inroads by amateurs, but also that they are actually dishonest, and when confronted with conflicting evidence they will suppress and if necessary destroy it.*

Harold S. Gladwyn believed unshakeably that the professionals were plotting to distort the truth about the American Indian. Wheeled toys, for instance, never ceased to rankle where Gladwyn was concerned, and he joined forces with the Verrills in alleging that their discovery had been concealed by an act of 'dastardly deception'. As a butt for his ridicule of the archaeological profession he used the famous Dr Phuddy Duddy (derived from Ph.D.), who even slept with his window closed for fear that a new idea might fly in. Yet Gladwyn himself was an amateur archaeologist of note and director of the Gila Pueblo Archaeological Foundation, under whose auspices the first traces of the important Hohokam civilization were found in the American south-west. Moreover, this author, who missed no opportunity to make fun of university professors and museum curators, had no compunction in asking Dr Ernest A. Hooton, professor of anthropology and curator at the Peabody Museum of Harvard, to write a preface, in order to give academic weight to his book.

Gladwyn is nowadays remembered more for his detailed site reports than for his book, *Men out of Asia*, published in 1947. This work pretends that after the death of Alexander the Great in 323 B.C., part of his fleet, of whose fate nothing is recorded, eventually reached America and bestowed the blessings of civilization on the natives of that continent. The same role had already been accorded to fugitives from other historical catastrophes; as long ago as 1827, John Ranking, the English author of a book published in London entitled *Historical Researches on the Conquest of Peru and Mexico in the Thirteenth Century by Mongols, Accompanied with Elephants*, stated that the Inca Empire of Peru was founded by the crews of some of Kublai Khan's ships, after escaping from the storm that wrecked the great emperor's armada, sent to ravage

Japan in the thirteenth century. Authors who ascribe New World culture to refugees from wars between worlds in the outer cosmos have now bestowed a new vitality upon the same notion.

Harold Gladwyn, notwithstanding the outsize chips on his shoulder, never lost his sense of humour; his book is enlivened by many a good quip, but its most appealing feature is the series of cartoons poking every kind of fun at poor Dr Phuddy Duddy and his entrenched dogmas. The first part of the work is not concerned with Greek castaways but deals with the racial background of Ancient America, on which its views closely concur with mine. Gladwyn insists that people with black skins did not necessarily come from Africa and stresses that they could better be described as Negritos than Negroes. Only half way through his book does he launch into theories about the origins of New World civilization, with which he refuses to credit those uncouth Indians who made their way across Beringia. As in so many works, great play is made of the presence of bearded white gods in America. Finally, the fate of Alexander's fleet is introduced and the text merely states:

> All that we have to go on is that some of the ships were very large for their day; that there was a large number of such ships; that they were manned by competent seamen from the eastern end of the Mediterranean; that they were fully supplied and equipped; that hell had broken loose on the shore; that the date was summer 323 B.C. The rest is guesswork.*

The author is munificent in supplying this guesswork. Alexander's ships, minus a few vessels lost in wrecks, are described as still ploughing their way through the Micronesian Islands as late as 300 B.C., nearly a quarter-century after Alexander's death. Gladwyn, to add weight to his theory that the fleet managed to cross the Pacific, then introduces Dr Nordensköld's famous list of customs and traits shared between the islands of Oceania and South America. From this point onwards, the book is less concerned with links between Greece and America and becomes a comparative study of Oceania and Peru, a subject which I shall treat in a later chapter. On the whole, Gladwyn fails to present a cogent case concerning the American origins. The impression remains that the author only believes half of what he writes, and gets more satisfaction from lampooning Dr Phuddy Duddy than from seeking alternatives to the Doctor's theories.

*

So far in this chapter the dogma of a well-endowed church and the views of a familiar if unorthodox figure in the archaeological world have been considered. But the number of potted solutions linking the Near East with America is infinite, and they cannot all be dissected. Of necessity we must confine ourselves to a small selection, choosing for the purpose a few works that are representative of the rest or that merit attention for a particular reason.

For instance, theories are omitted that favour American contacts with the Scythians, though three hundred years ago the idea was advanced that, when Julius Caesar wrote of the fierce Scythians of the Black Sea coast, he was also referring to the American Indians since they had surely come from that region. Only brief comments can be devoted to the Etruscans, sometimes seen as the founders of American culture. A reverse migration was even mooted, whereby the Etruscans are credited with a Peruvian origin. When I was in Venezuela recently, a friend kindly gave me a book by Natalia Rosi de Tariffi entitled *American Fourth Dimension*. The author devotes ten pages to links between two Andean tongues, Quechua and Aymara, and such diverse European languages as Italian, English and Magyar. No additional reasons for connecting Etruscans with America are given, and the book well illustrates the pitfalls of playing with mere word similarities, without paying heed to the basic structure of the languages in question.

The Phoenicians, a typically seafaring people, inevitably enjoyed a long run of popularity as a source of speculation on New World origins. The devout churchman and scholar Sir George Jones, in his *Original History of Aboriginal America*, dedicated to the Archbishop of Canterbury and published in 1843, described in lurid detail a Phoenician landing in America. According to Jones, the arrival of Phoenician sailors in the New World occurred as follows:

> . . . still the star-tracery on the azure wall of the external Dome, and their Apollo daily sinking on his Western couch, and with his last glance, beckoning them [the Phoenicians] as it were, still to follow his path – this knowledge and their religious adoration directed them in safety to that Virgin land where the glorious Sun from Creation's dawn, had never beamed upon a human foot-print, until their own had kissed the untouched Floridian shore! There Flora and her attendant Nymphs in all their peerless beauty, and Nature's own attire, were grouped on every hill; from their coloured lips, smiling Welcome breathed forth her ceaseless incense.

As a more sober specimen of the same viewpoint, I prefer *Fair Gods and Stone Faces*, written by Constance Irwin and published in 1963. Irwin's book is methodically written and begins with an admirable summary of the original trek of Ancient Man to America over the Beringian landmass. Even so it reveals the dangers inherent in simple solutions to complex problems. As the very title implies, the author's case rests squarely upon the bearded white god theory. She quotes the usual passages from Alva Ixtlilxóchitl and Fray Sahagún, both of whom she oddly describes as 'discredited historians'; Ixtlilxóchitl, the prophet and preceptor of the Mormons, scarcely deserves the epithet, while Sahagún, who is not principally a historian, is so far from being discredited that a distinguished gathering assembled in Santa Fé, New Mexico, in 1972, was dedicated to the sole purpose of studying his voluminous work. To support her theories, Constance Irwin draws attention to a passage from Sahagún describing the Plumed Serpent Quetzalcóatl as having a long beard 'yellow as straw'. When I managed, in spite of a confusing reference, to locate the Sahagún text in question, I realized that the English verse rendering used by Irwin was not a true translation of the original. Had she checked the Spanish text, she would have found that Quetzalcóatl is described as having an ugly face, a long head, and a beard; in Sahagún's Nahuatl version of the same story, the god is at least credited with having a *long* beard. In neither account is there mention of a *yellow* beard – more characteristic of a white man.

Although Irwin's book refers to supposed New World contacts made by Etruscans and Hittites, most of the book concerns the belief that Phoenicians or Carthaginians made landings in America and left their stamp upon its culture. Illustrated on the cover is a tiny head found in Mexico, with an odd kind of square beard, which the author compares with statues of Melkarth, God of Tyre and Carthage. However, Alfonso Caso also published a picture of the Mexican piece and placed beside it not the Phoenician Melkarth but a Merovingian figure from Ratisbon, in Germany, to which it bears an even closer, if coincidental, likeness.

Irwin also draws attention to Olmec reliefs depicting bearded people and to the many figures with Negroid lips and noses. The conclusion is reached that the Phoenicians must have brought black slaves when they came to America. In this continent, the slaves unaccountably became the masters since Negroids are portrayed much more frequently than men with aquiline features. Infant sacrifice, practised by both Phoenicians and Olmecs, is also cited as evidence, though the true significance of this custom among the Olmecs is unknown. As additional proof that the Phoenicians crossed the Atlantic, a single Olmec relief is shown, in which a bearded figure wears pointed and upturned shoes, also worn in the eastern Mediterranean.

One-track theories depend on the chronological data available at the time. In 1963, Olmec dates did not go beyond 800 B.C., but since then the figure has been pushed back, first to 1200 B.C. and now to nearer 1400 B.C. Olmec culture therefore predates the great age of the Phoenicians by an ample margin, and cannot have been created by them. Phoenician oceanic voyages are believed to have begun in the sixth century B.C.; even if they had ventured beyond Gibraltar long before this, they could not possibly have done so before the rise of the Olmecs.

The author of *Fair Gods and Stone Faces* rightly states that the Phoenicians, unlike many earlier peoples, possessed the maritime skills needed for ocean voyages. A Phoenician expedition that reached Cornwall in search of tin is mentioned – presumably a reference to the 450 B.C. journey of the Carthaginian captain Himilco to a destination called the 'Tin Isles'.* Possibilities of sailings round the coast of Africa in both an east–west and a west–east direction are also discussed. During their ascendancy, which ran from about 1150 to 850 B.C., the Phoenicians monopolized the local seaborne trade; they ranged far and wide and were the first people of the eastern Mediterranean to penetrate beyond Sicily and Sardinia; they even passed the Straits of Gibraltar to trade with Tartessus, probably situated on the Spanish coast west of Gibraltar.

The African voyages to which Constance Irwin refers came relatively late, when the Phoenicians were past their prime and when their Carthaginian colony was beginning to outstrip them. The first known Phoenician voyage to Africa was commissioned by the Pharaoh Necho II (610–594 B.C.). The king remade the canal originally dug by Senruset in the twentieth century B.C. to join the Nile to the Red Sea. Herodotus tells how the expedition reached the Red Sea by this waterway and then sailed out into the Indian Ocean. In the course of their circumnavigation of Africa, the explorers put in to land at a suitable point each autumn, sowed crops and remained until they were harvested. Pursuing this leisurely mode of travel, the Phoenecian navigators eventually passed through the Pillars of Hercules, entered the

Mediterranean, and returned to Egypt in the third year after their departure.* The voyage was expected to be much shorter, since it was commonly believed that Africa formed a rectangle running from east to west; ships reaching Ethiopia would then have turned right and followed the bottom of a smaller African continent, skirting a shore that ran parallel to the Mediterranean coast.

Herodotus writes of another African expedition, this time by the Carthaginians, undertaken probably between 500 and 480 B.C. Arguments never cease as to how far they sailed, but they certainly reached Cape Verde, the westernmost extremity of Africa. Sixty ships took part, with 30,000 men and women on board, which resembles a migration more than a mere expedition.*

Constance Irwin stresses that Phoenician ships, though small and only partially decked, were reasonably seaworthy. Some vessels may have been entirely wind-propelled, in contrast to those of other Mediterranean peoples, who relied on a combination of sail and oar. Gerhard Herm in a recent book points to the limitations of these Phoenician boats, and to those of their forerunners, the Cretans and the 'Peoples of the Sea' mentioned in Egyptian records. Since voyagers across the Mediterranean met with very large waves at times, Phoenician seamen preferred to avoid a direct route over the open sea; because their ships would not, in Herm's opinion, have survived for long in a storm, journeys were arranged in such a way that the ships could put into safe harbours in case of need. In Roman times the capabilities of Carthaginian ships were greatly increased; some exceeded 1000 tons and were, therefore, much larger than the English boats that crossed the Atlantic in the seventeenth century; the *Mayflower* weighed 180 tons.

The Phoenicians stand out as the first people of the Old World to develop craft that might have been capable of surviving ocean crossings to America under optimum conditions. Accordingly the possibility at least exists, as for the Chinese a thousand years later, that Phoenician boats were occasionally blown off course, lost their bearings and reached the New World.

Phoenician records tend to be scant. The African voyages are described by Greeks, and no equivalent accounts of Phoenician travels to America survive. However, Phoenician feats are not necessarily fictitious because they are not recorded. Even so, grave doubts persist regarding planned voyages to America, leading over the boundless ocean, with no friendly coast to hug, when the circumnavigation of Africa entailed such difficulties (including the need to spend the winter on shore).

If landings were made, whether by accident or by design, dependable traces of Phoenicians are lacking in America. The fallacies of the bearded god argument have already been exposed; the Negroid faces in Olmec art have been rejected as proof of racial links with Africa; and when examined closely, the remainder of Constance Irwin's reasoning carries even less weight. Infant sacrifice was practised in many lands and may have prevailed at the time of Pekin Man, at least half a million years ago. As for upturned shoes, the author herself illustrates their presence among Hittites as well as Phoenicians. This type of footwear was worn in England in the Middle Ages and is still at times worn by the typical Oriental who appears in newspaper advertisements for carpets and rugs.

I have considered *Fair Gods and Stone Faces* in some detail because the Phoenicians are among the first potential oceanic voyagers, and the book avoids some of the worst extravagances in dealing with the question. In certain respects, the author provides an excellent example of how *not* to write a work on the prickly topic of American origins; her case may provide an illusion of serious presentation, but the basis is flimsy and the reader is offered nothing but a few coincidental likenesses, such as the presence on two continents of infant sacrifice and of upturned shoes.

Recently a much more ambitious attempt has been made to derive New World civilizations from those of the Old. The book in question, entitled *America B.C.*, was published in 1976, and its author is Barry Fell, Professor of Invertebrate Zoology at the Harvard Museum of Comparative Zoology. Fell's work in the classification of Echinoderms is outstanding, but his studies of human civilization are open to question.

The distinguished zoologist claims a universal expertise in the field of epigraphy, or the deciphering of scripts, and his theories are based on that claim. One of the chapters of *America B.C.* is entitled 'Alphabets Galore', and it is indeed hard to find a form of ancient writing for which he will not provide a rendering. Using these talents to the full, Fell deduces that not only Celts, but Basques, Carthaginians, Libyans, Phoenicians, Egyptians and Etruscans were present in the New World and more particularly in New England. Since then, he has added Arabs and Cretans to his list. The Algonquins of the east coast of the United States spoke a language said to include words derived from Siberians, Egyptians, Celts, Iberians and Norsemen. In this versatility, Fell differs from other self-appointed experts on American origins, who doggedly plead the cause of a single Old World people who supposedly brought civilization to the New.

The *New York Times Book Review* (13 March 1977) described *America B.C.* as rubbish. Fell's outraged followers leaped into the fray and accused the reviewer of ignoring the hard facts that support such notions. Facts tend to be elusive, since it is so difficult to prove that something did *not* happen. However, in purely general terms, the facts do deny Fell's reasoning.

America B.C. lacks any proper archaeological basis and relies for 'proof' on linguistics of a kind. The book does mention bronze weapons, found in North America and supposedly brought in from the Old World. Nonetheless Jeffrey Brain, the Harvard archaeologist, has pointed out that laboratory tests at M.I.T. showed that these weapons were made of native copper, not bronze, which was unknown in Ancient America.

Fell blithely ignores the negative archaeological evidence; not one single artefact has been found to support his views. Like von Däniken's Martians who visited the Maya, Fell's Celts and Phoenicians packed their bags very meticulously and left not a single utensil behind. By way of contrast, as we shall see later, Helge Ingstad's painstaking digs *did* prove a Viking presence in Newfoundland. Moreover, either Fell's interminable succession of voyagers to the New World were poor teachers, or the local Indians were idle pupils. Presumably bewildered by such a wide choice of ancient forms of writing, they promptly forgot them all and reverted once more to semi-savagery. By the time the Vikings landed on the north-east coast of America about A.D. 1000, they found only the wild native skraelings that are described in the Norse sagas.

In addition to provoking such doubts of a general kind, Fell's selection of 'hard facts' bristles with detailed omissions. In the first place, the true specialists in each of his many chosen fields of study have shown that his epigraphy is often wrong, and his knowledge of the language defective. A leading authority on Algonquian, Dr Ives Goddard, formerly of Harvard and now working for the Smithsonian Institution, says that Fell's work on that tongue is full of errors of analysis and interpretation.

Before he turned his attention to the presence of Celts and others in Vermont, Fell wrote about voyages from the Near East across the Pacific to Polynesia. But Ross Clark, senior lecturer in linguistics at Auckland University, states in an article in the *New Zealand Listener* (16 April 1977) that Fell and his leading New Zealand apostle, Dr R. A. Lochore, are both deficient in their knowledge of Maori and other Polynesian dialects. Another New Zealander, Dr A. K. Pawley, of the Department of Linguistics of the University of Hawaii, writes that Fell's rendering of a Maori chant makes little sense to him. Dr Kenneth P. Emory, of the Bernice P. Bishop Museum, Honolulu, the father of modern Polynesian studies, regards Fell's incursions into his field as ludicrous and told me that what he portrays as Polynesian writing has never been seen in Polynesia.

Both the Celtic Ogham and the Libyan scripts consist of simple geometric patterns and offer the decipherer a great deal of latitude, of which the author of *America B.C.* has taken the fullest advantage. In certain instances he goes farther and resorts to invention or to the citing of inscriptions that are known to be fakes. As Ross Clark also points out in his article, Fell produced an Egyptian–Libyan rendering of a set of rock carvings from Pitcairn Island, working from a version of these carvings published as long ago as 1870 in Richard Taylor's *Te Ika a Maui*. But Otago University archaeologists recently obtained an accurate copy of the glyphs, which showed that the Taylor version had been much altered and rearranged to fit onto a single page. Fell's deciphering would not work on the correct version of the inscription, and was withdrawn.

Clark goes on to relate how the editor of a Canadian anthropological journal, himself a champion of the unorthodox, was interested in Fell's work and sent him a sketch of some rock markings which he had received from a local priest. Fell promptly responded with a Phoenician deciphering of the markings. However, soon after this, the Canadian editor had a chance to examine the original stone and found to his surprise that the 'inscription' was a set of cracks made by nature.

Not content with using rock texts that have been doctored or that are merely written in nature's own handwriting, Fell avails himself of inscriptions that professional epigraphers have shown to be frauds. In

1877, the Reverend Jacob Gass found several tablets in an Indian burial mound at Davenport, Iowa. One of these, known as the Davenport Tablet, was once compared by the *Reader's Digest* to the Egyptian Rosetta Stone. Much more recently, however, officials of the Smithsonian Institution established that the tablets in question were frauds, planted alongside authentic Indian artefacts. And in 1970, Marshall McKusick, state archaeologist of Iowa, actually wrote a book called *The Davenport Conspiracy* in which he assembled massive evidence of trickery, including testimony by Davenport residents that the tablets had been made in the basement of the Davenport Academy, belonging to one of those many amateur scientific societies that flourished in America in the nineteenth century.

None of this deterred Barry Fell from writing in 1976 at some length on the Davenport Tablet, which he calls one of the most important stelae ever discovered and describes as a priceless national treasure. Whatever one may think of his other endeavours, to write in such terms without even mentioning McKusick's book is surely unscientific.

To sum up, Fell's ideas, far from being new, are mere variants on well-worn themes. The notion of people from the Ancient Near East cruising among the Islands of the South Pacific was first mooted at the beginning of the nineteenth century; the translation of the Pitcairn rock carving is taken from an 1870 copy; the Davenport Tablet has been discussed since 1877.

Progress in archaeology and linguistics is constant, but Fell ignores the new archaeological discoveries in Polynesia, to be discussed later, or the strides made in the last ten years in reconstructing the original or proto-Polynesian language. His reasoning on the Maori tongue is of a type more current fifty years ago. The Harvard professor merely offers a rehash of Harold Gladwyn's theory that Alexander the Great's fleet sailed across the Pacific and substitutes Libyans for Greeks. This theory is based on yet another inscription, reputedly found in Chile in 1885, which is said to record the visit of a band of Libyans in 23 B.C. Gladwyn at least made a joke of the whole business, but Fell writes in deadly earnest. Really, von Däniken's belief that astronauts were at work in A.D. 800 on Easter Island (now, incidentally, a Chilean possession) is no wilder, and spacemen are a good deal more entertaining to write about than Libyans or Celts.

Like so many other eccentrics, the sponsor of all these weird if unoriginal ideas works in isolation from professional colleagues. As Peter J. Frawley writes in an article in the Harvard *Crimson* (15 February 1977), none of the leading professional archaeologists and linguists of Harvard had been consulted by the zoologist on his doorstep, and none took his work seriously. These American scientists had not heard of a single one of the so-called experts in European museums and universities whom Fell listed as believing in his work.

Like so many of his kind, Fell is a champion player of the word-list game; a mere fifteen allegedly common words prove that Algonquian derives from Egyptian, and a further eight words link Algonquian with Norse. To illustrate the absurdity of this approach, Ross Clark has challenged him to name a language that is *not* related to Maori, and Clark will produce a list of words common to Maori and that tongue.

As in other instances, the quest for frivolous solutions to serious problems is endowed in *America B.C.* with the status of a cause. 'I have had to call upon my colleagues and other associates [i.e. pesudo-experts]', we are told, 'to undertake more of this work, that is assuming something of a ministry; for it is plain that the word we bring is something that young people have longed to hear.'

Professor Fell is surely indebted to Noah, who pressed into his ark every species of the animal kingdom and thereby preserved them for study by future zoologists. His own feat, in assembling every breed of Old World Man in Ancient New England, if not comparable to Noah's, is so remarkable that it must be the work of a crank or a genius. But alas! for every crank who turns out to be a genius, there are ninety-nine who remain cranks.

An allegedly Phoenician tablet found in Brazil also requires mention. On 11 September 1872, Joaquin Alves da Costa wrote a letter to the President of the Instituto Historico in Rio de Janeiro enclosing the copy of an inscription in strange characters, engraved upon four broken pieces of stone and reportedly found by slaves on his property of Pouso Alto, described as 'near the Paraiba'. Dr Cyrus H. Gordon of Brandeis University in Massachusetts relates what followed. The Emperor Don Pedro II had an amateur passion for Near Eastern studies, but no one else in Brazil claimed to know anything of such topics. Quite undaunted by the shortcomings of his subjects, the Emperor assigned the task of examining the text to Dr Ladislau Netto, Director of the National

Museum in Rio de Janeiro. This scholar was not a philologist but a naturalist; he plunged boldly into the study of Hebrew and Phoenician, however, and finally deduced that the Paraiba tablet described a sailing to Brazil from the Red Sea port of Ezion-Geber.

Netto's announcement that the inscription was authentic produced a storm of international proportions and provoked Ernest Renan into declaring the text a forgery. Netto, who could not hold a candle to the famous French scholar in the knowledge of Canaanite linguistics, became the butt of merciless ridicule in Rio de Janeiro. His agony, moreover, was long drawn out and not until 1885 did he publish a retraction entitled 'Letter to M. Ernest Renan'. This communication actually provided a list of five people in Brazil who might have been capable of composing the bogus text.

Notwithstanding Netto's retraction, Cyrus Gordon now maintains that the inscription is perfectly genuine. It reads as follows:

We are the sons of Canaan from Sidon, from the city where a merchant [prince] has been made king. He dispatched us to this distant land, a land of mountains. We sacrificed a youth to the celestial gods and goddesses in the nineteenth year of Hiram, our king. Abra! We sailed from Ezion-Geber into the Red Sea and voyaged with ten ships. We were at sea together for two years round Africa. Then we got separated by the hand of Baal and we were no longer with our companions. So we have come here, twelve men and three women, into one island, unpopulated because ten died. Abra! May the celestial gods favour us!*

Gordon insists that the text could not have been invented in 1872 since it contains peculiarities of language that were first discovered in other north-west Semitic texts unearthed long after that date. Any assumption that the tablet is the work of a nineteenth-century forger implies that such a person was familiar with twentieth-century developments in the study of Canaanite religion.

Few would question Gordon's expertise in Canaanite texts; but his views concerning those of Ancient America are more open to doubt. For instance, in the book in which Gordon discusses the Paraiba inscription, he also defends the authenticity of the Viking Vinland Map, now proved to be a forgery. In the Paraiba case, all that we possess is Netto's transcriptions of the lost master copy, taken from the original stones by Da Costa, who claimed to have discovered them, who did not know a word of any eastern language and who was never heard of again. A number of places in Brazil are called Pouso Alto, and two widely separated Paraibas exist; no one, therefore, has any idea where the find occurred, if at all. In other words, the stone tablets, whose place of origin is untraceable, have vanished into thin air, together with their discoverer and his original copy of the text. The sceptics can hardly be blamed for their doubts.

Moreover, Gordon's general views on pre-Columbian matters do not inspire confidence. An unfailing sponsor of the white god theory, this author is also a player of the word-list game and happily assumes a relationship between Latin and Nahuatl, based on three Nahuatl words that are said to resemble their Latin equivalents.* He accepts Alexander von Wuthenau's dubious contention that Negroids in America derive from Africa, and also states as a fact, not an opinion, that Japanese pottery was found in Ecuador, a theory that is at best controversial and provides a flimsy basis for dogmatic statements. As far as Paraiba is concerned, Gordon agrees that the inscription could have resulted from a chance Phoenician landing rather than a planned expedition. Phoenician culture made no lasting impact on Brazil; despite Man's antiquity in that vast territory, signs of higher civilization, whether of local or Phoenician inspiration, are absent.

The Paraiba inscription serves to show that some people, if given an inch, will take a mile. Gordon wrote of a single tablet, but other authors, indulging in wilder flights of fancy, convey the impression that scarcely a rock is to be found in all Brazil that lacks its Near Eastern text. For instance, another self-appointed expert on Ancient Brazil, Peter Kolosimo, shows no compunction in describing 'thousands of inscriptions on South American menhirs and dolmens which contain letters from early European and Mediterranean alphabets'.* Writing specifically of Brazil, Kolosimo even dreams up cuneiform texts, which unfortunately could not be read.

Matters have not radically changed since Le Plongeon's day and efforts to link Egypt with America continue unabated. Certain endeavours of this kind are based on the so-called science of pyramidology, whereby arbitrary measurements taken from Egyptian and other pyramids enable students of the occult to prove any theory that they wish. Similarities between Ancient Egyptian and American words are cited, and attempts are also made to link Quetzalcóatl and Osiris, but the fair god legend offers scant proof that the bronze-skinned inhabitants of the Nile Valley visited the New World.

Of the countless twentieth-century writers who attempt to link Egypt with America, two who are methodical, if not totally convincing, stand out. The first is the distinguished brain anatomist, Sir Elliot Smith, originally renowned for a book entitled *Essays on the Evolution of Man*, which ran into many editions. In *Human History*, published in 1915, and in later works, Smith evolved a theory that all civilization derived from Egypt; this 'Heliolithic' culture, as he named it, had first spread to Asia and thence was carried to America a little after 1000 B.C., during the rule of the Egyptian 21st Dynasty.

Smith points to the many similarities of style between Egypt and Asia. He then makes comparisons between Asian and American art, offering some of the more familiar examples, such as the 'lotus' frieze in the Chichén Itzá Ball Court and the 'elephant' in Copan; the feathered headdress that adorned Queen Ahmes in Egypt thirty-four centuries ago was now worn, he claimed, by Indian braves in Arizona, from where it had even been copied by English schoolboys.

Central to Smith's theme is the practice of mummification, originating from a single focus in Egypt and spreading to other parts of the world. The ritual of embalming the dead is fundamental to the Heliolithic civilization, and its diffusion across Africa, to Indochina, India, Polynesia and finally America is described in detail. This custom admittedly is lacking in China, but Smith maintains that the influence of mummification is implied by the use of jade, pearls and gold in tombs, in the firm belief that they preserve the body from putrefaction.

Most works of this nature create not a ripple in the academic millpond and are quietly ignored by professional Americanists. But the painstaking erudition of Smith was hard to ignore, and in particular spurred Dr Roland B. Dixon of Harvard University to retaliate. Robert Wauchope describes Dixon as the archetypal college professor of his day, complete with pipe and tweedy clothes. This learned anthropologist now entered the fray and devoted his energies to the demolition of the thesis of Elliot Smith and his principal disciple, W. J. Perry.

By examining every known instance of mummification on earth,

Dixon ridiculed the belief in 'secret' processes known to the ancients but long since forgotten; he denied that the Egyptians held the key to mysterious techniques without which mummification could not have been practised in other lands. He meticulously examined the different procedures for embalming bodies, particularly those of Indonesia, whose islands were an obvious stepping-stone from Egypt to Polynesia and ultimately America, and put down to coincidence any similarities between Egyptian and Indonesian mortuary methods, such as the casting of the viscera into the sea, which was merely the most obvious place of disposal. He insisted that no true mummification existed among the Peruvians, who simply desiccated the bodies.

At the completion of his detailed research, Dixon was prepared to admit that in one instance only, in certain islands in the Torres Strait situated between New Guinea and Australia, mummification truly followed the Egyptian pattern; in this minute and remote corner of the globe, nine out of twelve specifically Egyptian traits were present, including occipital removal of the brain, painting the body red, and using artificial eyes.

So Dixon showed that human civilization was not simply an Egyptian invention. But if Smith overstated his case with regard to mummification, Egypt certainly exercised an influence on Greece, and elements of Hellenistic culture in their turn reached India in the wake of Alexander the Great's invasion; equally, many Indian traits are visible in South-East Asia. But the transfer of Egyptian influences to America is quite another question. The problem of Asian–American links was discussed at some length in connection with the views of Heine-Geldern and Ekholm, whose arguments on this theme are more weighty than those of Smith and Perry. Elliot Smith's reasoning simply brings us back to the start of the discussion; for if South-East Asian culture really reached America, as Heine-Geldern and Ekholm insist, then certain Egyptian influences, much diluted by time and distance, were indisputably included in the package. But these would not necessarily be the common traits selected by Smith; like many who opt for a single explanation, his theories have been upset by later discoveries. Since the Olmec and Chavín civilizations have now been traced back to long before the tenth century B.C., they precede the Egyptian 21st Dynasty, which Smith claimed brought Egypt to America.

Last but not least among those seeking links between the New World and the ancient Near East comes a book by R. A. Jairazbhoy published in 1974. The title is *Ancient Egyptians and Chinese in America*, but of the two peoples the work concerns mainly the Egyptians. Unlike many authors on such topics, Jairazbhoy, who was born in India and now lives in England, is refreshingly free from any chip-on-shoulder attitude towards archaeologists; on the contrary, he goes out of his way to consult them. He avoids the common error of quoting only authorities of bygone centuries, and of clinging to outdated terms, but provides his book with an up-to-date bibliography; and instead of blindly accepting second-hand reports of the original sources, Jairazbhoy studiously consults them for himself.

As his basic theme, this author favours the possibility of contact between Egypt of the time of Rhamses III (1195–1164 B.C.) and the Olmecs of Mexico. Drawing attention to the alleged existence of two Olmec racial elements, one Negroid and the other Caucasian in appearance, Jairazbhoy opts for the fallacious argument that the Negroids were Africans and the Caucasians Semites. This part of his work, including his identification of the Babylonian semi-divine hero Gilgamesh with the central figures of an Olmec mural, is the least acceptable.

Jairazbhoy points to certain similarities between Olmec and Near Eastern culture, such as the presence of dwarfs in the royal court, the building of stepped pyramids, the practice of wrestling, the prevalence of a phallic cult, and the use of similar incense burners. But such humdrum parallels, so often cited, carry little conviction. Moreover, Jairazbhoy is sometimes mistaken, as for example in his assertion that the Egyptians introduced the technique of irrigation, which had existed in Mexico for many centuries before the Olmecs.

But in the field of Mexican and Egyptian religion, Jairazbhoy is on stronger and more original ground. A few examples may be cited of the parallels that he offers between the gods of the two regions: a text from the Book of Gates in the tomb of Rhamses VI tells of the double twisted rope which comes out of the mouth of Aken; in the Museum of Jalapa, Mexico, a squatting Olmec figure has two twisted ropes emerging from its mouth. In certain statues of Osiris, the god's body is extended along the earth, but he is reviving and raises his head; in an Olmec sculpture from Santiago Tuxtla, a Negroid figure also lies prone and lifts its head in exactly the same way as the resurrected Osiris. The Mexican goddess

Tlazolteotl would 'eat' the sins of men when they confessed to her once in their lifetime; similarly, the Egyptian monster Amemit was called the 'devouress' and consumed the hearts of condemned sinners, after the dead had confessed to her at the last judgement.

In all twenty-one likenesses between Mexican and Egyptian deities and myths are cited. To these, a number of interesting similarities in ritual are added, such as the Mexican custom of delivering bunches of paper to the dead, while in Egypt they buried people with small sheets or strips of papyrus. In this part of his study Jairazbhoy produces comparisons that have not, as far as I know, been made before.

One basic objection to this approach arises, however: some of the author's comparisons with Egyptian culture concern Olmec times, when contact between the two regions is assumed to have taken place. But others of Jairazbhoy's ritual parallels with Egypt are related, not to archaeological data on the Olmecs, but to accounts by Spanish writers, describing Mexican religion in the early sixteenth century. Admittedly something can be learned about earlier Mexican deities by studying the Pantheon of Conquest times, since so much more is known of these later gods. However, this game has to be played with infinite caution since between 1200 B.C. and A.D. 1500 Mexican religion changed a great deal. For instance, before comparing Tlazolteotl with the Egyptian monster Amemit, we must be sure that this Mexican goddess existed in Olmec times, a point on which no evidence exists.

Where Mexico is concerned, Jairazbhoy's book is full of unusual comparisons, though the section devoted to South America is shorter and less interesting. But quite apart from the problem of changing patterns in Mexican religion, chronology as usual raises its ugly head. The author affirms in a footnote that the very earliest Olmec dates now available go back as far as the mid-fifteenth century B.C. and that this may entail some readjustment of his own theories in a further volume.

Egyptian power, after a prolonged period of weakness, was reasserted with the establishment of the 18th Dynasty in the mid-sixteenth century B.C., and any major Egyptian expansion into new territories is more likely to have taken place at that moment since the early rulers of the 18th Dynasty, such as Tuthmosis I and Tuthmosis III, were great campaigners and fought many successful wars. By the time of Rhamses III and the 19th Dynasty — of whom Jairazbhoy writes in connection with Mexico — Egypt was already on the defensive. The 'Peoples of the

Sea', the forerunners of the Phoenicians, penetrated right into the Nile Delta during the reign of Rhamses III, though he managed to beat off their assaults as well as those of the Libyans.

But to all speculations concerning Egyptian wanderings a more fundamental objection exists. As already noted, it is Thor Heyerdahl's view that Egyptian craft from earliest dynastic times onwards were basically designed for river and coastal travel. Study of the subject is greatly aided by copious and detailed illustrations of boats from 2900 B.C. onwards. From these early times Egypt had imported considerable quantities of wood from the famous cedar forests of the Lebanon. However, flat-bottomed vessels were employed for this purpose, of a kind that could be easily beached at the onset of bad weather; such craft were not remotely suited to sailing the open sea.*

In addition to the need for timber, huge quantities of incense, myrrh and frankincense had to be supplied for burning on Egyptian altars every year. These products were available only from southern Arabia and from the African coast below the Red Sea, an area which the Egyptian scribes called Punt; and from a period coinciding with the known beginnings of American higher civilization, an account of one such great maritime expedition survives. In the Valley of the Kings, on the opposite side of the Nile to the royal capital of Thebes, Queen Hatshepsut erected a huge temple shortly after 1500 B.C. and on its walls the record was carved of a large-scale trading voyage to Punt. No detail is omitted: the fleet can be seen entering the harbour of Punt, including three ships with their great sails swelling in the wind, while two others have doused their canvas and are ready to moor. Later, the fleet departs, the ships' decks now piled high with cargo, among which are souvenirs listed as native spears, apes, monkeys, dogs and even 'a southern panther alive, captured for her majesty'.*

Undoubtedly such vessels were a great advance over the boats of one thousand years earlier that first brought Lebanese cedar-wood to Egypt. The ships of the Punt expedition are cleaner and faster; they have great broad sails, not used previously, and their lines have the graceful curves of a racing yacht. But in spite of their fine appearance, they had serious weaknesses as they were directly descended from the earlier craft designed for use on rivers, where they would face no violent winds. Even the largest were built without a keel and with few very light ribs; planks were pinned to one another rather than to a skeleton. The artist draws Hatshepsut's boats so precisely that every detail of their construction is visible, including the way in which such craft were adapted from the original river-going prototypes. This feat was achieved by looping round both ends of the boat a huge hawser that acted as a substitute for keel and ribs. But the keel of a ship has been likened to the spine of an animal; without this backbone, the Egyptian boats were graceful and speedy, but they lacked sturdiness.* Such, then, were the vessels available to the Pharaohs at the dawn of American civilization; they could make the journey to Punt, but hardly to Panama. The Cretans of the same period were certainly skilled mariners, as were the 'Peoples of the Sea', with whom Rhamses III had to contend. But neither of these two peoples is known to have penetrated into the western Mediterranean, let alone into the Atlantic Ocean. All early navigators, including even the first Phoenicians, preferred to limit themselves to the shortest possible stretches of open sea when they planned their voyages.

Discussion in this chapter has centred upon the first and second millennia B.C. and upon the supposition that peoples of the Near East created American civilization. But all the gallant attempts to prove a connection between the New World and the eastern Mediterranean during the period yield meagre results.

The rather jocular assertions by Harold Gladwyn that Alexander the Great's fleet arrived in California can hardly be taken very seriously. And if the mysteries revealed in the golden tablets of Mormon are excluded from the discussion, we are left with Egypt and Phoenicia as the leading candidates for incursions into the New World.

As we have seen, the Phoenicians at least had boats that could, at a pinch, have survived an ocean crossing, and the possibility cannot be denied that an occasional Phoenician vessel *might* have ended up on the Atlantic coast of America. But if any such chance landings occurred, they brought little cultural baggage in their train, and no traces of Phoenician influence have been found in America; in fact only the most trivial similarities are cited, such as the common wearing of upturned slippers. A copy of a copy of a lost inscription, whose place of origin is unknown, whose discoverer has disappeared, and which was later branded as false by its original decipherer, is all that remains as evidence of a Phoenician presence in the New World.

With Egypt the situation is different, and specific elements of the Nile Valley civilization may have an American equivalent. The rather meaningless generalities sometimes put forward, such as the construction of stepped pyramids in both continents, signify little. Even Elliot Smith's case for the bringing of Egyptian-style mummification to the New World was well answered by Dixon. But the more exact parallels listed by Jairazbhoy and others cannot be lightly cast aside. However, in the absence of any clear notion as to just how Egyptian culture could have been borne across the ocean, in face of the evidence that Egyptian boats were unfitted for the task, such studies lead nowhere.

Some of those traits allegedly shared by Egypt and Mexico may also one day be found in Asia, perhaps in Indonesia or India. Of the various authors mentioned, both Gladwyn and Elliot Smith write of Mediterranean influences that reach the New World not westward across the Atlantic, but eastward via Asia — thereby avoiding the problem of Egyptian seamanship. If some of Jairazbhoy's Egyptian elements were also detected in East Asia, then Far Eastern rather than Near Eastern parallels with Mexico would once more be the point at issue; the fact that certain of these Far Eastern elements could be traced back to Egypt would be incidental to the problem. But the question still remains to be answered: did Asians reach America in the first or second millennium B.C.? Alternatively, if they did not do so, how can similarities between peoples on both sides of the Pacific best be explained?

CHAPTER EIGHT

WORLDS IN CONFUSION

The great rich land was intersected and watered by many broad, slow-running streams and rivers, which wound their sinuous ways in fantastic curves and bends round the wooded hills and through the fertile plains. Luxuriant vegetation covered the whole land with a soft, pleasing, restful mantle of green; bright and fragrant flowers on tree and shrub added colouring and finish to the landscape. Tall fronded palms fringed the ocean's shores and lined the banks of rivers for many a mile inland. . . . Over the cool rivers, gaudily-winged butterflies hovered in the shade of the trees, rising and falling in fairy-like movements, as if better to view their painted beauty in nature's mirror. Darting hither and thither from flower to flower, humming birds made their short flights, glistening like living jewels in the rays of the sun.*

This purple passage is not taken from a travel brochure, describing a new tourist paradise, but from a description of the lost continent of Mu. In lyrical terms the account goes on to tell of the myriads of lotus flowers, the feathered songsters vying with each other in their sweet lays, and the lively crickets whose chirpings filled the air; herds of mighty elephants roamed the land, 'flapping their big ears to drive off annoying insects'; only a mention of primaeval forests reminds the reader that this Eden is long since lost to Man.

Colonel James Churchward, to whom we are indebted for such details of the fabled continent of Mu, or Lemuria, was already serving in India in 1868, but he devoted fifty years to his researches, and his book did not appear until much later. Churchward claims to have gained his information from two sets of sacred tablets. The first were the Naacal writings, so-called because they had been written by the Naacals, either in Burma or in the vanished motherland itself; only three priests in India could read their language, one of whom reluctantly revealed its hidden mysteries to Churchward. Then, to complete his story, the English colonel had recourse to a large collection of stone slabs discovered by his friend William Niven in Mexico; by now the Mormons no longer enjoyed a monopoly of secret tablets deciphered by divine inspiration.

With Churchward we enter a new dimension in which authors no longer look for links between the New World and the existing continents of the Old. Instead, the origins of Indian civilization are attributed to some kind of cosmic catastrophe that smote both hemispheres. Certain works describe volcanic upheavals, violent enough to submerge whole continents that had previously formed a bridge between America and Eurasia; others speak of errant moons or planets, whose movements caused South America to be alternately flooded and drained of water. Some books offer speculations on wars between planets lying outside our solar system, with the losers seeking refuge on earth, and more particularly in the Western Hemisphere.

Such theories savour more of science fiction than of science and might therefore seem irrelevant to any serious study of New World origins. However, authors who can claim the attention of millions of readers, and whose appeal is, in fact, worldwide, cannot be ignored. Furthermore, having accepted the existence of a sunken landmass called Beringia, I cannot fairly remain silent upon the lost continents of Atlantis and Mu.

Atlantis was described by Plato, but the concept of a continent called Mu or Lemuria is barely a century old. Surprisingly, beneath the trappings later added by disciples of the occult lie arguments that were tenable at the time and accepted by prominent scientists. In the middle of the nineteenth century, remarkable similarities were seen to exist between the animals, plants and rock formations of lands now separated by thousands of miles of ocean. A fellow of the Royal Society, the zoologist P. L. Sclater, first put the case for Lemuria (of which Mu is merely a shortened version), in order to explain the continued presence of the lemur in Africa, south India and Malaysia. Logically, if a continent had once existed, stretching across the ocean from Malaysia towards Madagascar, it could be regarded as the lemur's first habitat, from which he then spread to Africa and Asia.

Distinguished scientists supported Lemuria's case, including the evolutionist T. H. Huxley and the naturalist Alfred Russell Wallace. In Germany, the lost continent received the backing of Ernst Haeckel, who proposed that it also housed more sophisticated beings than the lemur and went so far as to state his opinion that it was 'the probable cradle of the human race, which in all likelihood here first developed out of anthropoid apes'.*

But alas! Lemuria, once the happy hunting ground of eminent scholars, soon shed its privileged status and fell prey to every kind of mystic. On taking possession of their new-found promised land, the occultists moved its locality to serve their quest for novel theories on Ancient America. The flamboyant Madame Blavatsky and her fellow-members of the Theosophical Society now insisted that Lemuria was not to be sought in the Indian Ocean but had extended across the Pacific, whose archipelagoes were the surviving traces of the great continent. Churchward even provides a map, in which Mu occupies much of the Pacific Ocean and links the New World with the Old.

Helena Petrovna Blavatsky founded the Theosophical Society in New York in 1875 and thirteen years later published *The Secret Doctrine*, in which she sought to reconcile the speculations of P. L. Sclater with her own peculiar brand of mysticism. Madame Blavatsky took her data on America from 'secret annals', in which the social and political history of the Lemurians had been recorded. Unfortunately, only very few people (of whom Blavatsky was naturally one) could interpret these occult writings.* Before Modern Man, Earth had been successively inhabited by five races, of which no less than three had lived in Atlantis or Lemuria. Of the master race of Mu, Madame Blavatsky gives some lively details: its people had four arms and an extra eye in the back of the head; they reproduced themselves by laying eggs; their limbs were so fashioned that they could move forwards or backwards with equal ease. According to another account, the Lemurians were said to be thirty feet high. Madame Blavatsky died in 1890, somewhat discredited by a disastrous episode in which her so-called shrine, used to deliver messages from the masters, was found to have been fitted with conjurers' apparatus. The Theosophists, however, continued to prosper and to elaborate fresh theories on the Lemurians.

The great latter-day chronicler of Mu, or Lemuria, was James Churchward – his account, already cited, omits no conceivable detail. Mu had sixty-four million inhabitants; fifty thousand years ago they had developed a culture from which our own descended, vastly inferior to that of Mu. In addition to his Naacal tablets, Churchward also uses (or rather invents) Chinese and Japanese records, and with their help provides genealogies of the dynasties of Mu and Atlantis.

No refinement of civilization was lacking in Mu, including a network of super-highways: Churchward describes broad smooth roads running in all directions, like a spider's web. But if one reads between the lines, even Paradise had its problems. Quite apart from irksome details, such as the 'annoying insects' that plagued the elephants, society was patently racist; the author makes it clear that a white race dominated the scene and lorded it over people with black or yellow skins. In addition, Mu was class-ridden, and its wealthy people were festooned with precious jewels and attended by countless servants.

About twelve thousand years ago, according to the same account, Mu was torn asunder by a great catastrophe and sank beneath the waves. Some inhabitants managed to reach America, bringing those other 'secret' tablets later discovered in Mexico by Churchward's friend Niven. In support of his theories, Churchward cites the Codex Troano and the Codex Cortesianus (which are really two parts of the same document) and gives his romantic renderings of otherwise undecipherable passages. As a teller of tall stories this author outpaces all rivals: Mexico City was founded two hundred thousand years ago and then stood at sea level: the city of Lexington, Kentucky, was built of the dust of a dead metropolis belonging to a lost race. Towards the end of his book, *The Lost Continent of Mu*, Churchward adopts a tone of the deepest reverence in quoting Le Plongeon, his true peer in sheer inventive capacity. Le Plongeon's Queen Moo should not be confused with the lost continent of Mu, however; it was Atlantis, not Mu, that this fugitive Mayan heroine visited on her way from Mexico to Egypt.

Another champion of Mu is George Hunt Williamson, who gets the best of both worlds by combining in the same text a story of Lemuria and a description of the arrival of Venusians from outer space. Williamson relates in his book, *The Secret Places of the Lion*, how a prominent (but unnamed) 'historian' of Mu was exploring a remote region of his country when he was surprised by 'great ships of light coming down from the heavens'. The local population became jubilant when they learned that the gods had come to live among mortals. Williamson's interplanetary visitors had landed in the eastern regions of Mu, known as Telos, which managed to survive the coming catastrophe and now form the western part of the United States. Shortly after the Venusian incursion, the great disaster occurred; the winds howled as if all the night gods were shrieking and most but not all of Mu sank beneath the waves. However, another 'historian' of Mu, called Mutan Mian, determined that this priceless heritage should not be lost forever and recorded every feature on yet another set of secret tablets, made of indestructible telonium. These plates have never been found, but some at least were left in Telos and now await discovery in the American south-west.

After his brief revelation of past events, Williamson's book tails off into a tedious attempt at biblical reinterpretation; however, an appendix gives a fascinating table of 'reincarnational patterns'. For instance, Joseph Smith, the founder of the Mormon Church, was a reincarnation of King David, as well as of Merlin, the magician of King Arthur's court, and — believe it or not — of Moctezuma II of Mexico. Joseph Smith's brother, however, Hiram Smith, was Rhamses I of Egypt in a previous existence. Nefertiti became, in another appearance upon earth, Mary Baker Eddy.

As in the case of Mu, speculation on the lost continent of Atlantis has both serious and frivolous aspects. The discussion started with Plato, and still continues twenty-three centuries later. We are not immediately concerned with theories that place Atlantis in the Sahara desert, for instance, but with works linking the lost continent to the peopling of America; they are so numerous that J. O. Thompson's epigram still rings true: 'In a sense Plato may be said to have invented America.'*

Plato's original and much-quoted account is divided into two parts. The shorter of the two occurs in his *Timaeus*, in which Critias tells of the statement made to Solon by an Egyptian priest. According to this version, Atlantis was larger than Libya (Africa) and Asia combined; it lay beyond the Pillars of Hercules, i.e. the Straits of Gibraltar, and had possessed a great and wonderful empire; having first occupied part of the Mediterranean shore of Africa, it had tried to conquer both Egypt and Greece, but the Greeks saved the day and repulsed the Atlantean invasion. After this, Atlantis was destroyed and disappeared into the depths of the sea: this event occurred about nine thousand years before the date of the narrative.

Another Platonic dialogue, the *Critias*, gives a much longer account, including a genealogy of Atlantean rulers, who descended from the sea-god Poseidon and a mortal maiden called Cleito. A description of Atlantis follows, almost as vivid as Churchward's writings on Mu. Rich minerals, luxuriant flora, and exotic fauna abounded; as in Mu, elephants roamed in herds. Plato even provides a plan of the metropolis of Atlantis; it was circular in form, built upon a hill, and surmounted by the royal palace, 'a marvel to behold in size and beauty'. His account also mentions a religious cult of the bull and states that the king himself was obliged to hunt and capture a bull, which was then sacrificed. However, unlike the people of Mu, who were peaceable and pleasure-loving, the Atlanteans were a martial race and so organized that the whole population was available for war. Their arsenal included ten thousand chariots. Spartan virtues were honoured, and the privileged classes were not sated by luxury, nor did their wealth deprive them of their self-control.

Speculation on Plato's Atlantis is a time-honoured pursuit. Voltaire and Buffon both believed in its existence and it was marked on Toscanelli's chart, used by Columbus. Spanish sixteenth-century chroniclers of the New World write of the lost continent: Bartolomé de las Casas mentions Plato's story and says that it inspired Columbus to undertake his voyages; López de Gómara insists that Columbus had read Plato's *Timaeus* and *Critias*.

However, an entirely new impetus was given to the cult of Atlantis by Ignatius Donnelly, a writer most influential in moulding modern opinion on the subject, particularly in the United States. His book, *Atlantis, the Antediluvian World*, was first published in New York in 1882; it had run through eighteen editions by 1889, was translated into German in 1894 and was still thought worthy of reissue in 1949. Donnelly, who was not only a prehistorian but also a novelist, Congressman and a Shakespearean scholar, set forth in detail every argument serving to show that Atlantis had formed a bridge between the Old World and the New. The book includes a map, showing the lost continent as joined on the eastern side to Africa and reaching westwards as far as a Cuba that then formed part of the North American mainland. Donnelly's search for connections between Old and New World civilizations is lengthy but superficial. As a sample of his reasoning, the statement may be quoted that Panuco, a name that occurs frequently in Mexican legend, was Panopolis, the city of the Greek god, Pan. But Panuco is merely a Spanish corruption of the Nahuatl name, Panotlan, meaning 'Place of Crossing'.

Donnelly may be regarded as the father of a modern craze for the lost continent; for if a vast landmass were to rise out of the sea tomorrow, it could scarcely attract more attention than has been accorded the legendary Atlantis. Studies fall into distinct categories, and many have nothing to do with the peopling of America. The mystics and occultists who fastened upon the notion of Atlantis first deserve mention. For instance, Donnelly greatly influenced Madame Blavatsky, the prophetess of Mu, who eagerly welcomed the existence of two lost continents instead of one; she simply joined them together and maintained that Atlantis was connected to Lemuria by a huge tongue of land stretching round southern Africa. Rudolf Steiner, who became leader of the German section of Madame Blavatsky's Theosophists, used clairvoyant vision to elaborate on their original teaching on Atlantis.

Steiner claimed to possess special powers whereby he could interpret the Akashic Record, a brand of mystic information that derived not from further sets of buried tablets but from the peculiar notion that all events, including every thought and idea, are somehow preserved in the astral light.* Steiner was therefore able to add colourful touches to Critias' original description; for instance, the Atlanteans thought in pictures, possessed extraordinary memories, and used the energy latent in plants to drive a kind of hovercraft. Steiner declared that he was pledged not to reveal the occult sources of his knowledge of Atlantean conditions; he also stated that the Lemurians had lived before the Atlanteans, and were very different because, having absolutely no memory, they promptly forgot anything that they were told.*

According to Steiner, the early priest-kings of the Aryans were descended from the élite of Atlantis, and his ideas were accordingly used by authors intent upon giving a racist orientation to current thinking on the lost continent. In *The Myth of the Twentieth Century*, the leading Nazi theorist, Alfred Rosenberg, adopted Steiner's notions and improved on Plato by insisting that Atlantis, as home of the Aryan race, had to be situated in the north. After the publication of his book in 1930 an exhibition of trance paintings of Atlantis was held in Berlin. The vanished Aryan homeland had not only its painters, but also its poets; the best known was Edmund Kiss. The cult of the lost continent as the seat of a master race received official recognition with the establishment in 1935 of the Deutsches Ahnenerbe, literally 'German Ancestral Heritage'; its curator was Hermann Wirth, another leading Atlantis theorist.*

Such speculations proved to be a two-edged weapon, however, since they could be used by the enemies of the Third Reich as well as by its friends. In 1941, Lewis Spence published *The Occult Causes of the Present War*, which prophesied that the struggle would end when Germany and much of Europe were submerged and became by that means a second Atlantis. Spence methodically sought links between Atlantis and America; he connected the Mexican rain-god, Tlaloc, with the submerged continent, while Quetzalcóatl, the Plumed Serpent, personified Atlas. Spence's pseudo-scientific musings are imbued with occultism, and part of his information is claimed to derive from 'men of insight who had strange visions'.

The notion of a Nordic Atlantis did not die in 1945. During the 1950s Jürgen Spannuth, the German writer and man of adventure, maintained that it was really situated in the vicinity of Heligoland and sent divers down to look for it. Spannuth had previously written a *History of Atlantis* in which he added his own embellishments to previous accounts, such as the suggestion that the elephants mentioned by Critias were probably used for war.

Atlantean enthusiasts have sought the lost continent in such unlikely places as Morocco, Tunisia or even Corsica. Recently, sounder but less spectacular theories that entirely divorce Atlantis from the history of America have been advanced. During the nineteenth century, Cretan civilization was still virtually unknown; however, as studies of Minoan culture progressed, scholars began to suggest that the Atlanteans who made war on Athens were really Minoans. According to this hypothesis, the story of the final cataclysm derives from the fate of Thera, or Santorini, as it is now usually called, an island which lies about sixty miles north of Crete. About 1500 B.C. it suffered a catastrophic volcanic eruption, which destroyed most of it; today an active volcano still exists on a small island facing the main harbour, and only a few years ago Thera was badly damaged by another earthquake. The eminent Greek archaeologist, Professor Marinatos, discovered the remains of an important Minoan city on Thera and took charge of its excavation until his death in 1975. The Minoan site lay buried beneath a mountain of volcanic ash, and Marinatos became convinced that the eruption on that island was of such violence as to cause a great mass of this volcanic dust to descend on Crete, destroying the original Minoan civilization. A catastrophe of such titanic proportions could have given rise to the legend of Atlantis because we know that Crete was in close touch with Egypt. Stories of the destruction of Minoan civilization by the explosion in nearby Thera would have been thoroughly garbled over the centuries and come to relate, not to the real and smallish Crete, but to the huge if mythical Atlantis.

The tale of Atlantis could equally have been a mere after-dinner yarn, told by the Egyptians to amuse their visitors. Some of the Greeks were themselves highly sceptical about the story, which Aristotle described as a poetic fiction. Greeks were given to the writing of Utopias; Aristophanes portrayed his 'Cloud-Cuckoo-Land', and Plato described his ideal 'Republic'. Even if the legend is partly factual, it cannot be one-hundred-per-cent exact. If, for instance, as Plato states, the Athenians were involved, then his dates must be hopelessly wrong since no Athens existed nine thousand years before his time. But if a more recent date is accepted for the catastrophe, then Atlantis could well be Thera. The distance from Egypt to Atlantis was probably overstated in Plato's account, since in ancient history numbers are very often exaggerated. Egyptian records tell of wars with Cretans; the Mycenaeans, the predecessors of the Classic Greeks, invaded Crete, where the cult of the bull, mentioned by Plato, definitely prevailed; some great catastrophe did occur in Thera in Minoan times. As an explanation of the Atlantis riddle, the Minoan theory is the best available.

Suggestions that Atlantis or Lemuria acted as a stepping-stone to the New World invite scepticism. Not a shred of archaeological evidence supports this viewpoint, and geologists find no traces of sunken continents in either the Atlantic or Pacific Oceans. A huge mid-Atlantic mountain ridge indeed exists, running from Iceland far down into the Southern Hemisphere, and even comes to the surface at isolated points, such as the Azores. But most of the submerged range lies over five thousand feet below the surface, while to its east and west the ocean depth is about sixteen thousand feet. No scientist believes that the sea level rose by anything like five thousand feet, although much smaller changes are known to have occurred during the Ice Ages.

The general contours of the mid-Atlantic ridge were revealed by soundings a quarter of a century ago, but only recently has a more exhaustive search become possible. Participants in a three-year Franco-American project, aided by new types of equipment, succeeded in reaching the sea bed at selected points and have taken large quantities of pictures, using new photographic techniques.* The area of their descent lies between 36° and 37° north, some three hundred and seventy-five miles south-west of the Azores. At this point, the ridge consists of two parallel ranges of steep mountains, located about nineteen miles apart and divided by a depression or valley whose bottom lies far below their crest.

There is not the faintest suggestion in the explorers' reports that part of this great range emerged from the sea in the last twelve thousand years. The ocean floor in that region is indeed rocked by continuous volcanic activity, and titanic forces are constantly tearing it apart. But mere millennia count for nothing in geological terms and, according to the author of the report, the Atlantic ridge took two hundred million years to form. From two 'obviously very young volcanic extrusions' rock samples were taken which were described as 'no older than 100,000 years – a mere blink in geological history'. The rise of *Homo sapiens*, therefore, came after the creation of two rather insignificant 'young' volcanoes, whose peaks never rose to within a mile of the surface. More spectacular changes in the mid-Atlantic mountain ridges involved many millions of years and have absolutely nothing to do with Ancient Greeks – or Ancient Americans.

The Deutsches Ahnenerbe did not confine its efforts to the search for Atlantis, but launched into other speculations about lost continents and global catastrophes. 'Glacial Cosmology' was invented by the Austrian Hans Hörbiger, whose system rested on the belief that Earth possessed several moons before the present one. These satellites had previously been independent planets, orbiting between ourselves and Mars, before they were 'captured' by our planet. One after the other the captive bodies crashed upon Earth with catastrophic consequences, and on each occasion a great civilization perished. The fall of the last moon created the universal legend of the *Flood* and caused the submersion of Atlantis.

In the general tradition of Hörbiger was Immanuel Velikovsky, whose principal work, *Worlds in Collision*, was published in 1950 and caused a sensation, though his theories were quickly repudiated by leading scientists. Velikovsky's predictions as to the surface temperature of Venus and its manner of rotation have lately been proved unexpectedly near the mark, though the same cannot be said of his other prognostications. He wrote copiously, if inaccurately, about Ancient

America in order to prove his points on cosmic events. His views can be stated briefly since they do not bear directly on American origins except where they influenced others who have ventured into that field. Essentially the author seeks to prove that the Old Testament is a perfectly literal account of historical events: the supernatural incidents in the Bible occurred exactly as described and were caused by cosmic catastrophes.

The chain of disasters began with a gigantic comet that became detached from the total mass of Jupiter: each time this breakaway monster approached Earth, the effects were dramatic. The first shock came in 1500 B.C. and caused the waters of the Red Sea to part at Moses' command, when the Israelites left Egypt. Mars and Venus were originally both comets; the greatest catastrophe of all came when they collided, after Mars had shifted its orbit nearer to the earth. The clash of the comets brought ruin upon the armies of the Assyrian king Sennacherib in 687 B.C., when 185,000 men perished, smitten, according to the Bible, by the angel of the Lord. Cataclysms of such magnitude shook the New World to its foundations and produced upheavals, one of which prompted the Aztecs to abandon their homeland – in the same year that the Assyrian army was destroyed.

Velikovsky simply makes up Aztec history: not a shred of evidence suggests that the tribe even existed at this early date. He also writes of 'wars between Toltecs and Aztecs', which he states 'must have taken place earlier than is generally supposed', and connects such events with his clash between the planets. But these wars are an invention of the author, for though the Aztecs and Toltecs both rose to be the dominant power of central Mexico, they did so at different periods: the Toltec Empire collapsed in the twelfth century A.D., while the Aztec Empire came into existence in the fifteenth. Conceivably the Aztecs had already appeared upon the scene before the fall of the Toltec capital, but they were then nothing but humble migrants.

Hörbiger's theories about Earth's possession of a whole series of moons are closely followed by his disciple, H. S. Bellamy. In his book *Built before the Flood*, Bellamy applied these notions to the great Bolivian archaeological site of Tiahuanaco, insisting that it had first been destroyed in the dim past when a previous satellite crashed upon Earth. The ruins visible today belong to a second Tiahuanaco that came into being at a time when Earth's present satellite had approached so close that it swung round the globe three times in every 48 hours. The Moon's proximity drew off all the waters of the oceans into equatorial regions and flooded most of South America. Therefore the second Tiahuanaco was built at sea level on land, jutting out as an island refuge from the waters that covered the rest of the continent. About thirteen thousand five hundred years ago things returned to normal, the sea sank, the Tiahuanaco region was left high and dry, and nearby Lake Titicaca was formed at its present altitude of 13,500 feet.

Writers who seek bizarre explanations of America's past are drawn to Tiahuanaco as bees to honey. Bellamy, guided by little but his own imagination, is one of several who invented calendric interpretations of the symbols carved on Tiahuanaco's famous Gate of the Sun. The site has apparently mesmerized the minds of mystics simply because of its very high altitude. Searchers after occult messages from the ruins obviously puff and blow when they breathe the rarefied air of the Bolivian Altiplano – or read of others who suffered in this way. Then, judging by such experiences, they take for granted that the great blocks of stone could not conceivably have been dragged to their site by any human agency, so great would be the physical effort required. To complete the magic aura with which they surround Tiahuanaco, the mystics then conclude that the archaeologists err as to its dating and that it was really built, not two thousand but two hundred thousand years ago. Even Arthur Posnansky, long regarded as the father of Tiahuanacan archaeology, indulged in occasional flights of fancy and wrote that Tiahuanaco was 10,600 years old.

But people sometimes forget that the effects of altitude are relative. Occultists who pontificate about Tiahuanaco would have been precious little help in the task of dragging enormous blocks of stone across the Altiplano. But the Indians who live there – and who did so long ago – are perfectly adapted to such dizzy heights. As a result, their bodies would not function normally at sea level: Inca records confirm that troops recruited in the Altiplano were ill-fitted for fighting on the coast, and vice versa. In a mining village, south of Orouro, called Totoral, situated at 15,800 feet – or far above Tiahuanaco – football is played with enthusiasm. The present Bolivian capital, La Paz, is situated only slightly lower than Tiahuanaco, and the highest parts lie at about 12,000 feet; yet strenuous manual labour of every kind is carried out there, precisely as in other parts of the world. Even people adapted to

Stone figures, representing Toltec warriors, which supported a pyramid temple to Quetzalcóatl. The objects held in the right hands, probably swords, have been interpreted by von Däniken as ray-guns. Tula, 7th–9th centuries A.D.

Egyptian ship of the Punt Expedition.

Phoenician ship, C. 700 B.C.

Viking ship from Oseberg.

Greek galley, 4th century B.C.

Polynesian double sailing canoe.

Seriated columns set into a wall, Uxmal, Mexico.

Seriated columns set into a wall flanking a doorway to the temple of Banteay Srei, Angkor, Cambodia.

Niched pyramid, El Tajin, Veracruz.

Niched terraces at Borabudur, central Java, Indonesia, 8th century A.D.

Mexican wheeled toy, Museo Nacional de Antropología.

Wooden horse on wheels. Egyptian toy of the Roman period, A.D. c.200, *from Akhmun. British Museum.*

Red tiger spotted with jade.
Pyramid of Kukulkan,
Chichén Itzá, Yucatan State.

Tiger's head of bronze inlaid with silver. Chou Dynasty, 1027–221 B.C.
Ostasiatische Museum, Cologne.

Maori carved wooden pilaster, New Zealand. British Museum.

Carved wooden totem pole from the Haida village of Kayang, Queen Charlotte Island, northwest coast of America. British Museum.

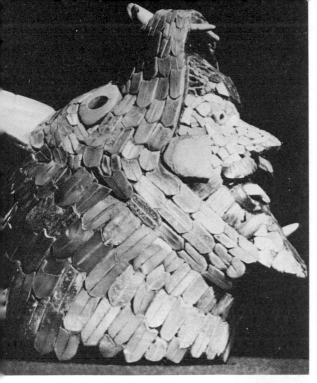

Shell mosaic image of Quetzalcóatl emerging from the jaws of a monster. Toltec, 7th–9th centuries A.D. Museo Nacional de Antropología.

Chinese bronze ritual vessel in the form of a man being protected by a tiger, 14th–12th centuries B.C. Musée Cernuschi, Paris.

Easter Island statue, Polynesia. British Museum.

Olmec head, La Venta.

Stone heads, Angkor, Cambodia.

Split–image designs on the façade of one of the buildings of the Nunnery Quadrangle at Uxmal.

Split - image designs on a Chilkat weaving, north–west coast of America.

'Hocker' figure. House screen in the form of a bear from the house of Chief Shakes of Wrangell Islands. Tlingit, A.D. 1840. Denver Art Museum.

'Hocker' figure. Hohao plaque, Papua New Guinea. Buffalo Museum of Science.

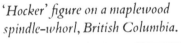

'Hocker' figure on a maplewood spindle-whorl, British Columbia.

Totonac goddess of subsistence and fertility, Veracruz, A.D. *300–800.*

Head of Queen Nefertiti. Egypt, 14th century B.C. *Berlin Museum.*

Bearded Olmec figure.

lower altitudes do not cease to function at such heights, though their energy may be reduced.

There is nothing particularly odd about Tiahuanaco. An initial phase, running from 200 B.C. to A.D. 600, has been established by radiocarbon for Pucara, which lies to the north of Lake Titicaca. This early Pucara unquestionably coincides with the early Tiahuanaco, whose larger buildings date from the later part of this period, running from A.D. 200 to 600. The next Tiahuanaco phase ran from A.D. 600 to 1000 and Tiahuanaco-type pottery designs of this era have been identified in many regions of Bolivia and Peru. Tiahuanaco dates are thereby firmly interlocked with those of other civilizations of Peru; if the site was really ten thousand years old, let alone two hundred thousand, then all the radiocarbon figures for Peruvian cultures become sheer nonsense, together with most of the writings of Peruvian scholars.

This book would not be complete without some reference to Erich von Däniken, who is rather different from those already mentioned in the present chapter; for while a vein of mysticism runs through his writings, he is not basically an occultist. Von Däniken's hypothesis is too well-known to require detailed description; in *Chariots of the Gods* and other works he suggests that on a number of occasions this planet was visited by extraterrestrial beings who engendered *Homo sapiens* and inspired human civilization.

Certain antecedents to such views exist. Literal explanation of the supernatural or miraculous in the Old Testament is a time-honoured pursuit. George Hunt Williamson, writing in 1958, quoted von Däniken's favourite passage from the prophet Ezekiel and treated it as a description of biblical aviators: 'When they were lifted up from earth, the wheels were lifted up' (Ezekiel I: 14–20). Williamson also developed the theme of invasion from outer space, affirming that a spaceship lay buried under the Pyramid of Cheops in Egypt; this author, like von Däniken, rejected out of hand the accepted dating of the Great Pyramids.

Nevertheless, von Däniken far and away leads the field among authorities on visitations from the stars, and in this domain stands out as a giant among pigmies. His following among the general public is vast, and he has been imitated or even outdone by numerous authors, of whom Robert Charroux is typical. In *Lost Worlds*, published in 1971, this

French author omits no conceivable fantasy; not content with stressing the extraterrestrial genesis of mankind, he writes of eight heart transplant operations performed one hundred thousand years ago. Like von Däniken, Charroux has no time for archaeologists: 'But for those of us who dare to be men of tomorrow, conventional prehistory is only adulterated and foolish fiction.' Most archaeologists would consider that the words 'foolish fiction' better described Charroux' own efforts. But scholars are in good company as the butt of his strictures that also includes the Twelve Apostles, who are accused of drug abuse as the only possible explanation of their somnolence on the Mount of Olives. The competition in extravagance is unending: recently another book called *Mystery of the Ancients* was recommended to the reader on the grounds that its theories make von Däniken seem 'prosaic'; in face of such rivals, he seems in danger of becoming just another Dr Phuddy Duddy.

The average specialist readily ignores or ridicules von Däniken because his work errs in matters of detail. But von Däniken and his imitators can only be understood as high priests of a cult, not as proponents of yet another theory of ancient history. Many people, intrigued by the possibility that we are not alone in the Universe, become ecstatic when this possibility is moulded into a dogma, offering a romantic version of Man's origins. Such views may offend certain churchmen, who are no more amused at the idea of Adam and Eve being descended from Martians than from monkeys. Yet part of the rage for von Däniken's views may spring from people who shrink from the thought that they are related to the orang-utan and are relieved to learn that their ancestors were really astronauts. The cult of which von Däniken is the leading prophet has crystallized into an official movement. *Der Spiegel* (9 June 1974) reports a meeting of 285 members of the Ancient Astronaut Society held in Zürich, and describes the typical attendant as belonging to the 'middle management' level of society. The account stresses the fervour of those present, who seemed as if they were votaries of a new faith. The reactions to von Däniken's theories can only be comprehended in this light; his audience is not made up of students of science but of disciples of a Messiah. For members of the Ancient Astronaut Society, as *Der Spiegel* points out, orthodox science is cast in the role of the enemy, or the Devil; they see themselves as potential Giordano Brunos, ready to be burned at the stake rather than deny their beliefs.

Von Däniken's dogma has created such a stir that he has acquired plenty of detractors as well as admirers, and a number of books have been written with the object of debunking his theories. Such works appear from unexpected quarters. For instance, *Some Trust in Chariots* was published in Australia; another book from Brazil is entitled *The Truth about Astronaut Gods*. These publications go to great lengths to refute von Däniken, criticizing his lack of accuracy and listing, systematically if monotonously, his errors in matters of undisputed detail. But, somewhat ironically, von Däniken's detractors are also at times inaccurate. For instance, the outer cover of *Some Trust in Chariots* is clearly intended to illustrate the famous Aztec 'Stone of the Sun'; but the picture is taken not from the authentic stone but from a metal reproduction that is to be found in every tourist shop in Mexico. The signs in this metal version differ from those of the original, of which it is not therefore an exact replica. Von Däniken himself does better in this respect and provides a photograph of the actual stone in one of his books.

Furthermore, the only section of *Some Trust in Chariots* that concerns American archaeology is written by Gordon Whittaker, a disciple of Dr Cyrus H. Gordon, already mentioned in connection with the Paraiba Stone of Brazil. To put it mildly, some of Cyrus Gordon's notions on ancient America are most questionable, so it is not surprising that Whittaker, in seeking to refute von Däniken, himself makes debatable statements.

Von Däniken is clearly more at home with physicists, some of whom he knows, than with archaeologists, whom he does not. His preface to *Chariots of the Gods* warmly thanks the personnel of NASA, but no similar bouquets are handed out to the poor archaeologist. Von Däniken's acceptance of the findings of one scientific discipline does not deter him from rejecting the achievements of another. He writes of orthodox archaeologists, 'The story of Man's origins is instilled into him in the form of a pious fairy story.' Not for the first time, the specialists are accused of dishonesty: von Däniken 'doubts the integrity' of those who deny that the famous stone relief of Palenque offers 'proofs' of his theories; on another occasion he refers to 'the tricks of scholars'. But while everyone may be entitled to his own interpretation of the Palenque relief, charges of trickery verge on the ludicrous when levelled at such eminent Mayan scholars as Sir Eric Thompson or Dr Alberto Ruz Lhuiller, who discovered the relief.

Using a very selective method of approach, von Däniken rejects outright the Egyptologists' dating of the Great Pyramids and their dynasties and produces a special chronology for Tiahuanaco that is totally at variance with radiocarbon dating; however, he is strangely willing to accept the orthodox scholars' dates for the Sumerians, who were the contemporaries of the Pyramid-builders. But point-by-point analysis serves no purpose in dealing with the arguments of people who happily ignore the unanimous findings of science and who prefer to devise their own rules and to invent their own dates. One might as well argue with the prophet Ezekiel himself as contest some of von Däniken's categorical pronouncements. For instance, if Mayan reliefs are stated to lack vegetation, what is the use of pointing to photographs of stelae whose carvings drip with foliage? If the existence of a bird-cult in Colombia is denied, what purpose does it serve to call attention to the rows of double-tailed birds displayed in the Gold Museum of Bogotá?*

Differences of principle here transcend points of detail. Von Däniken, like Faust, seeks one answer to every question: every shaven head is a spaceman's helmet; every outstretched hand clutches a spaceship's lever; every stylized moth becomes an aircraft. Underlying such notions is the basic tenet that, because no other sure explanation exists for a phenomenon, von Däniken's own hypothesis must be right.

But the flaws in this argument are patent. The famous lines and animal patterns drawn in the coastal desert near Nazca, Peru, serve as an example. Scholars freely admit that they cannot say for sure what the purpose of these lines was, but the lack of a clear-cut answer cannot be taken as 'proof' that they served as airstrips for spacecraft (that might be expected to land vertically, rather than on runways, let alone on strange animal shapes). In this instance, it would be wiser to trust the findings of Maria Reiche, who has spent her whole life studying the problem; she believes that each line bears on the point at which a certain star rose on the horizon at a given date; such directional points would alter in the course of centuries and thereby account for the not-quite-parallel lines starting from one point and forming a tangle more apt to confuse than to assist approaching astronauts; some patterns are not even visible from the air, but only from low mounds in their vicinity.*

Von Däniken's favourite thesis denies that ancient peoples, whether Egyptians or Olmecs, could have cut and moved huge stone blocks with the sole aid of equipment and techniques discovered by archaeologists. But an ample assortment of Ancient Egyptian copper tools is displayed in the Cairo Museum, and we also possess a detailed hieroglyphic description of the moving of a statue nineteen feet high belonging to Prince Tuthotep, who lived in approximately 1870 B.C., during the 12th Dynasty. This text is accompanied by a relief that shows exactly how the task was accomplished and illustrates the statue as it is pulled along by means of ropes, drawn by no less than 172 men, among them priests and soldiers, but no astronauts.

Von Däniken, thorough after his own fashion, tells how he and his friends tried to carve stones with ancient tools found on Easter Island and failed dismally. But Stone Age Man was highly trained in many skills not practised in Switzerland today. Who, for instance, would have been the winner in a contest between von Däniken and a herd of bison if he and his friends had pursued them for days on end, armed only with primitive javelins?

Another detailed report on the moving of megaliths comes from Mexico. The chronicler Father Durán relates how, a few years before the Spanish conquest, Moctezuma II ordered that the largest possible stone should be brought to his capital to serve as a new sacrificial platform. To obey the Emperor's command, peoples of many towns and villages were recruited, together with an appropriate cohort of priests and magicians; quails were then sacrificed, and their blood poured on the stone, before the attempt to move it began. The ropes, wedges and levers used for the purpose are clearly described; however, the task proved so hard that the stone was only finally heaved to its destination after an even larger force had been mustered.*

Sahagún gives a good description of Aztec methods of carving stone statues, as told to him by native informers who had actually performed the work.* Eyewitness accounts therefore show that the Aztecs at the time of the arrival of the Spaniards were perfectly capable of cutting big stones and moving them, aided solely by Stone Age tools and techniques. No possible grounds, therefore, exist for any belief that the earlier peoples of Mexico could not have performed similar feats without extraterrestrial assistance. Technical progress marched at a snail's pace in Ancient Mexico, and Aztec techniques in A.D. 1500 were no advance on those of A.D. 500. And, just in case Father Sahagún were to be charged with telling nothing but 'pious fairy tales', consider the removal of the Stone of the Sun to the new archaeological museum in Mexico City. The huge stone was successfully borne to the street from its previous resting place in the old museum by only ten men, using ropes; this solemn occasion was marked by the presence of a mariache band.

Even writers who outrival von Däniken do not suggest that the Aztecs were aided by astronauts in the last century before the Conquest, and the Spaniards' detailed accounts tell of no spacemen in New Spain. On the contrary, the European invaders were themselves greeted as returning gods. The conquerors had no chariots, but rode on horses, which the natives had never seen before.

Nevertheless, von Däniken claims that the Aztecs' immediate predecessors, the Toltecs, received assistance from the stars, though their empire crumbled barely before A.D. 1200, as established by year-by-year chronological records running from the end of the Toltec period until the Conquest. But the earlier civilizations of Mexico were no more in need of aid from outer space to complete their public works programmes than were the Aztecs, whose methods were the same and were observed by the Spaniards. Aztec sculpture and building were on a much grander scale than that of the Toltecs of Tula, where much of the work tends to be slipshod and poorly executed, despite the alleged use of laser appliances. Von Däniken even proposes that the famous Atlantid statutes of Tula hold ray guns in their hands and says that the Toltecs used laser appliances to melt the rocks by the emission of radiation. But, as to so many of this author's rhetorical questions, a simple answer is available.

The archaeologists are credited by von Däniken with the suggestion that the mysterious objects held by the Atlantids are symbolic keys. Such a statement probably came from a tourist guide since every archaeologist knows that the Ancient Mexicans did not have locks and keys. The Atlantids, in fact, hold in their right hand an *atlatl*, or javelin thrower, the main Toltec weapon, of which countless examples survive and are plentifully illustrated in Mexican codices. Had von Däniken also photographed the objects held in the Atlantids' left hands, he could scarcely deny that these were javelins, which were commonly used as ammunition for the *atlatl*.

Von Däniken's own calculations may serve to establish the odds against extraterrestrial visits. He offers a perfectly acceptable estimate of 180 million planets capable of supporting life situated in the Milky Way, the galaxy to which our own solar system belongs, and proposes that only one per cent (i.e. 1,800,000) of those bodies actually contain living beings, of which one per cent (i.e. 18,000) might in turn contain inhabitants comparable to *Homo sapiens*. Therefore, according to these calculations, there is a chance of only one in 10,000 (a hundredth of one per cent) that any planet whose conditions were suitable might in fact house beings of superior intelligence.

Von Däniken nevertheless maintains that such calculations allow for a reasonable selection of planets lying 'comparatively close' to earth and inhabited by potential space travellers. But this reckoning rather depends on what is meant by 'comparatively close'. Our galaxy is 26,000 light years in diameter, and according to Professor Stephen H. Dole, the American astronomer who has written at length on the possibilities of life in outer space, probably only fifty habitable planets – or a tiny fraction of the total – are situated within a radius of one hundred light years from Earth.* Accordingly, taking von Däniken's own calculation to the effect that only 1 in 10,000 suitable candidates would in actual fact be inhabited by superior beings, we are left with odds of 200 to 1 (10,000 divided by 50) against the existence of a planet inhabited by possible visitors to Earth from which the journey to our planet could be made in less than one hundred years, travelling at the speed of light.

Scientists who attended the important conference in Green Bank, West Virginia, in 1961 (mysteriously described by von Däniken as a secret meeting), produced a less optimistic forecast of the possibility that any given star might possess habitable satellites. According to the Green Bank formula, the nearest planet capable of undertaking space travel was likely to be 300–400 light years distant from Earth.*

For a civilization to evolve spaceships able to travel at anything near the speed of light, a technology vastly superior to our own is needed. Pioneer 10, which will pass the planet Uranus in 1979 and Pluto in 1987, would take a hundred thousand years to reach the nearest fixed star, Proxima Centauri. Present hopes of contacts with other civilizations, therefore, depend upon radioastronomy rather than manned expeditions. Although the word 'impossible' should be used with the utmost caution, the giant obstacles confronting would-be visitors to the stars make the mind boggle. In 1973 the physicists and engineers of the British Planetary Society began a study which they named 'Daedalus'. The declared aim was to devise a spaceship that could reach a nearby star during the lifetime of its crew; the outcome was the design for a space vessel (it could hardly be called a capsule), weighing 67,000 tons. In its wake would be launched a trail of atom bombs weighing 150,000 tons; by exploding these at short intervals during a period of five years, the craft would attain a velocity of 16.7 per cent of the speed of light and reach its destination, about six light years distant, in forty years.

So, although Earth *could* have received extraterrestrial visitors, the difficulties are formidable, even with the help of a technology far more advanced than our own. Any such visitors to the Toltecs or Mayas might still be on their way home today, if their return journey involved distances of hundreds of light years.

A rather geocentric view, such as led to the burning of Bruno in 1600, is needed to explain why people from distant worlds chose the solar system as their destination, from a choice of the 200,000 million stars that our galaxy contains. If a model is made in which the whole of our planetary system lies a few feet from the sun, then, using the same scale, the nearest fixed star would lie about 120 miles away. Still harder to account for is the addiction of these astronauts to the most primitive tools; believers in visits from the outer Universe never cease to explain that the gold moth in the Bogotá Museum is really an aeroplane and repeatedly refer to the rudimentary 'battery' in the Museum of Baghdad. But to liken batteries or even aircraft used today to the gadgetry at the disposal of the supertechnicians who arrived from the stars is to compare a Bushman's blow-gun with a modern missile.

An equally geocentric view is put forward by Robert K. C. Temple in a recent book called *The Sirius Mystery*. According to this the mermaidlike inhabitants of a planet of Sirius, the brightest star in our firmament and only 8.4 light years distant, had been keeping a close watch upon Earth for some time before setting forth in space-tanks filled with water to call on the Early Dynastic Egyptians. Temple reached this singular conclusion after eight years of research; central to his belief is the worship by the Dogon tribe in Mali, not of Sirius, but of its tiny companion known as Sirius B or Digitaria, a star not visible to the naked eye. It was first discovered with the use of a telescope in 1862; it is what is known as a white dwarf, consisting of matter in its ultimate stage of degeneration, and is so dense that a matchbox of it would weigh about fifty tons.

Temple believes that the Dogons migrated long ago from Egypt, armed with the knowledge of the movements of Sirius B, with which the Egyptians were also familiar. As evidence of a connection between Sirius and the Ancient Near East, the author relies on the importance of the number fifty, representing the fifty-year period of revolution of Sirius and Sirius B. In the Book of Leviticus, Moses commands the Hebrews to observe a fast every fifty years; in Greek mythology we find the fifty Nereids, and Cerberus, the hound of hell, originally had fifty heads; in Sumeria, the hero Gilgamesh has fifty companions. In reality the Sirius rotation period is $49\frac{1}{2}$ years. Temple did not hit upon the 52-year cycle (another good approximation to $49\frac{1}{2}$) of the sacred Aztec calendar, in order to develop the idea that the same people also visited Mexico.

Temple displays great erudition in mustering his facts, but his proposed links between Sirius and the Near East amount to little more than the significance in antiquity of the number fifty. The intriguing news of the Dogon worship of Digitaria was formally recorded by two French anthropologists (who themselves drew no inferences as to space travel) and perhaps one day more reports of this kind may be gleaned from primitive peoples. The apparent familiarity of the Dogon with Sirius B could result from mere guesswork; their information was only partly correct, because they also believed in a second companion to Sirius that scientists have not been able to find.

Sirius B is of 7.1 magnitude. The Greek Hipparchus first divided the stars into six classes of magnitude, of which No. 6 is the dimmest that the naked eye can see. Accordingly, since its discovery over a century ago, this companion star has been a borderline case, as it is only one grade below the limit of visibility (the largest modern telescopes detect bodies of grade 2.4). White dwarfs consist of matter in a state of nuclear collapse, but the state is not constant and Sirius B is believed to be subject to further shrinkage.* Therefore it is possible that it formerly shone brighter than it does today and could sometimes be seen by Man.

Alternatively, the process of transformation of an ordinary star into a white dwarf is astoundingly rapid and can occur in a matter of hours (astronomers prefer to think in terms of aeons), but no one knows when Sirius' companion took on its present form. W. Z. Sagittae first exploded in 1913, before the astronomers' very eyes, and did so again in 1946; it has now only one hundredth of the luminosity of our sun and shows every sign of being another white dwarf.

At all events, we may not have long to wait before we know whether

Temple's theories are correct. He modestly remarks that radio and television reports about his book could be monitored in a planet of Sirius and that he may therefore have pulled a cosmic trigger and prompted a new intrusion by these intellectual manatees.

One submits, with due respect, that writers like Temple and von Däniken under-estimate the potentialities of both mankind and of peoples who might exist in other worlds. The idea that either *Homo sapiens* or human civilization sprang up suddenly has been shown to be outmoded. Scientists now think in terms of a more laborious process, painstakingly revealed by modern archaeology. Extraterrestrial intervention is no longer needed to explain the progress of Man, who trod his own hard road from cave paintings to computers. Anyone who dismisses the scientific record as a pious story merely displays his own ignorance of present-day research.

And if the emissaries of an advanced civilization indeed visited Earth, they would hardly have wasted their time teaching the Olmecs to move huge blocks of stone in order to make them into giant heads. The efforts of their human protégés would have been bent to more socially useful tasks. Taxpayers from a super-developed planet would have been roused to extremes of rage when they tuned their television sets to Earth and saw their highly-paid astronauts busy showing the Egyptians how to make useless pyramids instead of schools and hospitals.

Von Däniken does not always make it clear whether his astronauts personally lent a hand in such tasks or whether they merely provided the necessary tools and know-how. Spacemen were by implication present among the Sumerians in the third millennium B.C. and made a further trip to Mesopotamia during the second millennium in Babylonian times. The reader is also given to understand that space-travellers were present in person in Tiahuanaco in the first millennium A.D. as well as on Easter Island, where they themselves carved the famous heads.

Therefore, at the moment when Julius Caesar crossed the Rubicon, the foundations of Tiahuanaco were being laid with the aid of laser beams, and in the time of Charlemagne astronauts, marooned on Easter Island, mass-produced those stereotyped stone figures, while others bored into the rocks of Tula and then forever departed before the Spaniards appeared.

A once-and-for-all visit to Earth from outer space might be just conceivable, or at a pinch two visits, sufficient to account for the creation of *Homo sapiens* and of higher civilization. But no theory is tenable which proposes that every time earthbound beings started to build pyramids or move large blocks of stone, extraterrestrial visitors plunged in to help them. Besides, no explanation is provided as to why Earth's visitors steered so clear of Chinese, Arabs and Greeks, who would have kept accurate records of their doings; astronauts would have also caused a flutter in Europe if they had rushed to the aid of the Crusaders instead of merely helping the Toltecs build a rather unimposing capital.

No idea should be rejected out of hand, and those of von Däniken have helped to stimulate interest in the American past. But in order to carry conviction, any theory of interstellar visitors requires a closer scrutiny. The case for such notions is merely weakened if its supporters scorn the findings of the science of archaeology.

CHAPTER NINE

POLYNESIAN PERSPECTIVES

A vast stretch of empty ocean divides America from the islands of Polynesia, and even the outpost of Easter Island lies 2300 miles from the coast of Chile. But the nearest fixed star, Proxima Centauri, is 25,500,000,000,000 miles from earth. So in turning from outer space to Oceania, we once more deal with distances that our minds can measure and with people whose seamanship we can study.

Thor Heyerdahl, like Santa Claus, is known to everyone, and his feats therefore provide a springboard for viewing Polynesian–American relations, though new facts have come to light since he first became famous. *Kon-Tiki*'s triumph in crossing from Peru to the Tuamoto Islands was acclaimed by all the world; the raft is preserved in Oslo and immortalizes the memory of its captain. The design of *Kon-Tiki* was based on sailing rafts used in fifteenth-century Peru, of which it was not an exact replica; the voyage proved that balsa wood could float and convey men from America to Polynesia – a possibility that had often been denied.

Assessment of Heyerdahl's achievement must include theory as well as practice, since his main intent was not to display valour but to prove a thesis about Polynesian origins. His ideas were formulated in a work called *American Indians in the Pacific: the theory behind the Kon-Tiki expedition*, published in 1952. In his long and rather diffuse book, Heyerdahl did not confine himself to travel from America to Polynesia in pre-Columbian times – a feat now restored to the realm of the possible. He went on to declare that Polynesia was mainly populated by migrants from America. In recent statements, Heyerdahl has gone a little way towards meeting his critics and has conceded that some of the latest evidence runs counter to his opinions. However, his principal writings deny the consensus view that the inhabitants of Oceania, including Melanesians and Micronesians, originally came from East Asia.

In *American Indians in the Pacific*, Heyerdahl rejected well-established theories as to close links between the Polynesian language and those of South-East Asia: 'Some sort of parental contact between Polynesian and Malay languages must have existed, but apart from a number of common terms, the relationship is very vague, and exceedingly remote.'* Eminent but outdated nineteenth-century authorities were quoted in support of this opinion. In contrast to nebulous connections with the languages of South-East Asia, the author pointed to a uni-formity of speech throughout Polynesia so close that the Maoris of New Zealand could understand Tahitians or Hawaiians, though separated by thousands of miles of ocean. Heyerdahl belittled, but did not reject, the existence of a racial tie between Polynesia and Asia: 'It is not my intention to deny that Polynesians, to a certain degree, have distant relatives among the Malay people.'

Heyerdahl devoted many pages of his *magnum opus* to possible links between the Polynesians and the Indian tribes that inhabit the north-west coast of America, between Vancouver Island and Alaska. These people, like the Polynesians, have lighter skins and thicker beards than the average American Indian; their art forms and implements recall those of Oceania; both regions lacked weaving and pottery. Maritime currents lead direct from the north-west coast to Hawaii, and Heyerdahl suggested that certain tribes first wandered from Asia to North America, whence they continued their migration to the Hawaiian Islands; he saw Hawaii as the Hawaiki so prominent in Maori legends about their ancestral habitat.

For Heyerdahl, however, north-west America was not the original home of all Polynesians; their allegedly Caucasian traits – such as fair or reddish hair and aquiline noses – were derived from people who came from South America. As evidence, the flaxen-haired mummies of Peru were cited, as well as the familiar legends of white-bearded heroes, forming part of a kind of master race which first settled in Peru and Mexico and then left for Polynesia. This 'aristocratic body' had formerly been far more numerous than it was in Columbus' time, since most of its members had long ago sailed away into the Pacific: 'An ethnic group of the same peculiar Caucasian-like stamp is traced from Polynesia back to pre-Inca Peru and the earliest cultural levels of Mexico.' Migrants could accordingly have gone either to Hawaii from British Columbia, or from Peru to other parts of Polynesia, following the *Kon-Tiki* route. Any reverse migration from Oceania to America was described as entirely incredible, in view of the practical barriers of distance, wind and current.

In support of his thesis, Heyerdahl also invoked megalithic sculpture found throughout the Andes, from San Agustín in Colombia to Tiahuanaco in Bolivia, and compared such statues with those of Easter Island. According to the author, botanical proof of South American migrations into the Pacific was offered by the sweet potato, known as *cumar* in Quechua, the language of the Incas, as *kumara* in New Zealand and Easter Island, as *umara* in Tahiti and *unala* in Samoa. Heyerdahl provided an exhaustive list of all the rituals and customs common to both America and Polynesia, such as trepanning operations on the human skull, the practice of mummification, and the use of gourd whistles; the two regions share similar creation myths and a creator god known as Tici or Tiki.

Contacts between pre-Columbian America and Polynesia could therefore have occurred in three ways. Either Heyerdahl's anti-consensus theories are correct, and all traffic flowed in an east–west direction, resulting in the peopling of Polynesia from America. Alternatively, the Norwegian navigator is wrong: migrations in the Pacific occurred only from west to east, and Polynesia was occupied by people coming from Asia via the islands of Micronesia and Melanesia: a few of these settlers might even have reached America. Two-way traffic becomes a third possibility, whereby American rafts from time to time reached Polynesia, and Polynesian canoes occasionally landed in the New World.

The dark-skinned Melanesians and Micronesians inhabit the western part of the Pacific Ocean. Beyond these islands lies Polynesia, situated within a great triangle, whose apex consists of the Hawaiian group, and whose base is formed by a line drawn from New Zealand north-eastwards towards the outpost of Easter Island. The dimensions of this triangle are ably illustrated by Captain James Cook, who remarked that his voyage from New Zealand to Easter Island in 1772 covered about one quarter of the circumference of the globe.

Speculation about migrations from America to Polynesia began long before the *Kon-Tiki* expedition and had already been advanced by the English author William Ellis in the 1820s. Half a century later, in 1877,

Dr J. D. Lang published a book in Sydney entitled *The Origins and Migrations of the Polynesian Nation*, in which he maintained that all American Indians were of Polynesian descent. According to Harold Gladwyn, Alexander the Great's fleet had passed through the Pacific Islands on its way to America; Elliot Smith's Heliolithic theory of civilization was based on the notion that Egyptian culture had first spread to Asia, and thence via Oceania to America.

On a more serious level, at the turn of the century the Germans F. Graebner and A. Krahmer studied analogies between Polynesia and America, and in 1931 the Swedish ethnologist, E. Nordensköld, published a comprehensive list of traits and customs common to the inhabitants of America and Oceania. The much-publicized *Kon-Tiki* expedition focused world attention on the problem, and was followed by other voyages. Heyerdahl himself tells how, since 1947, seven different rafts have left the coast of Peru and landed safely in Polynesia. Among the most spectacular ocean crossings were those of Eric de Bisschop, who started off from Tahiti in 1956, drifting and sailing southwards until he reached a latitude of 35°; from this point he went east to the Juan Fernández Islands, lying some four hundred miles from the Chilean coast, having covered a distance of five thousand miles in six months. De Bisschop's second voyage started in south Chile; he reached Callao in Peru and then drifted north and west until wrecked in Manihiki (about one thousand miles north-west of Tahiti) six months later, after a journey of seven thousand miles.

Drift voyages such as those of de Bisschop and Heyerdahl were not in themselves new, but they differed from previous ventures because they were intentional. In the course of the nineteenth and early twentieth centuries, in sixty known instances Japanese junks were inadvertently carried off into the Pacific; of these, six reached North America between Alaska and the Columbia River, while another six were wrecked on the Mexican coast or encountered just offshore. Many accidental voyages had occurred long before this, and Japanese slaves were held by the Salmon Indians of the north-west coast of America when the Europeans first arrived.*

Polynesia calls to mind visions of coral reefs and sun-baked islands with palm-fringed beach and luxuriant interior. The islanders are seen as indolent beings, dependent for their needs upon the bounty of nature and occupied only in dancing, feasting and lovemaking. But the real

Polynesia has contrasting facets. In the first place, its landscape is far from uniform. At the northern apex of the triangle lies the Hawaiian group, whose largest island is a great dome of black lava, formed by the oozings of its towering twin volcanoes. Nearer to the centre of the triangle is Tahiti, with its fairy-tale scenery that surpasses every dream of Pacific island beauty. At the south-western extremity lies New Zealand, whose North Island reminds one of Switzerland (apart from its exotic native ferns), while the undulating pastures of the South Island recall England or Ireland. And at the third corner of the triangle, bleak little Easter Island juts from the ocean.

The Polynesians are full of paradox, and their nature has a dark as well as a light side; they are capable of extremes of generosity and one Tahitian chief even wanted to give Cook his pet shark, which he kept prisoner in a creek, having cut off its fins to prevent escape. Cook thought the shark would be a nuisance on board and declined the gift, accepting in its place a giant turtle that its owner bestowed more reluctantly, since he was thereby depriving his people of a bumper feast.

Polynesian women were notoriously uninhibited, and early European visitors were quick to take advantage of their easy-going attitudes. The people of the Marquesas advanced the ingenious notion that the white race consisted solely of men, who had to travel all the way to the Marquesas in order to have intercourse with women; only their voracious sexual appetite could account for repeated and otherwise inexplicable visits by Europeans.

But the Polynesians expected a good deal in return for their bounty; their obsessive pilfering did not always endear them to early discoverers, in fact it led to ugly incidents. Captain Cook relates how natives of the Marquesas tried to make away with one of the iron stanchions of the ship's gangway and a Tahitian chieftainess actually stole the anchor from a Spanish vessel, while other Tahitians filched Cook's stockings from under his pillow, though he swore he had not been asleep.

Moreover, these playful and fun-loving natives were bloodthirsty warriors, and the isles of paradise witnessed endless and ruthless wars of aggression; the victors sacrificed and ate the vanquished, after submitting them to tortures that make the Aztec treatment of captives seem humane. In islands where cannibalism prevailed, chiefs preferred to eat war prisoners or members of other tribes; even women from neighbouring villages would be kidnapped for the purpose. But if no outsiders were available, a chief would think little of eating his own people, picking on any commoners who were in his bad books.

Even tiny Easter Island was racked with dissension, and tribal conflicts lasted for decades. Besides, in proportion to their manpower, Polynesians fought total wars. Cook witnessed the manoeuvres of a fleet of three hundred vessels in Tahiti, manned by eight thousand resplendent warriors and destined for the invasion of the neighbouring island of Moorea; the operation, planned on a scale recalling D-Day, was not due to be launched for another ten months. When Cook returned to Tahiti three years later, the war still raged; he refused to participate as an ally, but accepted an invitation to witness the elaborate ceremonies culminating in human sacrifice, which were held to propitiate the gods.

Cook and other explorers gleaned much information on island history. They were usually told that the people of a particular island or group had descended from a god or hero who had arrived a number of generations earlier. With the aid of this Polynesian gift of memory, rough estimates could then be made of the date when an island had first been settled, though genealogies often underestimated the length of human occupation: for instance, the Hawaiians told of thirty to forty generations of ancestors, scarcely amounting to 1000 years, allowing twenty-five years per generation, while radiocarbon dating now suggests that the islands have been occupied for at least one thousand four hundred years.

Until recently, notions of Polynesian chronology rested on these rather vague foundations. However, in the past twenty years, following digs on a few of the twenty-five thousand Pacific islands, science has come to the rescue and provided a much clearer picture. The Polynesians lacked pottery when the Europeans arrived, and it was therefore assumed that they had never known the potter's art. But in 1956, John Colson, a British archaeologist living in Auckland, New Zealand, excavated a large flat-topped mound on Nuku'alofa, an island of the Tonga group, and was surprised to discover rather primitive pottery of a type named Lapita after a site in New Caledonia, situated about half-way between Australia and Tonga. This Tonga pottery was the first to be located on a purely Polynesian island and was virtually identical with Lapita ware already found in Fiji.* Dates for the earliest

Lapita pottery in New Caledonia go back to 2000 B.C.; by 1300 B.C. it was also being produced in the Fiji Islands. From Fiji it spread to Polynesian Tonga, where it flourished as early as 1140 B.C., and thence to Samoa, where the first radiocarbon date for Lapita is 800 B.C.*

Parts of Polynesia were therefore settled far earlier than had previously been proposed. However, a whole millennium was to pass before, about A.D. 300, these first Polynesians from Tonga and Samoa sailed eastwards for a distance of one thousand eight hundred miles and settled the Marquesas, where small quantities of Lapita pottery have also been located. Laboratory analysis of materials used in these sherds from the Marquesas shows that they were made in Fiji, whence they were presumably transported to Tonga and then on to the Marquesas. But pottery never took root in East Polynesia, and shortly after A.D. 300 the Tongans and Samoans – acting with scant consideration for future archaeologists – ceased to make pots.

Tahiti was next settled by people who doubled back in a south-westerly direction from the Marquesas. Radiocarbon dates suggest that Easter Island was occupied (also from the Marquesas) about A.D. 500, followed by the Hawaiian group in A.D. 600. New Zealand was then populated in about A.D. 1000 by migrants coming from the Society Islands, to which group Tahiti belongs; very recent excavations in New Zealand have revealed burials exactly recalling those of the western part of the Society Islands.

It had long been appreciated that the East Polynesians differed considerably from the West Polynesians. Since language showed that the peoples of Oceania had come originally from Asia, it was also generally assumed – notwithstanding Heyerdahl's opinion to the contrary – that the East Polynesians derived from the West Polynesians of Samoa and Tonga. This supposition was confirmed by the plainly Asian derivation of Polynesian plants and animals, with the exception of the sweet potato. With the aid of archaeology, a picture has emerged that fully supports this reasoning concerning East Polynesia. Using Fiji as a staging post, the ancestors of the Polynesians sailed from Asia to Tonga (though Samoa now has an almost equal claim to be regarded as the homeland of their culture).* After a thousand-year interval, battling against prevailing winds and currents, a group of people made their way from West Polynesia to the Marquesas, which became the focal point of East Polynesia; from this nucleus, between A.D. 300 and 1000, Tahiti,

Easter Island, Hawaii and New Zealand were settled by East Polynesians.* In these islands the potter's art never flourished, but in its place stone masonry attained heights unknown in West Polynesia.*

The languages of Polynesia were studied for a century before the archaeologists entered the field and are now accepted as an unquestionable part of the Austronesian group, previously called Malayo-Polynesian, a name coined as long ago as 1856 by Wilhelm von Humboldt. This linguistic family includes Melanesian, Micronesian and Indonesian, as well as the aboriginal languages of the Philippines and of Taiwan, and stretches almost continuously from Easter Island westwards across the ocean to distant Madagascar. Linguists demonstrated in the 1930s that Polynesian was linked with the many different tongues of Melanesia, and more recently exhaustive new studies have proved the point more precisely; outstanding is the work of Isidore Dyen, who drew up 371 lists, representing an estimated 275 languages of the Austronesian group and demonstrating their relationship one to another.*

People sometimes talk of Polynesian as if it were a single tongue, but a number of different dialects, so varied as to form separate languages, have evolved. Only sixty-one per cent of the words are common to the most divergent of these Polynesian dialects. From this percentage figure, linguists can deduce that the peoples of East Polynesia split from those of Tonga-Samoa about two thousand years ago – a calculation that tallies with the findings of archaeology.*

In contrast to the close ties binding Polynesia to Asia, language studies provide scant evidence of links with America. In addition to the use of similar words for the sweet potato in Polynesia and parts of South America, Heyerdahl stresses the sharing of *Tici* or *Tiki* for 'prince', he also calls attention to the Mayan word *Ahau* for 'lord', which he relates to the old Hawaiian name of *hau* for 'king' or 'supreme chief', but he offers no parallel for such a title in South America. Heyerdahl cites the place-name Tula as occurring in both Mexico and Samoa and states that from Tula were derived the Nahuatl or Aztec names *Tollan* and *Toltec*. But in fact the reverse is true: Tula is merely a Spanish corruption of Tollan, meaning 'Place of Rushes'. *Apai* is also sometimes cited, since in parts of Polynesia and in South America it means 'to lift or carry a burden'.

Attempts to detect similarities between Polynesian and American languages have been generally unproductive. The numerals from one to ten used in the languages of Madagascar, Indonesia and Polynesia alone suggest a close identity; by contrast, only a handful of words from all the two thousand tongues of South America remotely coincide with their Polynesian equivalents. Languages, moreover, take a long time to change, and the marked variation in speech between different parts of Polynesia helps to prove that the islands were settled over an extended period – invalidating the notion that they were more recently peopled from America in the course of a few centuries.

The physiology of the Polynesians affords no stronger grounds for thinking that they came from America. Detailed studies of blood group genes have been made, but have failed to reveal who the Polynesians were or whence they came.* Carleton Coon, a leading writer on Man's origins, believes that they descend from a blend of Mongoloids and Australoids; the same is of course true of the American Indian, who probably has more Mongoloid blood since he is shorter and less hairy.*

Early travellers were so struck by the difference between the dark-skinned Melanesians and the Polynesians that they possibly exaggerated the latter's relative fairness. Moreover, lightness of colour was artificially cultivated as being physically attractive. Noblewomen in Tahiti were periodically sent to be bleached in the shade of Tetiaroa islet; certain chiefs also sent boys for cosmetic bleaching along with the women.

Comparisons between Oceania and the New World in tribal customs, artefacts and equipment have yielded some more positive results. Outstanding is the work of Erland Nordensköld, who as long ago as 1931 compiled his compendium of traits common to the two regions, while Thor Heyerdahl provides an exhaustive study of such similarities in his *American Indians in the Pacific*, written twenty years later. Nordensköld's list included stone maces with star-shaped heads; plaited fans; wooden pillows; raincloaks made of leaves; panpipes and blowguns of remarkably similar design; knotted string records (known in Peru as quipus); fishing with poison; the making of cloth out of tree bark. From a total of 49 elements common to Oceania and America a few occur in North America, more particularly on the north-west coast, but a much larger proportion are found in Panama and Colombia. Items such as panpipes were already highly developed in Peru in the early centuries of our era, and Nordensköld was convinced therefore that most of his similarities related to a remote past: unlike his fellow-

Scandinavian Heyerdahl, he doubted whether Oceania had really influenced America (and vice versa); he points to the absence in the Pacific Islands of such typical American artefacts as weaving and pottery, quite apart from the Asian origin of animals and plants that were basic to the Polynesian economy. If elements of Oceanic culture were indeed introduced into America, Nordensköld thinks that they were brought by vessels arriving at widely different times; contacts were not close enough to cause the transference of *all* the most useful elements of one region to the other, but only of a random selection. As the Swedish scholar aptly puts it:

> As is well known, we find in South America a number of cultural elements of which parallels are found in Oceania. These we may call 'Oceanian', though this certainly does not imply any proof that they have been imported into America from Oceania. These 'Oceanian' elements may derive their origin from the crew of some weather-beaten vessel . . . some may originate directly from actual immigrations of exceedingly remote date into South America from across the ocean, or, with one or two exceptions, these cultural elements may simply have been independently invented both in America and in the Old World.*

American plants are generally lacking in Polynesia. But to this rule the sweet potato is an exception and still provides the best evidence of pre-Columbian contacts with the islands of the Pacific. The plant is unquestionably native to America, from where it was brought home by Columbus on his first voyage, and sampled by King Ferdinand and Queen Isabella in Barcelona in 1493. A reasonable consensus prevails among experts that the sweet potato was cultivated in Oceania before Columbus, and its early presence was even accepted by Roland B. Dixon, that pillar of orthodoxy who derided Elliot Smith's notions of Egyptian influences in America, transmitted via the Pacific Islands. The rich variety of sweet potato species present in Polynesia militates against European introduction, since it is unlikely that so many strains would develop in only five hundred years. The numerous variations in the word for sweet potato throughout Polynesia also suggest that the plant had been there for a long time; words basic to a language change very slowly. Another sign of the early arrival of the sweet potato in Oceania lies in the discovery that certain parasitic weevils of Old World origin have become exclusively adapted to the plant – a process also requiring more than the five centuries since Columbus' discovery of America.*

Strong reasons therefore support the belief that the sweet potato reached Polynesia before the first Europeans; paradoxically, however, the most familiar argument in favour of its early arrival is the least valid. Heyerdahl and others have made great play of the resemblance between an American word for sweet potato, *cumar*, and its various Polynesian equivalents, such as *kumara*. But *cumar*, current among Quechua speakers in Cuenca, the Inca capital of what is now Ecuador, had been borrowed from another language of that region; it was not the *usual* word for sweet potato in Quechua, and Inca Garcilaso de la Vega cites only the standard name for the plant, *apichu*. Moreover, Quechua was not spoken in coastal Peru, and nowhere on the coast of either Ecuador or Peru did people cultivate the sweet potato under a name remotely resembling *cumar*.*

But despite reservations over the name *cumar*, the likelihood remains that the sweet potato came to Polynesia from America before the Spanish conquest. Moreover, certain other plants are common to America and the Pacific Islands; of these the most important is the coconut, which, as already explained, is able to float across the ocean and survive. One single specimen landing on a beach can breed a whole race since the species is capable of self-pollination, and flourishing groves grew on uninhabited islands such as Palmerston Atoll, visited by Captain Cook. So the coconut does not present the same problem as the sweet potato, whose normal means of reproduction is vegetal, and whose tubers therefore have to be cut for the purpose. Equally, the calabash, another potential floater, was found in both Oceania and America, but this plant, though native to the Old World, was already present in America in 7000 B.C.

Sir Peter Buck, a leading authority on Polynesia and himself part Maori, wrote a best-seller entitled *The Vikings of the Sunrise*. However, to do full justice to the Polynesian genius, I would prefer to reverse the sequence and dub the Vikings 'the Polynesians of the north'. Spectacular voyages to remote Pacific islands had been undertaken centuries before the Viking era. The Norsemen were great seamen, but crossed only hundreds of miles of ocean; while the Polynesians covered thousands. On the voyage to Labrador via Iceland and Greenland, the longest open sea crossing, from the Faroes to Iceland, measures 240 miles; but from Samoa to the Marquesas, and from the Marquesas to Hawaii, voyages of 1800 miles were made.

The gradual discovery and occupation of the Pacific islands was an astonishing feat and ranks among the noblest episodes in Man's conquest of the globe. The details of the story are lost in time, but with the help of archaeologists and linguists, its outlines are now being established. The difficulty of locating countless small islands is illustrated by the Spanish and Portuguese failures in that respect. Centuries elapsed between Columbus' first voyage and the discovery of most of the Pacific archipelagoes. From the strait that bears his name, Magellan set off across the Pacific on 27 November 1520, and reached Guam on 6 March of the following year. By that time his crew were eating the ship's leather chafing gear, and rats were being sold on board for half a gold ducat. During this epic voyage, only a deserted atoll of the Tuamoto group was sighted, and one other uninhabited island, Caroline Atoll, some five hundred miles north-west of Tahiti. The Spaniards first settled in the Philippines in 1565, and thereafter regular voyages were made from Acapulco to Manila. But the specks in the ocean inhabited by Polynesians were so small that the Spaniards ploughed endlessly back and forth across the Pacific, blissfully unaware of the existence of most of its islands.

Alvaro de Mendaña, when he was only twenty-five, was the first Spaniard to discover a major group. For many years, reports had been rife that the land of Ophir, whence came the gold of King Solomon, was a Pacific archipelago; accordingly in 1567 Mendaña was sent by the Viceroy of Peru to find King Solomon's mines. Ostensibly the aim of the expedition was not lust for gold but 'to convert all infidels to Christianity'. Eighty days after leaving Callao in Peru, Mendaña's ships reached the Solomon Islands, duly named after King Solomon, and inhabited by dark-skinned Melanesians. The Spaniards' relations with the inhabitants of the few islands they discovered usually ended in disaster: on this expedition Mendaña lost a watering party of nine men, who were duly cooked and eaten; but the natives made matters worse by producing a mock peace-offering in the form of a dummy pig stuffed with straw. The Spanish expedition, finding stuffed pigs a poor substitute for gold, left the Solomon Islands; after this momentary unveiling, they were lost to the sight of Europeans for more than two centuries.*

Thirty years later, in 1595, Mendaña led four ships in a further search for islands. After three months at sea, the expedition sighted Fatu Niva in the Marquesas – so named after Mendaña's patron, the Marquis of Cañete, Viceroy of Peru. On Fatu Niva, a lonely savage island of extraordinary beauty, the Spaniards were surprised to find a much fairer people than the Melanesians of the Solomons; no one on board was aware that they had discovered the Polynesians, a race hitherto unknown to the rest of mankind. The islanders were equally astonished at the Europeans, and dumbfounded by their wearing of clothing; only after the sailors had bared their breasts to show their skin were the Polynesians sure that their visitors were human beings like themselves.

Mendaña died during the expedition, which eventually reached Manila under the effective captaincy of his pilot, Quiroz. However, the dying man had named his wife, Doña Isabel, 'governess' of the ships, and the implacable governess showed no pity for her crew. While the bodies of men who died of thirst were thrown to the sharks, Doña Isabel brooded in her cabin and wasted quantities of water in laundering her dresses; when Quiroz remonstrated, she remarked that she was entitled to do as she pleased with her own property.

A further voyage by Quiroz, resulting in the discovery of the Santa Cruz Islands (lying south-east of the Solomons), completed the rather meagre list of Spanish finds. During the seventeenth century, the Dutch entered the field, and their mariners were the first to sight the great landmass of Australia and the tiny speck of Easter Island, reached by Jacob Roggeveen in 1722 on a voyage of discovery sponsored by the Dutch West India Company. But only in the second half of the eighteenth century, two hundred and fifty years after Balboa first gazed on the Pacific, was a more systematic exploration of its islands undertaken, and not until 1778 did Europeans first set foot on Hawaii. Tahiti was discovered by Samuel Wallace in 1767 and visited a year later by the French navigator, Bougainville.

However, the greatest explorer of the vast ocean was Captain James Cook, who made three voyages between 1768 and 1779. On the first voyage he planted the British flag on the east coast of Australia; on the third he was killed in Hawaii, one of the group that he named the Sandwich Islands. Cook, the leading discoverer of Polynesia, wrote admirable descriptions of his voyages, and much of our knowledge of pre-European Polynesia derives from his pungent and precise prose. Cook writes of his constant difficulties in preserving his gear and tackle from the light-fingered islanders and tells of the hard bargaining involved in restocking with food and water. During a visit to the Marquesas, Cook managed to peg the rate of exchange between pigs and iron nails, only to find his market upset by someone who offered the natives red feathers instead of nails, the price of which then plummeted. Red feathers became such a status symbol among the Polynesian establishment that, when Cook left Tahiti, the king asked him to take as passenger a young Tahitian, travelling for the sole purpose of cornering the European market in this form of finery. Cook thought well of the Polynesians and, by mixing firmness with tact, usually established excellent relations; however, he insisted that wrong must be requited, and a Tahitian thief was once given twelve lashes in front of his own people, since, as Cook explained, he could not punish his crew for misdemeanours if he did not also punish others. On another occasion, in Moorea, Cook felt compelled to destroy a number of houses in order to recover a stolen goat.

When the island of Nuku Hava in the Marquesas was occupied from Samoa about A.D. 300, the 1800-mile journey was made against the prevailing current, which flows in a west-south-westerly direction at a rate of between five and fifteen miles per day. How did the Polynesians cross such stretches of ocean? On the answer to this key question hinges the broader problem of Polynesian–American contacts.

Since Cook's day it has been assumed that the Pacific islands were gradually settled as a result of planned expeditions, though Cook himself never said this. However, in the 1950s, closer studies of method and motivation were begun; the New Zealander Andrew Sharp was among the first to refute the notion of planned occupation and to insist that the most productive voyages had been accidental. Fundamental to Sharp's case is the limited range of the islanders' knowledge of their neighbours when the Europeans arrived. In 1595, Quiroz had reported that the Santa Cruz Islands in Melanesia were in touch with Sikaiana, 250 miles away; and Cook found that the Tahitians exchanged occasional visits with the Rotumas, of which the largest island was 350 miles away. But two-way journeys over greater distances than this were then unknown. Admittedly the Tongans gave Cook a list of 156 islands, including those in the main Samoa group, but they could all be reached by crossing relatively short stretches of open sea.

Whereas purposeful two-way voyages on record were limited to a range of two to three hundred miles, Sharp points to many known cases of much longer journeys, made accidentally, without touching land on the way. Cook himself found on Atiu three Tahitians who had been blown off course and unintentionally travelled a distance of 700 miles from their native island, when they had only planned to go to Taiatea, 100 miles west of Tahiti. The missionary William Wyatt Gill tells of people from Moorea, also near Tahiti, who drifted as far as the Samoan island of Manau, a distance of 1250 miles; no lives were lost. Gill also refers to an unintentional voyage from Manihiki westwards to the Ellice Islands, a distance of one thousand miles; during their journey, half the party perished for lack of food and water.*

Sharp concluded that the gradual occupation of countless Pacific islands resulted from chance voyages; people who had intended to make a much shorter trip were driven off their original course, lost their bearings and sailed or drifted onwards to new and unknown destinations. Many such travellers failed to reach any destination at all and perished at sea. His views aroused much controversy; his critics insisted that he ignored the achievements not only of the Vikings, but of those Irish monks who preceded them, sailing over five to seven hundred miles of open sea to reach Iceland, and that he overlooked the recorded feats of Chinese and Arab sailors in the Indian Ocean.

Another New Zealander, David Lewis, who served in the Indian Civil Service and later became a leading expert on Pacific voyagers, has described the navigational skill of the Polynesians and believes in their ability to make much longer intentional voyages than Sharp thought possible. In his book *We the Navigators*, Lewis relates how he made a journey of 450 miles without instruments among the Mariana Islands of Melanesia and duly arrived at his destination. The native pilot, Tovake, had held course for eight solid hours by keeping a particular swell dead astern, at a time when Lewis' own sense of direction was paralysed by squalls. Lewis stresses that little is known about Polynesian maritime skills, although there is more data for Melanesia and Micronesia. Throughout Oceania, seafaring lore was a closely guarded secret, and knowledge was restricted to a chosen few. Valuable information on Polynesian techniques comes from Captain Cook, who was lucky in meeting Tupaiai, a deposed high chief and navigator-priest of Raiatea, and probably the only highly qualified Polynesian navigator interviewed by a European. Tupaiai gave Cook a list of 74 islands known to the Tahitians and guided him to Rurutu, 300 miles south of Tahiti.

Lewis explains that the same methods prevailed from one end of Oceania to the other with only local variations. Steering by the sun and stars were the main techniques of navigation; and people preferred to travel at night since there were then many stars to give guidance but only one sun by day. The Polynesians were undoubtedly familiar with the stars; they had their own names for the principal constellations in early times and did not adopt the European appellations. What Lewis calls 'expanded target landfall' helped sailors to locate islands before they sighted them: birds can often be seen from afar, and certain species, such as brown boobies, are only encountered within thirty miles of land and so indicate its proximity. Cloud colours vary as a boat comes near to the shore and patterns of ocean swell also give signs of approaching land.

But the major problems of long-distance navigation lie in the science of dead reckoning – the ability to estimate the distance and direction travelled; to accomplish this, the navigator must consider the element of drift, which affects all his calculations and partly depends upon the speed of currents, which are likely to vary from one day to the next. However consummate the pilot's skill, however vast his experience, any attempt at dead reckoning without the help of instruments becomes well-nigh impossible at times, especially after a storm. Even Columbus, who did have a compass, was subject to gross error in this respect. On his first voyage, he kept a true reckoning of distance travelled for his own personal use, and a false and smaller calculation for the benefit of his crew, in order to still their fears of sailing so far into the void. However, Columbus greatly overestimated the speed of his vessels, and the 'false' reckoning was nearer the mark than the 'true'.

In some respects, Sharp's views on Polynesian navigation are hard to refute: people who were not aware of islands more than three hundred miles away could not possibly have made precise plans to reach them. But Sharp offers no satisfactory explanation as to how mariners who had merely lost their way created new island settlements. Lasting occupation obviously depended upon the presence of women among the migrants, as well as pigs and chickens, found by Europeans on most islands (on a few islands pigs and rats were encountered, but no humans). Most accidental drift voyages would not have met such conditions: no fishing party, when caught in a storm, would have been stocked with plants and animals, ready to serve as a kind of miniature Noah's Ark.

But voyages may be deliberately undertaken, even if the voyagers do not know where they will end up – for islands easily became overpopulated, since a mere coral atoll can sustain relatively few people. Wars also caused departures into the void, and hostilities were frequent, not only between different islands but between rival tribes on the same island. To escape a sinister fate, the vanquished simply set off to find a new home, whose exact location was as yet unknown, even if a general notion prevailed that new land was to be found in a given direction. The migrants naturally took with them their womenfolk, some livestock, and seeds or tubers of their staple foods, such as taros, sweet potatoes, bananas and cane sugar, without which they would in the end have died of hunger. The exiles used their knowledge of the stars to steer a fixed course and, aided by their flair for spying land from a distance, sometimes hit upon the new home of which they dreamed. Thousands of such voyages surely took place over the centuries, and some led to the creation of an island community; many others failed, with all on board lost at sea.

Specific instances of voluntary departures may be cited: Captain Porter, commander of an American naval unit, visited Nukuhiva in the Marquesas in 1814 and was told of groups of deliberate exiles who from time to time set off from Nukuhiva for islands traditionally situated in the west. Such expeditions were quite frequent and Porter says that thousands had departed within living memory, though their fate was unknown.* To quote another instance, later in the eighteenth century a chief's son on the island of Uvea, west of Samoa, was accidentally injured during the building of a canoe. Fearing his father's anger, the boy decided to leave for lands unknown; he and his party reached an island in the Loyalty group, lying off New Caledonia and a thousand miles south-west of his point of departure. The island thus colonized was also given the name Uvea and is still so called today.

Departures into the unknown arose not only from wars, but from family quarrels, national calamities, and even sheer lust for adventure and prestige, combined with the desire to find a more fertile homeland. The islands were gradually settled over a very long period of time, more as a result of these intentional if hazardous expeditions than through accidental drift voyages, which would not normally carry women, plants and animals. The modern mind may boggle at the carelessness of human life among the Polynesians; all voyages were fraught with danger and even the regular nineteenth-century missionaries persuaded the natives to cut their travelling to a minimum and settle more permanently on one island or the other.

The likelihood of stray Polynesian vessels reaching America can only be weighed in the light of these known feats of seamanship. The boats – *canoe* is perhaps a misnomer – were well suited to the task. To quote the American archaeologist Charles E. Borden: 'The best sailing vessels of Micronesia and Polynesia were more weatherly, and despite their matting sails, could out-sail the ships of Captain Cook, Bougainville, Kotzebue and other late explorers.'* The dimensions of such craft were ample; the Marquesans' canoe with outrigger could accommodate forty to fifty men on fishing or warlike expeditions; the Tongan double canoe as many as one hundred. The carrying capacity of the big oceanic voyaging vessels was large, with facilities to store twenty days' non-perishable food and water.

If a group of Polynesians were able to make the 1800-mile journey from Samoa to the Marquesas at the outset of the Christian era, other vessels might occasionally have survived a crossing from the Marquesas to the coast of Mexico (the nearest part of the American continent to that group). Alternatively, to reach the north-west coast of America from Hawaii, or Chile from Easter Island, involves a 2000-mile crossing.

A merely accidental drift to America is well-nigh impossible, because people travelling from Hawaii to the north-west coast, or to Mexico from the Marquesas, have to face contrary winds and currents. In 1972 a computer simulation of pure drifts in the Pacific was undertaken, in the belief that drift voyages *could* account for the peopling of all Polynesia. Contrary to expectation, the results showed that while many island groups could be reached by accident in this manner, drifting could not account for certain key contacts. For instance, pure drift could not have brought people from the Marquesas to Hawaii, New Zealand or Easter Island, nor from Eastern Polynesia in general to America.

More probably, many eastward-bound voyagers were not mere drifters, but people who had left their original home intentionally, sailing in a fixed direction in search of a place of voluntary exile; if they found no other land, and simply pressed on in the same direction, they would eventually have reached America. Alternatively, the shores of the New World could have been encountered if a boatload on some routine west–east trip to a neighbouring island missed its objective and then just carried on, hoping to find other land. Voyages to America do not presuppose the presence of women and livestock; on the contrary, the general absence of Polynesian fauna and flora suggests that purposeful migrants from the islands did *not* reach America.

Controversy about the general effect of wind and current on west–east voyages persists, apart from sudden west–east cyclones and squalls of brief duration. The equatorial countercurrent is usually assumed to run from west to east along a fairly narrow strip of ocean, approximately following the 10° north parallel. Though Heyerdahl questions its very existence, Sharp insists that wind as well as current goes from west to east at certain times of year; he sees the seaward expeditions as taking place in the summer months, when these changes in wind and current occur. Easter Islanders assured me that the wind sometimes blows from the west, though the east wind prevails; most accounts of Pacific voyagers report changes in wind, rather than a uniform flow of air in one direction.

Nevertheless eastward travel was not easy at any time of year; the Spaniards were unable to sail from Asia to America until 1565, when they discovered the eastward-flowing Japanese current that runs well to the north of Hawaii. However, the assumption that simple craft could have made west–east crossings only in these higher latitudes is not valid. The people of Oceania seem to have been more skilled than the Spaniards and Portuguese in this respect: as late as 1910, the *Deutsches Kolonialblatt* wrote of canoes that had been carried off to the Philippines from the Caroline Islands and then made the long eastward return journey.* Both the archaeological record and the accounts of travellers show that west–east journeys did take place, even if in that direction the going was tougher and the pace slower. Cook's informant, Tupaiai, told him that the Cook Islands lay ten to twelve days' journey from Tahiti on the outward run westwards, but that thirty days were required for the return trip.

If America had been just another speck in the ocean, lying thousands of miles beyond Polynesia, the islanders might never have reached it (though they *did* find Easter Island). But a giant continent is very different: suppose a boat or convoy of boats missed every island in their path, and still pressed on eastwards; if only they could stay afloat, they must in the end hit upon some part of America. In the course of two millennia, thousands of travellers could have faced this predicament. The odds against the survival of any particular boatload were rather high, but almost inevitably a few would have been spared and landed in the New World. This possibility is accepted by scholars who are utterly sceptical about earlier contacts between Americans and Asians. Even Pablo Martínez Del Río, the great Americanist who rejected many other theories on transpacific travel, accepted the possibility of contact with Polynesians. Man has a great capacity to survive long and unforeseen voyages: there exists a nineteenth-century record of nine Japanese who lived through an accidental journey of eleven months, before reaching the Hawaiian Island of Oahu. In such crises, fish not only serve as food, but fish juices can be used as a substitute for water.

However, Polynesian castaways faced other problems: in pre-Columbian America they are unlikely to have received a rousing welcome. Much of the Mexican coast was quite densely populated, and chance visitors, if detected, would have been lucky not to end their days on the sacrificial stone. The killing of a crew would not have prevented strange trophies found on board, such as panpipes or blowguns, from being treated as sacred objects; the first gifts which Moctezuma received from Cortés were ceremonially buried in the Temple of Quetzalcóatl in Tula. Accordingly, some traits common to Oceania and America were perhaps not invented twice but imported, though the exact truth may never be known. Any visitors from Hawaii to the north-west coast of America could have run into the kind of trouble with marauding natives that beset the Viking visitors to the north-east and which drove them away from Vinland without forming permanent settlements and without making any impact on native culture.

If Polynesian visitors encountered hostile 'skraelings' – as the Vikings called the natives – they must, like the Norsemen, have had every incentive to stock up with food and water and attempt the return journey; by this time they were fully conscious that wind and current favoured westward travel. Concrete examples of Pacific islanders who *did* manage to return home from long accidental voyages are available. In addition to the recorded two-way trips between the Carolines and the Philippines, Captain F. W. Beechy, an English commander who visited

Polynesia in 1824 and wrote a two-volume narrative of his voyage, relates how in 1826 he landed on the atoll of Ahunui in the Tuamoto Islands, where he found a party of 46 people who had originally set off from Tahiti to visit another island 200 miles to the west. However, after completing three-quarters of their intended journey, they were swept off course by *westerly* gales and ended up on an uninhabited Tuamotan island 520 miles from the spot where they first lost their bearings; they recouped their strength, took on new provisions, and had already sailed 100 miles on their homeward route when Beechy met them in Ahunui. The distances involved in a return journey to Polynesia from America are vastly greater, and the obstacles more formidable, even for travellers who were not trying to locate their particular point of departure. However, the principle remains the same, and evidence is at hand of marooned mariners who did at times attempt a return journey.

After *Kon-Tiki*, doubts as to the possibility of ocean travel by American Indians as well as by Polynesians have vanished, and Heyerdahl performed the inestimable service of showing that journeys to Polynesia from Peru were at least feasible. Fairly copious data of the capabilities of pre-Columbian craft have survived: the very first Spanish caravel to reach Ecuadorian waters sighted a raft carrying 30 tons of cargo and 20 Peruvian natives; the Spaniards were amazed to see such fine rigging and cotton sails.*

We do not know exactly how such craft were constructed, but sixteenth-century Spanish chroniclers often mention sailing rafts and praise their efficiency. The shape of the sails is not recorded, except in one account by Pedro Gutierrez de Santa Clara, a *meztizo* soldier born in the New World, who relates that, since time immemorial, people had used 'rafts of light dry wood and cane, with triangular sail and a rudder at the stern'.* An illustration survives of an Ecuadorian raft of the mid-sixteenth century, but precise details are not shown. The Dutch admiral Jovis van Speilbergen led a fleet of Dutch ships on a voyage round the world between 1614 and 1618, and tells how he met rafts with triangular sails at different points on the South American coast.

The American Indians certainly reached the Galapagos Islands, about five hundred miles from the coast of Ecuador, and Peruvian pottery has been found there, though at the time of the Conquest these islands, as well as the Juan Fernández Islands off the coast of Chile, were uninhabited. Craft heading for the Galapagos could have been swept farther afield and hit upon a Polynesian island. However, the failure to occupy the Juan Fernández Islands and the abandonment of the Galapagos suggest that the urge to make such journeys was not strong; in proportion to the countless island-hopping voyages made by Polynesians annually or even daily, the frequency with which American Indian rafts abandoned the safety of coastal waters and faced the ocean was surely more limited. Given the demonstrable skill of the Polynesians and their ability to make crossings of nearly two thousand miles, the odds on Polynesian visits to America are much greater than on American trips to Polynesia. Moreover, supposing that American Indians *did* reach Polynesia, the prospects of a friendly welcome were also poor: on many islands the practice of killing strangers who landed prevailed. Many European visitors would have ended on the local chief's dinner table, had they not been protected by their firearms and their sturdy ships.

Accordingly, assuming that the sweet potato reached Polynesia before the Spaniards and Portuguese, I believe that it was imported by two-way Polynesian travellers rather than by American voyagers making a one-way trip. Of the three possibilities listed earlier in this chapter, I opt for the second, which presupposes that Polynesia was occupied by people coming from Asia via Melanesia who brought with them Asian animals and plants. I consider it likely that, on occasion, Polynesian boats following the more difficult west–east course overshot all islands, somehow survived the immense additional journey and reached America. The effect of such landings was limited, and the fate of the crew uncertain; a few travellers even managed to return, riding the east–west current, and found a new home on some Polynesian island, where they first planted the sweet potato.

The alternative possibility – the peopling of Polynesia from America – is totally unacceptable, and further argument on the matter is little more than a waste of time. Whatever faint possibility existed in the early 1950s that Polynesia had been settled from America (as opposed to occasional drift voyages in that direction) has since vanished. As we have seen, deeper studies of language show that the Polynesian tongue is inextricably linked to those of Melanesia and South-East Asia; these findings are upheld by the recent work of archaeologists, who have demonstrated the *eastward* movement of Lapita pottery from Fiji through Tonga to Samoa and onward to the Marquesas. The radiocarbon dates for the earliest Polynesians are now so early as to leave little room for serious argument that they came from America.

The culture of the north-west coast of America, which includes British Columbia and south-eastern Alaska, differs markedly from the rest of pre-Columbian America. Typical New World traits, such as agriculture, pottery, pyramid mounds, altars and priests are lacking. Instead of these, in the north-west we find an intricate and unusual economic system, peculiar forms of art, and an outstanding florescence of woodworking.

Certain north-western traits and artefacts are also present in Polynesia, including the carved wooden columns known as totem poles. Those of the north-west coast served various purposes, among the Tlingit Indians they were called coffins and acted as a repository for the dead, whose ashes were placed in a recess at the back. Poles had other uses; when Alaska still belonged to Russia, a man who visited the Russian cathedral at Sitka and was then converted to Christianity was entitled to erect a totem pole, placing on top a carving of St Paul, copied from an illustration in an old Russian Bible. Even the Czar Alexander II and a Russian secretary of the interior were portrayed on poles.

At the opposite end of the Pacific to Vancouver lies New Zealand, where a very similar type of woodcarving flourished, and it can also be identified in certain intermediate areas: poles of a comparable type are reported from Tahiti by an eighteenth-century visitor; smaller wooden posts were made in the Marquesas and in Hawaii.

Pine driftwood still floats westward to Hawaii from the coast of British Columbia and Indian canoes could also have made the crossing from time to time; the eastward journey from Hawaii to the north-west coast is more difficult. The Haida had canoes nearly seventy feet long, which could carry a hundred men, and sea travel was the region's principal means of communication. Heyerdahl therefore envisaged a very early migration from the north-west to Hawaii, which he sought to identify with Hawaiki. But islands bearing names similar to Hawaiki exist in the original Polynesian homelands of Tonga (Hapai) and Samoa (Savai'i), while Hawaii is now known to have been settled relatively late; the first immigrants came there from the Marquesas and Tahiti, bringing with them the pig, the rat and the chicken, together with their staple plants. Hawaii spoke a language similar to the rest of East

Polynesia, and Hawaiian culture in pre-European times was fundamentally Polynesian, though special forms of wood-carving and other elements such as the use of bark cloth *could* have been introduced from the north-west coast and then spread from Hawaii to other islands.

Since it was first discovered, Easter Island has usually been described as bleak and treeless; but there are in fact flourishing eucalyptus groves, so that at first sight the island seems like a tiny fragment of New South Wales moored in mid-ocean.

One's initial feeling is likely to be one of a serenity rarely attained except on the world's remotest island. But first impressions often prove illusory, and in Easter Island the tranquil present is pervaded by the tragic past, whose fallen idols lie strewn at every turn of the road. The jagged volcanic shore is studded with the ruins of ahaus, or mausoleums, each with its quota of stone giants, who now repose face downwards on the landward side of the monuments that they once adorned. A few statues have been re-erected, including one raised up by Thor Heyerdahl at Anakena, where the legendary discoverers first landed.

Several centuries ago, these legless giants all stood erect on their platforms, vacantly staring at the hill of Rano Raraku, the quarry where they were fashioned. As Alfred Métraux, the French archaeologist whose work on Easter Island has become a classic, writes in his study: 'This vertigo of the colossal in a miniature universe, such is the miracle of Easter Island.'

The squeezing of so many colossi into so small a setting has provoked an avalanche of speculation. Obviously the 'mystery' had to be explained by some outside intervention; all eyes were riveted on South America and its megalithic sculpture. Scholars, however, sceptical as usual, have lately done much to unravel the island's prehistory, and to account for its peculiar creations, without invoking the aid of astronauts or American Indians.

The occupation of Easter Island is now thought to have taken place before A.D. 500 by people coming from the Marquesas.* A radiocarbon date of A.D. 430 is supported by studies of language demonstrating that the Easter Island dialect is linked to that of the Marquesas, from which it became separated at a relatively early date.

William Mulloy, an archaeologist who participated in the Heyerdahl expedition of 1956, originally identified three distinct building periods. William S. Ayres, who has been working with Mulloy on the Island more recently, dates the first period from A.D. 400 to 1000; during this time the mausoleums or ahaus were already being built, but without statues. During the second phase, from A.D. 1000 to 1680, the ahaus increased in size; at the outset columns of dressed stone were placed on their platforms, but these were gradually replaced by the large and standardized stone images.

The third period runs from 1680 to 1868, when the last Easter Island pagans were received into the Christian Church and the old gods were officially declared dead. During this late or decadent era, which lasted nearly two hundred years, no statues were constructed, and most of the existing ahaus were destroyed or fell into ruin, though some were still used for burial.*

The ritual meaning of the stone figures is best explained by Métraux: they were placed on the ahau platforms to represent important chiefs or high priests of the many small tribes into which the population was divided. Defunct chiefs became tribal gods and the monoliths were receptacles into which their spirits entered, when invoked by the priests. Accordingly, the sacred character of the statues was provisional and depended on rites that caused the departed spirits to enter them. In daily life, and without the accompanying ceremonies, the colossi were mere ornaments, or lifeless blocks of stone.

These silent monuments tell little of the golden age of island history to which they belong. However, Métraux, with the aid of islanders who in 1934 still recalled certain traditions, was able to throw more light on Easter Island's subsequent era of agony. Informants told the French scholar of wars of attrition between the rival confederations of Tuu, occupying the eastern part of the island, and the Hetu-Iti, in its western extremity. Hostilities lasted for a whole generation and Métraux' informants thought that they had continued until a few years before the arrival of Captain Cook in 1774. Long wars offered continuous prospects of banqueting off the remains of vanquished enemies, and on Easter Island, where chicken was the only alternative animal protein, a taste for human flesh was provoked by sheer appetite; natives told the early missionaries that toes and fingers were prized as the choicest delicacies. A grim feature of such wars was the fate of the women and children of the defeated tribe; there was nowhere to flee in such a tiny island, and any who sought refuge in caves in the interior were soon tracked down and led to captivity.

The Easter Islanders therefore, like the Maya, fell into a state of decadence long before the arrival of the Europeans, who found a people no longer busy in the erection of monuments but in their destruction, in the course of suicidal warfare among petty tribes. During these iconoclastic struggles, the mausoleums were ravaged and the statues overthrown. The Dutch explorer Roggeveen was the first to discover Easter Island, on Easter Sunday 1722; Cook arrived in 1774 and saw some of the statues still standing erect. The Easter Islanders played a typically Polynesian prank on Cook: in return for precious pieces of iron, they sold him a quantity of sweet potatoes, most of which turned out to be pebbles. At the end of the eighteenth century the stone figures on the west side of the island were still upright, but by 1866, when the missionaries came, not one still stood on any mausoleum.

The monoliths, with few exceptions, are identical in form. Their angular features, seen in profile, have been endlessly cited by those who seek the presence of 'Caucasian' heroes, in both Polynesia and America. However, viewed frontally, their nostrils have a bulbous quality that is Polynesian or even Mongoloid, rather than Caucasian. Attempts to attribute these figures to a specific race seem particularly futile: they are so distinctive that I myself have never set eyes on a human face remotely recalling an Easter Island statue. Unaccountably an odd and angular prototype was adopted, and copied in the features of hundreds of figures carved over the centuries; all came from the quarry of Rano Raraku, where a few elephantine models, fashioned in the same image, still lie embedded in the virgin rock. About thirty other statues stand erect at Rano Raraku, half buried in the soil, and form a reserve platoon of future gods, vainly awaiting the passage to a nobler resting place. Some cataclysm evidently came to pass, grave enough to halt the output of new statues and even to prevent the conveyance to mausoleums of those already poised for the journey.

According to island tradition, the statues walked to their location, inspired by the priests' mana or sacred power. However, the monoliths have no legs, and their conveyance to their ahau platforms was a task more grinding than their creation out of the soft volcanic stone. The transportation of these great hulks by a small population is a remarkable feat, but did not require the aid of South American Indians. The movement of a statue was a most sacred undertaking, in which the main resources of manpower were deployed, just as for the building of pyramids and the erection of giant statues in Ancient Egypt. Easter

Island is so small that if a monolith was shifted a mere 35 metres per day, it could reach any part of the coast within a year.

The famous Easter Island script has also given rise to endless speculation and has been attributed, among others, to Ancient Indians and Etruscans. But the first known inscribed tablet was originally the blade of a European ash oar: neither the Spanish visitors of 1770 nor Cook in 1784 mention the script, which was first reported in 1864.

A brilliant piece of research by two Russians, N. A. Butinov and Y. V. Knorozov, has shown that the beautifully carved signs represent a primitive hieroglyphic system based on a Polynesian-type language. The tablets constitute a kind of aide-mémoire and could only be read by people already familiar with a particular chant or tradition. Similar signs were developed in parts of the Inca empire *after* the Spanish Conquest.

Easter Island recalls in miniature the more general arguments about Polynesian origins. Traces of American influences, when analysed, prove meagre. The language of the island has been scientifically identified as an early breakaway from the dialect of the Marquesas; its plants, including taro, yam, sweet potato and banana, are typical of all Polynesia. Missing are the breadfruit, which would not grow, and the pig, which apparently never arrived.

The great statues have been taken as evidence of an American presence, with special reference to Tiahuanaco, but the austere figures of Easter Island bear absolutely no resemblance to the monoliths of the Bolivian site, incised from head to foot with complex and enigmatic symbols. Mortarless masonry, using carved polygonal blocks, is found in a few ahaus, particularly Vinapu, and has been cited as another link with South America since this method of construction faintly recalls the masonry of Cuzco, the Inca capital. But the great building work in Cuzco began in A.D. 1440, and Easter Island dating now makes nonsense of such comparisons since the earlier ahaus were built centuries before Cuzco became a great city.

In other parts of Polynesia, particularly in New Zealand, wood was the principal medium for the expression of the carver's art, which formed an integral part of his religion. Polynesians who were stranded in a place where wood was scarce and stone plentiful did not abandon their creative activity, but inevitably turned to the best available material, a softish volcanic stone, ideal for cutting with tools made from the abundant supplies of obsidian.

Similar mausoleums existed in other parts of Polynesia and were known as *marae* on Tahiti and in the Tuamotos and as *meae* in the Marquesas. Cook also saw a pyramid on Tahiti, and large stone statues were erected on Pitcairn, the nearest inhabited place to Easter Island, as well as in the Marquesas. Therefore the element of mystery lies less in the building of outsize monuments than in the original discovery of the island. Kenneth P. Emory, the well-known Polynesian scholar, states that his first-hand knowledge of the archaeology and language of the Marquesas convinces him that Easter Island culture could have evolved from a single landing from the Marquesas, fully equipped to settle a virgin island possessing no native edible plants.* This explanation makes sense, though the occupation was probably a once-and-for-all venture; bereft of wood for making larger canoes, the Easter Islanders lacked the capacity to make return journeys towards their point of departure, let alone to undertake onward trips to America.

CHAPTER TEN

THE VINLAND VIKINGS

By the edge of the sea, in Oslo Fjord, the Vikings built three great mounds, one on the eastern shore at Tune and the other two on the west side at Gokstad and Oseberg. In each mound a ship was buried; the three vessels have been unearthed and can today be viewed in all their splendour.

A visit to the Ship Museum on the Island of Bygdoy, a few minutes' boat ride from Oslo, is an unforgettable experience. Bygdoy is no mere repository of bygone trophies but a national shrine, dedicated to Norse genius. For the ship was the Viking's supreme achievement, his source of strength and ultimately his tomb.

The largest of the three vessels, the Gokstad ship, was excavated in 1800. The timbered burial chamber, built athwart the stern, contained the bones of a chieftain, elegantly dressed and armed. Near the body were found fragments of fine textiles, embroidered with gold thread, and just outside lay the remains of a peacock. Amidships, an abundance of kitchenware was stored. The burial dates from about A.D. 900.*

In 1893 a replica of the Gokstad ship successfully crossed the Atlantic, on the occasion of the Chicago World's Fair. Captain Magnus Andersen, who captained this facsimile vessel, remarked that her rudder was a work of genius and her performance remarkable, both for flexibility and for speed; on 15 May 1893, she outpaced steam vessels of her day by covering 223 knots in 24 hours, at an hourly average of 9·3 knots. A replica of Columbus' *Santa Maria* also sailed to America in the same year, but never averaged more than 6½ knots per hour.

The Oseberg ship, also displayed in the lofty hall of Bygdoy, was the last resting place of two women, whose burial chamber was found complete with beds, pillows, eiderdowns, exquisite wall-hangings and four magnificent carved headposts, adorned with animal heads. In the bows lay other fine trophies, including a wooden carriage and four elaborately carved sledges. The Oseberg ship is lightly constructed and was not designed for ocean travel; such boats belonged to chieftains, who used them in coastal waters and rivers. The Gokstad vessel was also built to serve some ruler or prince; she was not a warship but was admirably suited for long-distance trading.*

In all about five hundred Viking craft have been discovered. The most spectacular ships are those found in Skuldelev in Denmark; they were constructed about two hundred years after the Oslo boats and are even stronger. However, the Gokstad ship more closely resembles the vessels of the Vikings who sailed to Iceland and Greenland, and onward to Vinland, since it was built at the very time when Iceland was first colonized.

Boats like these were unrivalled in their day not only for speed but for flexibility; their shallow draft permitted their use in rivers and they could be beached even in shallow waters. They were, however, rather small for ocean travel and in comparison with Columbus' ships provided poor shelter for crew and cargo, though a tentlike wooden structure seems to have been erected amidships. No cooking could be done on board, and the crew had to depend on cold food. On the other hand, the Vikings' westward journeys into the Atlantic could be completed in a matter of days: the voyage from Iceland to Greenland averaged four days, while six were required for the crossing from Ireland to Iceland.*

Much more is known about Norse ships than about how they were handled. In the absence of compass, chart and sextant, bearings were taken from the sun and stars, though when possible captains preferred to follow a coastline, judging their whereabouts from known landmarks. Because of the mountainous landscape of many North Atlantic Viking settlements, high peaks visible from afar often helped to guide mariners to their destination. In good weather, a ship could almost travel from Iceland to Greenland without losing sight of land; the summits of Snaefellsnes in Iceland and Angmagssalik in Greenland stand out from a great distance, and modern sailors assert that both are occasionally visible at one and the same time.*

Like the Polynesians, the Vikings used ocean swell and wind direction as aids to navigation, as well as the flight of birds. As in Oceania, ships often lost their bearings in a storm and had to rely on the pilot's instinct and good luck to reach land. The Norsemen paid close attention to ocean currents and on their journeys to Vinland virtually followed the prevailing current. Because of dangers presented by large ice-masses in high latitudes, the summer sailing season was unlikely to have started before July.

Direct crossings were also made from Bergen in Norway to Cape Farewell in Greenland, a distance of 1500 miles. The Icelandic Landnamabok (Book of Land-taking) contains directions for sailing to Greenland that are practical if imprecise:

> From Hernar in Norway one is to keep sailing west for Huarf in Greenland and then you will sail north of Shetland so far that you can just sight it in very clear weather; but steer south of the Faroes so that the sea appears halfway up the mountain slopes; farther on, pass south of Iceland so that you may have birds and whales from it.*

Before they ventured across the Atlantic, Norse boats had already approached the limits of the known world; some had thrust down the great rivers of Russia to the Caspian and Black Seas, while others ranged far and wide over the Mediterranean.

The Vikings started their career of expansion as raiders, not settlers. In A.D. 793, descending like a bolt from the blue, they devastated the church and monastery of Lindisfarne, an island off the Northumbrian coast, and slaughtered its monks. News of the assault caused consternation in the court of Charlemagne, where the great Irish scholar, Alcuin, was then living; he wrote in horror to King Aethelred of Northumbria, lamenting that the heathen Vikings were the instrument of God's wrath, visited upon the sins of His people.

France soon became the target for these marauders, and in 799 islands lying off the coast of Aquitaine were pillaged. In the first half of the ninth century, raids by Norwegian and Danish Vikings became more frequent. The year 842 witnessed a combined attack on France and England: great massacres took place in London and Rochester, while other Vikings attacked Nantes and on 24 June, St John's Day, slew many of the devout and merry celebrants of the Baptist's feast. In 845 a Viking army defeated King Charles the Bald and on Easter Sunday entered and plundered Paris.

But by the latter half of the ninth century the Vikings became settlers more than plunderers and occupied large parts of northern France,

England and Ireland. The Danes who came to Normandy were the forebears of the Normans, best known as the conquerors of England and the founders of the Norman kingdom of Sicily.

Meanwhile, Swedish Viking traders and settlers penetrated deep into Russia; in the land that still bears their name they were known as Rus. The Vikings pushed down the Dnieper as far as Kiev, and in 839 these 'Rus' sent ambassadors to the Byzantine Emperor in Constantinople. A century later, other Swedish Vikings followed the Volga as far as the Caspian Sea and even came into conflict with certain Arabs. Ibn Fadlan describes the exploits of the Rus, some of whom in 921 crossed the desert to Baghdad; quantities of Arab silver coins found in Sweden bear witness to such contacts. These Vikings displayed an almost Polynesian lack of sexual inhibitions: Ibn Fadlan relates how a man would have intercourse with his slave girl while his companions looked on. Sometimes whole groups would come together in this fashion. Nor were the Vikings averse to human sacrifice, before they embraced Christianity. Adam of Bremen tells how an important festival took place in Uppsala every nine years, involving the slaughter of nine males of every creature: the bodies of the human victims, as well as those of the dogs, horses and other animals, were hung in a grove near the temple.*

To the Vikings, whose ambitions knew no bounds, the challenge of the wild and unfamiliar western ocean was irresistible. From Norway, which had long suffered from a dearth of good land, first Iceland and then Greenland were settled. Political events gave added cause to emigrate, as a means of escape from the oppressive rule of Harold Finehair, who made himself sole king of Norway in A.D. 900.

In A.D. 861, the Swede Gardar Svarvasson was sailing from Norway to the Hebrides when he was blown off course in a gale and eventually landed on the coast of a large uninhabited island. A few years later, the Norwegian Flake Vilgardsson crossed from the Faroes to the recently discovered land, where he spent the winter. Because of failure to store up fodder, Vilgardsson lost all his cattle; in the report on his voyages he named the new territory Iceland.

The first settlers arrived in Iceland in the 870s; they found a volcanic island a little bigger than Ireland, with huge black mountains and silver glaciers. A quarter of the surface was covered by lava or permanent ice-caps, but in the many fjord valleys crops could be grown, while uplands in the interior offered summer grazing. Lakes and rivers were filled with trout and salmon. Contrary to expectations, Iceland was not virgin territory. Celtish anchorites from Ireland had settled there centuries before the Norsemen. These solitaries preferred to abandon the Vikings to their heathen ways and returned to Ireland; according to the Landnamabok, they left behind them 'bells, books and croziers'.

The population of Iceland increased and by 930 numbered about sixty thousand. The community became a republic, governed by an elected assembly and a council; free democracy befitted a people unchallenged by native inhabitants and immune from threat of foreign invasion. The Icelanders soon developed a rich and varied literature. As Gwyn Jones puts it, poetry became a national industry, and poets a national export; from this harsh and riven island a continuous flow of poetry, history and saga poured forth. By the 960s the office of court poet in the kingdom of Norway had become the exclusive preserve of Icelanders, and remained so until the thirteenth century. The family sagas, telling of the occupation of Iceland and of the onward voyages to Greenland and Vinland, were not recorded in writing until several centuries later but provide a wealth of detail on earlier times.

But despite its cultural achievements, Iceland was no Tahiti. The inhabitants could clothe themselves, but lacked timber and produced insufficient wheat to meet their needs; on more than one occasion, they endured a cruel famine. Such privations created the urge to push even farther westward.

Eric the Red, discoverer of Greenland, came from an adventurous family. His father Thorwald fled to Iceland after committing manslaughter in Norway; Eric was outlawed in his turn, following quarrels with Icelandic families that culminated in a fight in which he killed two men. Expelled from his home, Eric sailed boldly westwards, found a huge island, and spent the next three years exploring its coastline. On his return to Iceland, the explorer tried to make this arctic wilderness sound attractive by calling it Greenland; in 986 he assembled an armada of 25 vessels and again set out for the new land, accompanied by 500 migrants, including women and children, and a full complement of provisions, implements and livestock. The voyage proved hazardous, and only 14 ships reached their destination, while the remainder were wrecked or forced to turn back.

Two colonies were established in Greenland, the East Settlement on the south-west coast and the West Settlement somewhat farther north. More colonists arrived, and a new community was founded which survived for five hundred years and then unaccountably vanished.

Eric the Red chose for himself one of the pleasanter and more fertile areas of the East Settlement, built his home there and called it Brattahlid. The main building, which has been excavated, consists of a great hall, surrounded by stables and storehouses; from this manor Eric's son Lief was to set forth in search of a new continent.

Helge Ingstad, the discoverer of the Viking settlements of the New World, gives a vivid description of the Greenland base:

> A strange country, along whose coasts drift-ice and bluish-white Icebergs move slowly northward, where green fields are bright spots in an otherwise rocky and treeless landscape, and towering peaks seem to be striding eastward, towards the gleaming white shield that is the great inland glacier.*

Climatic conditions in Greenland were probably better in the tenth century than today, and in a good year apples were reported to ripen; birds and fish abounded but the Norse farmers could not acclimatize wheat. The arctic made great demands upon the settlers, confined for eight months of the year in their dark dwellings, and condemned to a precarious existence that lacked bread, fruit, vegetables, wood and iron. Such conditions were a poor reward for those who had set forth with high hopes. Little succour could be expected from Iceland, where wood and corn were also in short supply.

Though their country produced no literature, the story of the Greenlanders' epic voyages into the unknown survives in two Icelandic accounts, the Greenlanders' Saga and Eric the Red's Saga. Both documents are rich in historical material, handed down by word of mouth and finally recorded in writing in the fourteenth century.

The first European known to have sighted America is Bjarni Herjolfsson, who spent the summer of 985 in Norway when still a lad of twenty. On returning to Iceland in the autumn of that year, Bjarni learned that his father had gone to Greenland and immediately went off in pursuit. After three days' good sailing a storm threw the ship off course; four days later the sun reappeared and a westward route was again followed until land was sighted; it could not have been part of

Greenland, because it had no great glaciers or mountains, but only small hills. Bjarni sailed on for two more days and once more came to a flat and wooded coastline that also bore no resemblance to Greenland.

Bjarni had seen the New World, but he returned to Greenland without setting foot on its shores. However, Lief Ericsson, son of Eric the Red, heard of these exploits and determined to learn more of the strange new lands. Some time after Bjarni's return, Lief bought his boat and, in A.D. 992, set forth with a thirty-five-man crew. Not much is known about Lief except that he had visited Norway and met King Olaf, who received him with honour and assigned him the task of converting his native Greenlanders to Christianity; his mother, Thjorhild, was later baptized, but his father Eric remained a pagan to the end of his days. Lief had asked Eric to lead the expedition, but the old man excused himself, saying that he no longer had the strength to endure the hardships of such a voyage: 'It is not my fate to discover any more lands than the one in which we now live. We shall not travel together any farther.'*

Lief accordingly took command and followed a route that was the reverse of Bjarni's. The ship came first to an island that they called Helluland (Stone Land), where there were glaciers but no grass and which is thought to have been the southern part of Baffin Island in the Canadian Arctic. Lief next reached a flat wooded country with white sandy beaches which he named Markland (Forest Land) and which probably formed part of the coast of Labrador. Finally the explorers came to the land named Vinland, where they decided to spend the winter, since grass was abundant and there was plenty of timber for building huts. In the rivers and sea the salmon were bigger than the Norsemen had ever seen before; the winter climate was mild, and the grass scarcely withered; night and day were of more equal length than in Greenland.

One evening, a man named Tyrkir, a German, was found to be missing. Lief, who had known Tyrkir when still a child and looked on him as a kind of foster father, was most distressed and immediately set out to look for his missing companion, accompanied by twelve men. The search party soon found Tyrkir, who was in a state of great excitement. Babbling in his native German, grimacing and rolling his eyes, he told how he had found grapes and vines. After this incident, Lief said to his crew: 'We shall gather grapes, and we shall cut vines, and fell timber, to make a cargo for my ship.' During the next few days the work was done, and in the early spring Lief and his companions sailed home.

The voyage to Vinland was eagerly discussed in Greenland. Thorvald, Lief's brother, thought that a wider region should be explored, and Lief suggested that his brother take the same ship and go westwards again. The new expedition, consisting of thirty men, found Lief's huts in Vinland and wintered there. The following summer was spent in exploring the coast, and after a second winter in Vinland, another voyage of discovery was made: the boat sailed down the shore as far as a wooded headland of such beauty that Thorvald declared that he would like to build his homestead there. Shortly afterwards, an ominous event occurred: on the beach, beyond the cape, the Norsemen saw what seemed to be three mounds. On closer inspection these proved to be skin boats and under each one lay three men. Of these nine Indians, the first of their kind known to have been seen by European eyes, eight were promptly massacred by the Vikings, but one escaped to tell the tale. The natives were described as small, with ugly, unkempt hair, large eyes and broad cheeks. Thorvald's men were then attacked by a large force of men in skin boats, who shot at them with arrows and fled. The Indians, however, achieved their purpose, for Thorvald was fatally wounded by an arrow; knowing he was going to die, he spoke to his men as follows:

'An arrow flew in between the gunwale and my shield, and under my arm. Here is the arrow, and it will cause my death. My advice to you is that you return home as soon as possible. But first you shall carry me to the headland where I wish to make my home. Perhaps I spoke true when I said that I should dwell there awhile. Bury me there and put crosses at my head and feet, and call the place Crossness for ever more.'*

The remainder of the party then returned to their Vinland base, where they joined their companions and sailed off to Greenland.

The third expedition to Vinland was launched on a more ambitious scale and differed radically from its predecessors, since the objective was not merely to explore but to colonize. The leader was Thorfinn Karlsefni, a man of great riches, who had been spending the winter with Lief Ericsson at Brattahlid. The Greenlanders' Saga says that the migrants numbered 160, including some women; all kinds of livestock were taken. The party arrived safely in Vinland and passed the winter there. But when spring came the skraelings once more appeared; the encounter is vividly described in the same Saga:

> After that first winter came summer. It was now that they [the Vikings] made acquaintance with the skraelings, when a big body of men appeared out of the forest there. Their [the Vikings'] cattle were close by; the bull began to bellow and bawl loudly, which so frightened the skraelings that they ran off with their packs, which were of grey furs and sables and skins of all kinds, and headed for Karlsefni's house, hoping to get inside there, but Karlsefni had the doors guarded. Neither party could understand the other's language. Then the skraelings unslung their bales, untied them, and proffered their wares and above all wanted weapons in exchange. Karlsefni, though, forbade them the sale of weapons. And now he hit on this idea; he told the women to carry out milk to them [the skraelings] and the moment they saw the milk, that was the one thing they wanted to buy, nothing else. So that was what came of the skraelings' trading; they carried away what they bought in their bellies, while Karlsefni and his comrades kept their bales and their furs.*

After another winter had passed, an incident occurred of a kind which so often marred the relations between European pioneers and newly discovered natives of America or Oceania: a skraeling was killed because he tried to steal weapons. A battle ensued, and many Indians were slain before they fled in disorder. However, Karlsefni was unnerved by this attack, and the ship returned to Greenland the next spring.

A further expedition, the last known to have been undertaken, came to grief, not because of skraeling attacks, but because of quarrels among the crew. Freydis, an illegitimate daughter of Eric the Red, set out for Vinland with two boats, accompanied by the Icelandic brothers Helgi and Finnbogi. After they had wintered in Vinland, trouble broke out among the settlers, and the pitiless Freydis, not content with murdering the two brothers, felled with an axe all the five women of the party.

Until recent years, the accounts of voyages to Vinland in the Sagas were looked upon as little more than fairy tales. Only a few scholars were bold enough to suggest that Vinland might conceivably be identified with Newfoundland. This large island lies farther to the east than any other territory of the North American continent; its physical characteristics fit the Sagas' description of Vinland as being a hilly country with large forests, interspersed by lakes and rivers. The maritime climate makes the winters much milder than those of continental Canada to the west. Moreover 'skraelings' were present in Newfoundland; it was once inhabited by Beotuk Indians, of whom a few still survive.

Nevertheless, theories on Viking voyages to America belonged strictly to the realm of speculation until the Norwegian Helge Ingstad went to work and made discoveries that rank high in the annals of modern archaeology. Ingstad was formerly governor of Spitzbergen and in the 1930s had already made a name for himself as a result of his researches in Greenland; here as elsewhere, his efforts were ably seconded by his wife, Anne Stine, a professional archaeologist.

After a further expedition to Greenland in 1953, Ingstad published a book called *Land under the Pole*, in which the belief was expressed that Vinland should be sought in comparatively northerly latitudes. The Norwegian explorer was convinced that *Vinland* really meant 'the land with the meadows' and agreed with the Swedish philologist, Sven Söderberg, in deriving the name from the ancient Scandinavian word *vin* meaning 'meadow', which had already gone out of use before the time of the Vikings. Previous writers, influenced by the repeated mention in the Sagas of the gathering of grapes and vines, had automatically assumed that Vinland meant 'Land of Vines'.

But no Norseman would have recognized grapes if he had seen them. Helge Ingstad saw the use of the German Tyrkir as the discoverer of the vines as a mere device to overcome this difficulty. The saga-teller displays his own ignorance when he claims that Lief Ericsson loaded his boat with both grapes and vines. No one in his right mind would have taken vines to Greenland, where practically no cultivation of any kind was possible; besides, this harvesting of grapes is said to have occurred in winter or early spring. The principal sagas do not state that Vinland meant 'Land of Grapes', and Ingstad accordingly came to the conclusion that Lief's 'grapes' were some kind of local berry. In an account of Nova Scotia written in 1624, William Alexander, Earl of Stirling, mentions 'red wine-berries', which were probably wild currants, but certainly not grapes, and Ingstad himself discovered in Newfoundland an astonishing variety of berries. The Norwegians of the tenth century were definitely familiar with the process of fermentation and probably made a kind of wine from the wild berries that abounded near the farms of Norway.

To prove his theories, in 1960 Helge Ingstad fitted out an expedition to look for Vinland. The voyage began with the exploration of the east coast of the American continent, starting with Rhode Island, which eminent scholars had identified with Vinland. Finding nothing, Ingstad continued his voyage, sailing slowly northward to Boston, New Hampshire and Maine, where he encountered only disappointment. Nova Scotia was equally unpromising and by this time the task of finding Vikings in America seemed as hopeless as looking for a needle in a haystack.

Ingstad eventually came to Newfoundland, where he was curtly informed in one small fishing village that if any treasure was buried in the vicinity, the villagers preferred to dig it up for themselves; he continued to question people about traces of old house-sites; no one knew anything, and some people thought he was out of his mind. But when the Norwegian expedition reached its last port of call, L'Anse aux Meadows, on the north coast of Newfoundland, their tide of fortune turned dramatically. At L'Anse a wide green plain terminated in low hills and the landscape answered exactly to the description of Vinland's first discoverer, Bjarni. The land had no mountains and was covered with woods and there were low hills, while a very pronounced cape pointing north also corresponded to the saga description. The scenery reminded Ingstad of certain Norse sites he had seen in Greenland, and when, at a short distance from the sea, he saw an ancient marine terrace with a few overgrown bumps on top, he was convinced that this was the place.

The first year's excavations offered no proof of a Viking presence, though dwellings were found, consisting of five or six rooms built round a large central hall, similar to the first Viking houses in Greenland; however, artefacts of any kind were lacking, whether Indian, Eskimo or Norse. Not until 1962, after six house-sites had been excavated, did a bone needle appear, the first artefact of recognizably Norse origin. Soon afterwards, a narrow piece of copper, about two inches long, was located inside a hearth; laboratory tests showed that the metal had been produced by a primitive smelting process unknown to

Indians or Eskimos. In the same hearth as the copper, charcoal was also encountered, which was dated by radiocarbon to A.D. 980, or very approximately to the time of the Vinland voyages. Lumps of iron slag and small thin pieces of iron offered additional proof of a Viking settlement.

Further exploration took place at L'Anse aux Meadows, and in 1964 a soapstone spindle-whorl of a type widely used in Viking times in Scandinavia was discovered. This find offered further evidence of the arrival of Norsemen and also indicated that women had accompanied their men and that wool was expected to be available for spinning.

In days when archaeologists were more often judged by the glamour of their trophies than by their contribution to history, a needle and a spindle-whorl would have been deemed a poor cache. But in terms of pure science, these humble chattels were worth all the treasures of Tutankhamen because they were indisputably Norse and therefore provided the answer to a major problem. Ingstad is convinced that the dwellings at L'Anse were built by Lief Ericsson. But if the houses were *not* those of Lief's expedition – which were also used by Karlsefni – then another Norse expedition, of which no report has survived, must have visited L'Anse.

Since there is now no doubt that L'Anse was a Norse settlement, saga reports of the Vikings' westward journeys can be taken at their face value. An increasing number of scholars consider that Lief's Helluland lies in the southern part of Baffin Island and that Markland was situated on the coast of Labrador. The identification of L'Anse with Vinland cannot be proved for certain and the claims of the St Lawrence Estuary, New Brunswick, Massachusetts, Rhode Island, Long Island Sound, Virginia, Georgia and Florida continue to find eloquent and vigorous sponsors. A new archaeological discovery in any one of these locations could change the picture overnight; however, in the absence of evidence to the contrary, I prefer to accept that L'Anse *was* Vinland; how far the settlers sailed beyond their Vinland base is not known, though during the summer both Lief Ericsson and Karlsefni made exploratory trips.

The Vikings therefore not only reached America in the late tenth century but even tried to make a permanent home there. But their settlement proved short-lived, in marked contrast to their five-hundred-year occupation of parts of Greenland. The American enterprise was basically unsound; Greenland itself, previously settled from Iceland, was little more than the colony of a colony, and its population amounted to only two or three thousand souls. Besides, Greenland and Iceland possessed the inestimable advantage of having no hostile natives; if it had not been for the opposition encountered in Vinland, there is no reason why a major part of the Greenland population should not have migrated thither, together perhaps with a number of Icelanders. From the point of view of a Greenlander, Vinland was a veritable paradise and would have provided handsomely for all their needs. However, the Norsemen's lines of communication were too stretched; the Greenland base was capable of sending out explorers and even settlers, but was too small and poor to contemplate the conquest of a new world in the face of opposition. The Vikings arrived before the days of firearms and therefore fought on almost even terms against hordes of natives. As soon as the skraelings appeared in force, the enterprise was doomed, and the Vinland game no longer worth the candle.

While L'Anse at present offers the only authentic proof that the Vikings reached America, a copious supply of dubious or fake evidence is also available, of which the best known example is the Vinland map. In 1957 Lawrence Witten, an antiquarian book dealer of New Haven, Connecticut, bought in Barcelona for $3500 an unassuming document, complete with four wormholes. The purchase was very profitable since in 1959 an anonymous benefactor acquired it for Yale University for a sum reputed to have exceeded $250,000.

The parchment in question, which gained fame as the Vinland map, included a map of Europe, together with a remarkably accurate tracing of the Island of Greenland. To the south-west of Greenland, at a distance approximately equal to that dividing Greenland from Ireland, another large territory is shown, described as 'the Island of Vinland, discovered by Bjarni and Lief in company'. A longer legend records a visit made to Vinland by Eric, Bishop of Greenland, in the last year of Pope Pascal (1117–18) – the first reported visit by a Christian prelate to America. The Viking map was bound together in a single volume with a manuscript describing the Franciscan mission of Friar John de Plano Carini to Tartary from A.D. 1215 to 1247, which has come to be known as the Tartar Relation.

At a symposium held in 1974 to discuss the authenticity of the Vinland map, Dr Helen Wallis gave an account of subsequent events.* The document had aroused passionate interest, especially among those who believed (at a time when L'Anse aux Meadows had not yet been excavated) that the Vikings had discovered America. However, from the very start many scholars were sceptical since the map did not fit into the general framework of European medieval cartography; in particular the outline of Greenland seemed too accurate to have been traced in the late Middle Ages. Early in 1967 the map made a tour of Europe and was exhibited in Scandinavia, Holland, and England (at the British Museum), and an examination made in London, though limited in scope, aroused further suspicions about its antiquity.

Then, deciding to resolve all doubts, Yale University commissioned the Chicago firm of McRone Associates, experts in small particle analysis, to make an investigation. Results released in January 1974 suggest that the Vinland Map is a plain forgery, made some time after 1920, whereas the Tartar Relation appears to be genuinely old.

Dr G. D. Painter, one of the original backers of the authenticity of the map, stuck to his guns in the 1974 symposium and said that he still believed that it was genuine. He proposed that a faded original had been cosmetically titivated with modern ink. However, Walter C. McRone contradicted Painter and explained in detail that the ink of the document contains a pigment called Anatase, available only in the 1920s; the material was the product of extensive research by several large laboratories and its process of manufacture is complex. McRone ruled out the possibility that Anatase had been used only in a retouching process: careful microscopic study revealed no evidence that the original lines had been retraced in modern times.

The importance of the Vinland map had been exaggerated by the press. The document told very little that was not known before; if genuine, it would have been significant not as proof of the Norse discovery of the New World, but as evidence that knowledge of this feat had survived until the first half of the fifteenth century and had been transmitted in map form to southern Europe, some half-century before Columbus undertook his first voyage.

The Navigation Map of the Venetian brothers, Nicolo and Antonio Zeno, has also attracted much attention. The document was published in Venice in 1558, with a commentary edited by a descendant of the Zeno brothers, also called Nicolo Zeno; the text that accompanies the map describes the voyages of his family in the fourteenth and fifteenth centuries to 'Frislandia, Eslanda, Engronelanda, Estotilandia and Icaria'. Attempts have been made to prove that Estotilandia was Newfoundland and a recently published book seeks to establish that Henry Sinclair, who was born in Edinburgh in 1345 and subsequently inherited the Norwegian earldom of Orkney, was the Prince Zichmni who supposedly visited Newfoundland and Nova Scotia.* However, the English sceptic F. W. Lucas demonstrated as long ago as 1873 that Zeno's narrative was mostly copied straight from other printed works of the sixteenth century.* According to the Nicolo Zeno who edited the text, it was put together from letters written by his forebear Antonio in the fourteenth century; however, Zeno's unscrupulous copying of other people's writings raises many doubts as to his accuracy and Dr R. A. Skelton, one of the two principal scholars who, before the 1974 symposium on the Vinland map, *was* prepared to accept it as genuine, is among the sceptics who think that the Venetian brothers never went beyond Iceland.

Finds of runic inscriptions have been reported from different parts of America and cited to prove a Viking presence. A freelance French anthropologist, Dr Jacques de Mahieu, has even traced Norsemen to distant Paraguay; near Amambay he unearthed ruins of a wall said to contain runic inscriptions, together with the remains of a Viking village. Mahieu affirms that seven Viking boats, each with eighty people on board, reached Mexico in A.D. 967. Twenty-two years later these adventurers undertook a new migration and eventually reached Paraguay, after passing through Venezuela and Chile. In Paraguay the Norsemen became the progenitors of a tribe whose sturdy womenfolk created the legend of the Amazons, and their last descendants still survive as the Guayaqui Indians. Mahieu admits that these Guayaquis are a sadly decadent breed of Vikings, since they measure only four feet, eleven inches in stature and some are cannibals. Such theories are treated as pure science fiction by leading Argentinian anthropologists, and although he has written no less than fifteen books on the subject, Mahieu has hardly proved his point.*

In the United States, the Columbus Day centenary of 1892 aroused the enthusiasm of believers in deep Norse penetrations into North America and may have inspired forgeries that came to light in the following decades. Of these, the best known is the Kensington Stone. In 1898, a

Swedish immigrant farmer called Olaf Ohman unearthed a stone in Kensington, Minnesota, measuring thirty-two inches by sixteen, and bearing inscriptions that he recognized as runes. Ohman, besieged by eager visitors, entrusted his find to a bank, where it was displayed in the window, and aroused keen interest. Dr George O. Curme, of Minnesota and Northwestern University, pronounced the stone to be a blatant forgery, and Ohman was so disappointed that he consigned it to his granary, where it remained until 1907. In that year it was 'rediscovered' by Hjalmar R. Holand, who was writing a history of the Scandinavian settlements in America. Holand spent the best part of his life in the attempt to prove that the stone was genuine and published three weighty volumes on the subject. According to Holand's translation of the inscription, thirty Vikings, on an exploratory voyage westward from Vinland in 1362, had settled in a place a few days' journey north of where the Kensington Stone was found.

Among other runic inscriptions, stones were discovered in 1971 at Spirit Pond on the coast of Maine, but the meaning of their writing is unclear and their authenticity doubtful. More recently, in New Hampshire and Vermont, yet another series of stones has been found which attributes the discovery of America to neither Lief Ericsson nor Columbus, but to the Celts; according to Dr Barry Fell of Harvard University they are inscribed in the Ogham script, used by the Celts from about 800 to 300 B.C.* Admittedly they had good boats, and the Irish sea-going curragh was not unlike the Eskimo uniak. However, the capacity of the Celts to reach the New World at such an early date is highly questionable. Moreover, Dr Fell's theories are not confined to Celts since he argues that Phoenicians also reached America about 400 B.C.; he claims that a stone inscription, discovered on Cape Cod by English settlers in 1653 and recently found by Hindus embedded in a flight of steps, is really Phoenician and proclaims the annexation of Massachusetts by the Phoenician Kin Hanna.* But Yale was wrong about the Vinland map, and much more information from Harvard would be needed before such finds could be accepted as genuine.

Claims that the English reached the New World before Columbus should be treated with equal caution. A book by David Beers Quin published recently in London attributes the discovery of America to Bristol cod fishermen in 1481.

F. R. Forbes Taylor of Bristol has also over the past few years assembled evidence that Bristol seamen discovered the New World.

Taylor discovered anomalies in the accounts of what individual ships exported from Bristol and imported from 1479 onward, as certified line by line by customs officials. Ostensibly these voyages were to Ireland but their duration was unaccountably long. Around 1479 a considerable but puzzling change took place in the pattern of cargoes. Until that date goods exported consisted mainly of cloths, salt, iron, wine and vinegar, but thereafter the emphasis changed to beans, honey and materials for dyeing cloth, together with the cloth itself. Return freights also changed at the same time: instead of importing salmon and Irish linen, cargoes included salt fish and white herring in barrels.* The subject provides full scope for the imagination, but little concrete information, and the changes in goods carried are not convincing. Salmon, not herring, abounded in northerly latitudes in America and farther to the south honey and textile dyes were freely available, not to mention beans. Admiral Samuel Eliot Morison, the biographer of Columbus, describes pre-Columbian voyages to America by Portuguese, Irish, English and Venetian as 'modern man-made myths, phantoms which left not one footprint on the sands of time'.

A few words must be added about the final great 'discoverer' himself. Columbus made the fullest use of skills acquired by those Portuguese pioneers whose prowess prepared the way for the voyages to America. Portugal was a small country that probably possessed less than a million inhabitants at the beginning of the fifteenth century. Like the Vikings, the Portuguese had a strong inducement to seek outlets from a cramping environment, and the health of their economy urgently demanded additional good land and gold. Portugal, moreover, happened to be ideally situated for maritime adventure in the Atlantic, and the winds off the Portuguese coast favoured exploration to the south and south-west. Ready use was made of these natural advantages, and Portugal became the first European country in which overseas exploration was actively supported over a long period by the government, largely as a result of the efforts of Prince Henry the Navigator.* At first Prince Henry could not persuade any captain to sail round Cape Bojador at the tip of the West African bulge; sailors feared that they could never return against the prevailing northerlies and assumed that any ship which went too far south would run into boiling water at the equator – a belief inherited from the Ancients.

However, in 1434, one of Prince Henry's captains was bold enough to round Cape Bojador; and within a few years Portuguese ships were trading in black slaves and gold dust, and a merchant factory had been built on Arguin Island near latitude 20°. By 1460, when Henry the Navigator died, ships had passed Dakar and reached Sierra Leone, only 10° above the equator. Finally, in 1488, Vasco da Gama rounded the Cape of Good Hope.

Such feats followed a revolution in ship design and in methods of navigation. Rudimentary forms of the magnetic compass are first mentioned by an English monk, Alexander Neckham, who crossed the English Channel in 1180 in order to lecture in Paris. Neckham writes that his ship was equipped with a pivoted needle which helped sailors to steer when the sky was covered by clouds. The oldest surviving maritime chart, the Carta Pisana, dates from 1275, and by the beginning of the fourteenth century an establishment had been set up in Genoa for the purpose of chart-making. In the course of this century, all the countries round the shores of the Mediterranean were charted, and navigational tables were already being used in 1382. In a Venetian manuscript of 1428 an actual copy of such tables survives.*

These advances in the art of navigation were consolidated during the fifteenth century, and by the 1480s Portuguese ships as a matter of routine carried not only a compass but also charts marked with latitude. Primitive but adequate ways had been developed by then for making the necessary measurements, based on the height of the sun at midday and by observation of certain stars; a table of African coastal latitudes reaching as far as the equator was compiled in this way; these were obtained by using a very simple form of quadrant to measure the angle above the horizon of a particular star. For measuring solar altitudes, the late-fifteenth-century navigator used a more sophisticated instrument, the astrolabe. Ships were being improved, as well as instruments, and the Portuguese caravel was a great advance over previous vessels. Little is known of its hull design and construction, but the caravel was able to sail much closer to the wind, and captains could therefore proceed as far as they wished along the African coast and still be sure of returning.

At a time when Portuguese pilots were eagerly sought by other maritime nations, Christopher Columbus served the King of Portugal and took part as a young man in expeditions along the coast of West Africa; in the journal of his first voyage to America, Columbus makes frequent comparisons between 'India' and 'Guinea'. He profited not only by Portuguese skills and inventions; in addition, the knowledge which Portuguese mariners had acquired of the western part of the Atlantic was crucial to his plans to sail farther west. The Portuguese had already in 1427 discovered the Azores, a third of the way to America. On his first voyage, the Admiral followed an established route to the Canaries and then made a right-angle turn to take advantage of winter winds known to blow from the east in that region.

Columbus was born in Genoa, though he has been variously presented as Castilian, Catalan, Corsican, Majorcan, Portuguese, French, German, English, Irish, Greek, Polish and Russian. Thorwald Brynidsen even demonstrated that the Admiral was a full-blooded Viking, directly descended from the founders of the eleventh-century Norse settlement: he had supposedly sailed back from America in a Viking ship and changed his name to Colón, his 'first voyage' was merely a return journey to the land of his birth.

The 'Enterprise of the Indies', for which Columbus sought backing first from the King of Portugal and later from Queen Isabella of Spain, was a practical project, based on the new maritime techniques learned from the Portuguese and on the knowledge of the eastern Atlantic Ocean they had acquired. But Columbus also possessed a copy of Marco Polo's book written nearly two hundred years earlier, in which he made many annotations. Polo had been the first European traveller to cross the whole longitude of Asia and to tell not only of China but of other East Asian nations, such as Laos, Thailand, Java and Sumatra, of which Europe had no previous knowledge. As a consequence of these reports, atlases could be produced that made a far better attempt to delineate Asia than ever before. Marco Polo greatly overestimated the size of Japan, which he placed at a distance of one thousand miles from the mainland and called 'the noble Island of Cipangu', whose temples and palaces were roofed with pure gold.

Fundamental to Columbus' plans were the reckonings of the Florentine physician, Paolo dal Posso Toscanelli, who argued in a letter to Don Alfonso V of Portugal that the Atlantic Ocean, which divided Europe from East Asia, was far narrower than anyone had supposed. (Methods of calculating longitude were still rudimentary: even as late as 1541, a concerted effort to determine the longitude of Mexico City resulted in an error of $25\frac{1}{2}$ degrees. (Columbus himself made calculations that further narrowed the ocean gap between Europe and

Asia; he concluded that the distance from the Canaries westwards to Japan, via the mythical island of Antilia, measured 2400 nautical miles; in fact it is over 10,000 miles.

Accordingly, Columbus was proposing a voyage from known islands off the African coast, the Canaries, to another island, Cipangu or Japan, known to lie beyond the coast of Asia. No question therefore arose of sailing off into the blue, in the hope of finding some unknown continent; a vague project of this kind would have stood a poor chance of acceptance by the authorities who were so hesitant to sponsor Columbus' more concrete plans. After endless frustrations, during which Columbus became the butt of the Spanish courtiers' clownish witticisms, Queen Isabella eventually relented and backed the enterprise. In doing so, the Queen ignored the unfavourable findings of a committee set up to inquire whether the Orient could be reached via the Atlantic Ocean; the committee (rightly) stated that the ocean was much wider than Columbus believed and insisted that God would never have allowed any important territory, such as Antilia, to be left uninhabited by His people.

The notion of the discovery of another continent, as opposed to mere islands, was never even mooted. Columbus was given a letter by Isabella to the Grand Khan (the Emperor of China). When the Admiral reached Cuba, he was so convinced that it formed part of the Celestial Empire – he knew that he had sailed too far south to reach Japan – that he sent an embassy into the interior, to seek the Chinese Emperor and present Isabella's letter.

Columbus' objectives were quite different to those of the Vikings, who had set off five hundred years before to explore unknown lands to the west, and who afterwards returned to the same place in order to establish not a trading post but a farming colony. However, Columbus, in his search for a new route to the exotic east, was faced with the same predicament as the Vikings, since both unexpectedly came face to face with the native inhabitants of America. On the Island of San Salvador, the first to be reached, the Spaniards found no Chinese mandarins, but immediately encountered natives of the Guanahani tribe, who were promptly dubbed 'Indians', as befitted a people whose territory was unquestionably part of the East Indies. To begin with, relations were most cordial and Columbus tells how the Indians invited his crew to share all that they possessed. But the honeymoon period was short: in

1495, when Columbus was on his second voyage, an all-out war broke out between the Indians of Hispaniola and the Spaniards. With only two hundred men, of whom half were armed with arquebuses, supported by twenty savage dogs who terrified the natives, a decisive victory was won in the first of so many one-sided battles between American Indians and Spaniards.

Columbus' achievements owed much to his genius as a sailor, but he was also fortunate to have been born at the right moment. The pioneer work of the Portuguese had made two-way transoceanic voyages a practical possibility for the first time in history, and the development of firearms enabled small numbers of Europeans to subdue hordes of natives in the lands that they discovered. If, like the Viking expeditions, the Enterprise of the Indies had not been backed by gunpowder, its outcome would have been uncertain.

CHAPTER ELEVEN

CAUSE AND EFFECT

ON 24 June 1876, on the banks of the Little Bighorn River, Montana, Major-General Custer is said to have exclaimed: 'Good gracious, look at all those Indians – where do you suppose they came from?' This question, viewed in a broader context, has been continually asked ever since Pope Paul III's Bull of 1537 conceded that the American Indian formed part of the human species.

The evidence of migrations across the Bering sub-continent during the latter part of the Ice Age is now too massive to be ignored, and provides most of the answer. Science, however, has failed – with one exception – to reveal a single trace of *other* visitors to the New World during the millennia that separate Columbus from the submerging of the Bering gateway. Doubts therefore persist as to whether the Ice Age hunters who crossed Beringia were later able to scale the heights of civilization on their own or whether the spark was ignited by later migrants from Europe or Asia.

Popular literature takes the second view, and prefers cut-and-dried explanations: out of dozens of possible candidates, ranging from Celts at one end of the Eurasian spectrum to Chinese at the other, each author makes his selection and writes his book, offering infallible proof that only through the aid of his chosen vehicle was the American Indian rescued from barbarism. By implication, all counter-theories are discarded since obviously Celts, Etruscans, Israelites, Scythians, and Cambodians – to name only a few – cannot *all* have converged upon the New World, bearing aloft the torch of civilization.

Books of this kind, not designed to unearth the truth but to flog a pet theory, confuse the issue by oversimplification. Such methods pay handsome dividends, and very often the more bizarre the writer's opinions, the more certain his success. The fascination of the far-out fringes of scientific theory, as *Time* magazine puts it, is not confined to Ancient

America, nor to such books as von Däniken's *Chariots of the Gods*, or Velikovsky's *Worlds in Collision*. *The Secret Life of Plants*, another super-seller, argues that plants are capable of extrasensory perception and may even possess souls. Charles Berlitz' *The Bermuda Triangle* is a more recent example of doctored science. To quote *Time*: 'Like its predecesssors, *Triangle* takes off from established facts, then proceeds to lace these with a hodgepodge of half-truths, unsubstantiated evidence and unsubstantial science.'* Would-be readers decline to be put off by the rebuttal of some of Berlitz' statements by the Coast Guard in Miami, or by the expostulations of such eminent authorities on the Spanish Main as Admiral Samuel Eliot Morison, who described the book as preposterous.

Since the days of the first shamans, Man has been mesmerized by the cult of the mysterious, which made renewed strides in the nineteenth century and remains a growth industry today. Faith in God may have faltered, but to many people the tedium of everyday reality cannot be borne unless leavened with whiffs of the supernatural; mysticism is blended with scraps of science to produce a satisfying brand of pseudo-science. Lacking loftier ideals, readers are avid for signs that plants have souls or that Easter Island during the reign of Charlemagne remained a resort for travellers from outer space.

The American Indian has offered unlimited scope for odd solutions to the riddles of history. As C. W. Ceram has pointed out, such attempts fascinate the layman since they affect problems which intrigue him, but which he has never investigated in a serious way. Books are written – and this is the secret of their success – that bathe the issue in a false aura of romance and mysticism and pretend to sell the reader a key that makes him one of an élite, a member of a group entrusted with special secrets and privy to hidden truths that escape the scientist, restricted within the framework of pure intellect. People in universities and museums who reject such revelations are treated as bigots.*

Until fairly recently, Ancient America admirably suited writers bent upon simple answers to complex questions since the available evidence was imprecise. Ideas remained vague as to when the first hunters reached the New World, and little was known about the beginnings of civilization; potted solutions were therefore hard to refute. But the picture has been transformed by new studies of Ice Age migrations, of the birth of New World agriculture and of the rise of civilization.

Previous theories become meaningless once it is shown that New World cultures are likely to predate the Old World prototypes from which they supposedly sprang.

Equipped with more knowledge and better techniques, the professionals can now afford to abandon overdefensive attitudes. During the first half of the twentieth century, many anthropologists ridiculed every notion of transpacific contact in their resolve to present a united front against wild theories; any hint that America had not produced its own culture was consigned straight to the wastepaper basket. But such reactions are no longer justifiable; more experts now prefer to keep an open mind, ready to alter their views in the light of new discoveries that are sure to be made. Thor Heyerdahl is therefore quite right in noting a tendency among modern scholars to abandon isolationist stances and steer a middle course.

In the present state of our knowledge, as outlined in this book, four stages may be discerned in the relations of pre-Columbian America with the Old World. During the first, running approximately from 40,000 B.C. to 10,000 B.C., small bands of hunters from time to time crossed the Bering landmass from north-east Asia, infiltrating southwards when conditions permitted. These migrants represented a cross-section of the peoples of East Asia and were therefore far from uniform in race and colour.

The second period, from 10,000 B.C. to A.D. 1, marks the improvement of hunting techniques and the gradual development of agriculture, following the extinction of the larger mammals such as the horse and mastodon; pottery began to be made in the fourth millennium B.C. In Chapter Two, evidence was offered that New World agriculture developed independently, and in Chapter Three assertions that the potter's art was introduced from Japan were shown to rest on fragile foundations. During the second millennium B.C., the first higher civilizations arose in America; with their kings, priests, pyramids and palaces, they are readily comparable to those of the Old World. The succeeding chapters of the book revealed Olmec and Chavín as contemporaries, not of the golden ages of Greece or Persia, but of the Egyptian New Kingdom and the Chinese Shang Dynasty, powers technically unprepared for transoceanic voyages. Many centuries later, the odd Phoenician vessel *might* have withstood an unplanned voyage to

America, but incursions of this kind have left no proven traces. Nevertheless, during this second stage, America was not totally isolated since Eskimos – or their predecessors – continued to cross from Asia to Alaska; but few of these migrants penetrated southwards, and the Eskimos developed their own pattern of life.

The third period embraces the first centuries of the Christian era and marks the apogee of the great 'classic' cultures of America: Teotihuacán and the Maya in Mexico; Nazca and Mochica in Peru. The development of these from their Olmec and Chavín predecessors can now be traced in some detail, and only in certain specific aspects does 'classic' American art recall that of Asia. Of such likenesses, pottery forms common to Teotihuacán and the contemporary Chinese Han Dynasty are an obvious example. Like the Phoenicians, the Han Chinese built ships that *might* have survived an accidental oceanic crossing, and a Chinese crew *might* conceivably therefore have given added inspiration to the skilled potters of Teotihuacán. However, the copious Chinese records of that period preserve a stony silence concerning such expeditions, and during this epoch America seems to have been left largely to its own devices.

Our fourth stage runs from A.D. 800 to 1492. In Chapter Nine it was argued that Polynesian boats very possibly reached America, and the arrival of Peruvian sailing rafts in Polynesia, while less likely, cannot be excluded. The effect of any such landings remains ill-defined, and the differences between Polynesian and American culture far outweigh the similarities. The picture would change overnight if Polynesian objects were found in a pre-Columbian context, or vice-versa, but so far nothing of the kind has occurred.

Meanwhile, only the Vikings are known to have visited America before Columbus, and L'Anse aux Meadows bears witness to their arrival; however, Viking influence on the North American Indian was nil. Finally, in the wake of the Portuguese revolution in navigation, Christopher Columbus inaugurated a final phase, which combined contact with conquest.

The degree of intensity of Old and New World links can therefore be expressed in a U-shaped graph. The top left-hand arm of the U represents the long period during which the first groups of humans entered America via the Bering land bridge. The U-curve then descends as a period of localized contact sets in in the form of early Eskimos who crossed the Bering Strait. Then, after centuries of virtual separation, representing the bottom of the U, the curve rises again, as isolated incursions into America were resumed by the Vikings from the east, perhaps preceded by Polynesians from the west. Columbus' first voyage, at the upper right extremity of the U-curve, marks the renewal of close contact.

The Polynesians and Vikings did not discover America – since it was already inhabited – even if they 're-discovered' it on several occasions. The 'discovery' of a fourth continent did not even enter into Columbus' calculations since he remained convinced that he had reached the great Asian archipelago. The full European discovery of America began when Amerigo Vespucci published his *Mundus Novus* in 1503 and formally recognized that the territory was not an Asian archipelago, but a new world.* In the fifteenth century, the belief was still firmly held that the division of the known world into three continents, Europe, Asia and Africa, reflected the threefold nature of the Holy Trinity and was therefore immutable. However, the principle was also accepted that the boundless ocean might contain other territories in the form, not of a fourth continent, but of an entirely new world.

The classical Greeks, recognizing that the earth was round, had already suggested that two more continents might exist, Terra Australis and Terra Occidentalis. Aristotle admitted this possibility, but at times assumed that the world was very small and that the distance from Europe to Asia across the western ocean was therefore limited – precisely the idea that Columbus adopted in planning his first voyage. Ptolemy's *Geography*, first translated from Greek into Latin at the beginning of the fifteenth century, is a treatise on the construction of maps and the use of fixed co-ordinates of longitude and latitude for the purpose. The notion of a round world and a new continent survived the Greeks; in the fifth century A.D. the Roman philosopher Macrobius wrote a book that was still widely read in the Middle Ages and contained maps of the world showing other lands beyond the ocean; medieval notions, however, had to conform not only to the 'Trinity' of continents but also the belief that Jerusalem was the centre of the world.

Roman and Greek speculations could only be tested two thousand years after they were first formulated, when the Portuguese made their dramatic contributions to the art of sailing. The Portuguese, not the

Ancients, developed the caravel, put the compass to practical use, employed a quadrant to determine latitude, and prepared extensive charts.

Theories of planned contacts between pre-Columbian America and the Near or Far East gloss over the problems of forging links across ocean barriers in ancient times. Furthermore, believers in such feats rarely reflect whether, supposing that the peoples of the Old World *had* been equipped to reach the New, they would have had any urge to do so.

Columbus' project was to sail from a known location, the Canary Isles, to another named territory, the island of Cibolla (Japan). Compelling commercial reasons then existed for opening up a new route to the East, since contacts made by the Crusaders had caused the spread of a taste for oriental goods in Europe. Following the earlier exploits of Marco Polo, Genoese merchants established residences in central Asia, India and China, and Franciscan missionaries built a *fondaco* for Catholic traders in Hangchow. But open traffic between Europe and Asia came to an abrupt end in mid-fourteenth century because of the Black Death, which made strangers everywhere unwelcome since any caravan might carry plague. Other barriers to commerce were also raised after the Khanate was overthrown by the Ming rising of 1368; even if European merchants could still have penetrated to Peking, the new masters of China would not have allowed them to trade, and the doors which had opened so invitingly a century before were now slammed shut.*

Supplies of pepper and other Far Eastern spices could now once more only be obtained through Alexandria. Prices became prohibitive; after the Pope had been persuaded to lift his embargo on Egyptian trade, merchants still had to deal with the representatives of the Sultan of Turkey, who was in a position to squeeze them dry by forcing them to buy at his price.

Columbus' project, therefore, if successful, offered untold advantages to its sponsors; even so he endured years of disappointment and ridicule at Queen Isabella's court before she consented to back him. An Egyptian Pharaoh or a Chinese emperor would have been slow to open his coffers to a would-be explorer, whose only proposal was to sail off into the blue in an unsuitable craft, without an inkling of what land he sought, in what direction it lay, or how to steer a straight course to get there.

Even before the Renaissance, modern Man began to develop a craving for boundless horizons that was unknown in the Ancient World. Morocco and Portugal were made into provinces by the Romans, who never used them as an obvious springboard for Atlantic exploration; the Canaries had remained uninhabited, and Madeira was first discovered in 1420. Oswald Spengler, who published his famous *Decline of the West* in 1918, saw the urge to conquer limitless space as the prime symbol of the 'Faustian Soul'. For Spengler, the seafaring Vikings were already imbued with the new spirit: 'The will-to-power (to use Nietzsche's great formula) that from the earliest Gothic of the Eddas, the cathedrals and the Crusades, and even the old conquering Goths and Vikings, has distinguished the attitude of the Northern Soul to the World.'* The contrast between the soul of the Classical cultures, which he calls Apollonian, and the new spirit is reflected in the spatial vaulting of vast cathedrals, undertaken by the Faustian Soul in its springtime.

The Greeks went carefully, point by point, on the known tracks of Phoenicians and Carthaginians, but their curiosity did not stretch beyond the limits of the Mediterranean. The city, or *polis*, was the centre of the Greek world; to settle far from the coast would be to settle in loneliness, out of sight of home, and exceeded the possibilities of classical mankind. The founders of Greek colonies clung to their old way of life as a child clings to its mother's apron strings; their ideal was to create a new city moulded on the old and in close contact with its parent. By contrast, the Spaniards and Portuguese were imbued with what Spengler calls the 'Columbus-longing' which had inspired the Vikings centuries before.

It was the spirit of the Viking and the Hansa, of those dim peoples, so unlike the Hellenes with their domestic funerary urns, who heaped up great barrows as memorials of the lonely soul on the wide plains. The spirit of the Norsemen drove their cockle-boats in the tenth century that heralded the Faustian birth – to the coast of America. To the circumnavigation of Africa, already achieved by Egyptians and Carthaginians, Classical Mankind was wholly indifferent.*

Spengler is seldom quoted nowadays – in spite of his flair as a prophet of doom – but he was ahead of his time in many respects and accepted at their face value the saga stories of the Viking discovery of America when they were generally treated as myths. In contrast to these

Norsemen, the Egyptians sailed in their oared boats far along the coast to Punt, but the idea of a high seas voyage, and what it meant as a liberation or a symbol, was not in them. The Phoenicians may have circumnavigated Africa, but if they did, their coast-hugging expedition offered no terrors comparable to those of the empty ocean. The Celestial Empire in particular had a soul that was far from Faustian. As a Chinese sage reputedly said: 'We invented gunpowder, which we used to make fireworks, and we invented the compass, but we did not use it to come to Europe.' And yet these were precisely the inventions on which the Europeans depended to reach and conquer America.

Admittedly, between 1405 and 1433, when the Portuguese were beginning to explore the African coast, formidable Chinese fleets, dispatched by the Grand Eunuch Chang Ho, ranged over the Indian Ocean as far as the Persian Gulf. But the will for yet more daring exploits was lacking: the Portuguese forged ahead but the Chinese held back and abandoned the practice of sending out such fleets because of the threat to morals and public order posed by free intercourse with foreigners.*

If planned voyages *had* taken place – though carefully expunged from ancient records – they would probably have failed if unsupported by firearms. All but the first of the Viking voyages were intentional, but the settlers came up against the native skraelings and were hounded out. If a Chinese or Phoenician expedition had landed in a highly populated region of America, the skraelings would have appeared in force; after a brief period of friendly interchange, some awkward incident would have occurred, and the visitors would have been duly expelled – or perhaps killed and eaten. Not only did firearms provide victory in battles against overwhelming numbers of natives; their very possession often made initial resistance seem futile. Fire and thunder were inseparable from divinity; not only was Cortés at first taken for a deity, but Captain Cook in Hawaii was identified with the god Lono. Alternatively, if an Old World expedition had hit upon a barren region of America, a foothold might have been gained, but the impact on any nomad hunters roaming in such wastelands would have been minimal. Viking chessmen have been found in Eskimo sites in Greenland, but the Eskimos did not learn the game and merely used the chessmen as children's toys.

If a ship had made an unintentional crossing to America, the effect of its arrival would have been even smaller. To quote a known instance, a Spanish boat with sixteen men and two women on board was wrecked on the coast of Yucatan six years before Cortés arrived; the crew were all sacrificed and ritually eaten, with the exception of Gonzalo Guerrero and Jerónimo de Aguilar who were instead enslaved by two local chieftains. Of these survivors, Guerrero had gone so far native that he adorned himself with the accoutrements of his adopted tribe, including elaborate nose plug and earrings, and refused on any account to abandon his new life to join Cortés; even Aguilar, when first found by the Spaniards, had become indistinguishable from an Indian.

Survivors of accidental landings are much more likely to adopt the local culture than to spread their own. Where planned expeditions are concerned, the absence of the urge to undertake them and the insufficiency of technical means would have rendered such feats unlikely in ancient times.

Books suggesting that civilization was brought to America from some part of the Old World on a once-and-for-all basis usually argue that American Indian culture sprang up overnight; the gift-wrapped package labelled 'civilization' *must* therefore have been imported since its contents lack native antecedents.

But the belief that higher civilization developed suddenly belongs to a bygone age of archaeology that confined itself to the study of artefacts and aimed to portray an ancient culture only at its apogee. The new archaeology lays more stress on the *processes* by which that culture developed; scholars are no longer content to examine just the fruits of its maturity, but want to know how the tree grew and then blossomed. As a consequence, many gaps in our knowledge are being filled in: the emergence of *Homo sapiens* is seen as more gradual and complex than had formerly been believed and it is now appreciated that neither the civilizations of the Old World nor those of the New appeared so suddenly.

The long-drawn-out processes that led to the birth of agriculture in Mexico have been studied in minute detail by Richard MacNeish: in Peru, the Chavín culture is now recognized to be the outcome of an extended period of development. The emergence from humble beginnings of the great city of Teotihuacán and its development during the course of a thousand years have been meticulously charted in the

Teotihuacán Mapping Project. As a culmination to this laborious task, a computer data file was created, one that stores 281 different items of information on *each* of the 5,000 sections into which the city was divided for the purpose. In the course of the research, no less than 400 obsidian and 100 ceramic workshops were found to exist. From the vast store of computer data a clear picture was produced of just how the city grew to maturity and then declined. Rochester University archaeologist René Millon, who directed the work, would think anyone demented who suggested that the building of Teotihuacán had been supervised by Chinese Han Dynasty mandarins. Even in their own country they possessed nothing comparable in scope or grandeur.*

The concept of adventurous incursions by Cambodians or Chinese, bearing a Pandora's Box replete with Asian arts and crafts, may appeal to the romantics, but such visions belie the findings of modern archaeology. At first sight, notions of a New World pulling itself up by its own bootstraps seem rather banal beside those of an America redeemed from savagery by the crews of Alexander's fleet or by the Lost Tribes of Israel. But seen in closer perspective, the American Indian's long and lonely path to progress provides a tale more enthralling than the mere donning of borrowed plumes.

Once ideas of the sudden emergence of American civilization are discarded, believers in Old World expeditions before the Polynesians and Vikings depend upon comparisons among artefacts, languages and customs to demonstrate their point. But such parallels offer no proof of contact if they can be readily explained by independent invention. Sheer coincidence may not account for every likeness between peoples separated by vast oceans. Nevertheless modern instances are on record that involve a whole series of coincidences more wildly improbable than, say, the independent invention of identical stirrup-spout jars by Peruvians in 800 B.C. and Africans in A.D. 1930. Where pottery is concerned, the uses to which a vessel is put and the nature of the potter's clay may cause certain features to be repeated at different times and places.

Attention has already been drawn to the odd parallels between the assassinations of Presidents Kennedy and Lincoln. The same point is brought out even more forcibly by the prizewinning entry in a London *Sunday Times* competition for the best example of the working of chance. In 1838, Edgar Allan Poe published a story called 'The Narrative of Arthur Gordon Pym of Nantucket' in which a Mr Pym was shipwrecked. The four survivors spent many days in an open boat before they decided to kill and eat the youngest of them, whose name was Richard Parker. Over fifty years later, in 1884, the British yawl *Mignonette* foundered; four survivors of the wreck passed many days in an open boat before the three senior members killed and ate the cabin boy, named Richard Parker. *The Times* of London reported the case in its issue of 28 October 1884.*

Another example of the force of coincidence may be taken from the same competition: in July 1940, a Mr D. J. Page was on active service as a young soldier with Troop 'B' of his regiment. But in Troop 'A' of the same unit was a man named Pape, whose army number was 1509322, while Page's own number was 1509321; as a consequence, a mix-up in their mail occurred quite often. Some time after the war had ended, Mr Page was employed as a driver with London Transport at its Merton depot, in south-west London. On one particular pay day, Page noticed that his tax deduction was unduly heavy; to his amazement he discovered that the Pape with whom his mail had been confused in army days was now working as a driver in the same garage; by the weirdest hazard, Page's bus driver's licence number was 29222 and Pape's was 29223.

Beside such staggering instances, parallels between Old and New World cultures may at times seem trivial – if attributed to pure chance – and few would have gained a *Sunday Times* award. For instance, the existence of a handful of Polynesian words having some vague parallel in one of the two thousand languages of South America would not even win a booby prize, while like methods of drawing scroll patterns in China and America would not qualify as a serious entry.

The conclusions hardly differ even if a whole series of parallel art forms are taken together. Comparisons between Mayan and South-East Asian art are often quoted: monster heads with no lower jaw; stylized cosmic trees; rows of stone colonettes to decorate buildings; human figures emerging from an animal's mouth. But the odds against the Mayans and the Cambodians developing the same type of cosmic tree or stone colonette are dwarfed by the wild improbabilities involved in the story of Messrs Pape and Page. It is quite on the cards that Olmecs and Phoenicians should separately adopt sandals with upturned toes, but the odds against a seaman Richard Parker being killed and eaten by his three senior companions on two different occasions are long indeed.

The coincidences given in *The Sunday Times* might be viewed by occultists as arising out of some hidden or mystic relationship, unrelated to pure hazard, but such ideas belong to the realm of parapsychology. Writers who link Mexicans and South-East Asians shun the idea of cultural telepathy and are adamant in their insistence that the two peoples were in physical contact.

Sheer coincidence can account for many likenesses, but instances arise when it cannot provide the whole answer. Yet in some such cases, historical contact must be ruled out as well, when civilizations are not only divided by thousands of miles of ocean but by thousands of years in elapsed time.

Robert Heine-Geldern's famous comparisons between early Chinese and Mexican art forms led him to insist that Asians must have landed in Mexico. However, towards the end of his life Heine-Geldern made a further set of comparative studies, between the archaic Chinese and the New Zealand Maoris. The Viennese scholar boldly rejected the possibility that Maori art derived from Polynesia; the New Zealand forms, with their wealth of spirals and curvilinear designs, were quite different from the styles of the Polynesian islands with their simple repetitive patterns.* He drew comparisons between Maori and Chinese quite as close as those he had discovered between China and Mexico; to justify his findings, he suggested that the time-gap between late Chou (600 B.C.) and the first settlement of New Zealand might one day be closed.

But since 1966, when this was proposed, the archaeologists have been hard at work in New Zealand and have, if anything, widened the gap between Maori settlement and Chou Dynasty Chinese. The Maoris first came to New Zealand from Tahiti in A.D. 900–1000 and then began to develop their elaborate forms, which Europeans first beheld in A.D. 1769 People of the Chou Dynasty, therefore, could no more have been in contact with the creators of Maori art than George Washington could have been visited by the Ancient Greeks. And if an exchange of visits between Maoris and Chinese must be ruled out the same proposition loses much of its force in the case of Chinese–Mexican parallels.

New Zealand tattooing designs have been compared not with Asia but with America; Claude Lévi-Strauss pointed to a striking likeness between Maori tattooing and the body-painting of the Caduveo tribe, situated in south Brazil, near the Paraguayan border. Both peoples use amazingly similar patterns, and no tattooing or facial painting is nearly as complex in any other part of the world. In seeking a solution to this riddle, Lévi-Strauss remarks that neither alternative of historical contact or independent invention is easy to accept.*

The problem of relations between the Old World and the New has been distorted by the insistence that similar traits or forms found on both sides of the Pacific were the outcome of improbable feats of seamanship and colonization. Contact often offers the simplest explanation, but if historians deny this possibility, likenesses between two cultures are not then reduced to a mere illusion. Nor is the process of investigation thereby to be condemned, though scientists must then look elsewhere for an explanation. To quote Lévi-Strauss:

> If history says no, we must have recourse to psychology or to structural analysis of forms, and ask if internal connections of a psychological nature cannot make such recurrences intelligible – of a frequency and depth that are unlikely to arise by sheer chance.*

The same author contends that mythology and history are products of the unconscious working of the mind and, like Freud, he gives pre-eminence to the subconscious in human development. Freud himself, in *Totem and Tabu*, compares the psychology of primitive peoples to the workings of individual neuroses as they are revealed in psychoanalysis. He draws attention, for instance, to the draconian precautions primitive peoples universally take to guard against incest. But psychoanalysis shows that the same incest-phobia is a prevalent form of neurosis among individual children today.

Jung, who was foremost in relating psychology to ritual and art, points to the same basic mythological themes among peoples throughout the world. He calls these themes archetypes, forming part of the collective subconscious as distinct from the individual subconscious identified by Freud. For Jung, both dogma and myth are based on dreams and present a picture that transcends reason. The near-identical forms in many religions were never 'invented', but were 'born' before human beings had learned to formulate thoughts based on logic. As an example, Jung cites the magic sign of the number 4, which plays a leading part not only in ancient religions but in patients' dreams in the form of a circle divided into four parts or a table surrounded by four chairs. Colours are also universal symbols of magical meaning: they play a leading part in the liturgy of all peoples, and experimental psychology stresses the role of colour in the subconscious of the modern individual.

This concept of a common heritage of the human mind, derived from the dreams of an unfathomable past, finds parallels in the animal kingdom. Innate in the nervous system of many creatures are instincts that cause them to react spontaneously and without teaching to the perils that beset them. Chicks with eggshells still adhering to their tails will dart for cover when a hawk flies overhead, but not when the bird is a gull, heron or pigeon; if a wooden model of a hawk is drawn over their coop on a wire, they react as though it were alive unless it is drawn backwards, when there is no response. And, just as the fearful image of the hawk is an inherent part of the nervous system of the chick, so other deep-rooted images are inherent to the human psyche in the form of archetypes, common to whole groups and pregnant with meaning in prehistoric religion and ritual.

The mystical aspects of Jung's teaching may have lost their appeal, but few people would contradict his belief that mythology and dogma derive in part from dreams, stemming from the human nervous system. Men were dreaming when they were little more than apes, and myth is the product of those dreams.

Before Freud and Jung, Nietzsche had already pointed to this significance of dreams: 'When we dream, we repeat once more the task of the earlier stages of human-kind . . . dreaming transports us back to distant stages in the development of human civilization, and places in our hands a means of understanding it better.'* Lévi-Strauss sees myth as the living reflection of Man's scientific discoveries, which enabled him to exploit the world for his own use: the transformation of weeds into cultivated plants and of wild horses into domestic animals; the fashioning of stout pottery from unstable clay; the elaboration of complex techniques to permit cultivation without soil and often without water. The myths and rituals involved are so closely linked to nature that they are often meaningless without a precise knowledge of the plants and animals concerned.

254

Plants have an additional role to play in the forging of Man's attitudes to the unknown: the Indians of North and South America discovered nearly a hundred hallucinogenic plants, capable of triggering an ecstatic vision of the supernatural. Such practices, derived from Asia, played a major part in New World religions. Fly Agaric grows freely in Eastern Siberia, and palaeo-Asiatic peoples devoted a veritable cult to this hallucinogen. The fungus's name derives from the custom of German housewives, who used to crumble it into a saucer and set it on the windowsill to kill flies; the same red-spotted mushroom was shown in Walt Disney's *Fantasia*. Georg Wilhelm Steller of Leipzig describes the use of the hallucinogen in the Kamchatka Peninsula in 1774:

> Among the mushrooms the poisonous fly-agarics are dried, then eaten in large pieces without chewing them, washing them down with cold water. After about half an hour the person becomes completely intoxicated and experiences extraordinary visions. . . . Those who cannot afford the fairly high price drink the urine of those who have eaten it and become equally intoxicated, if not more so.

The narcotic complex that astonished early European explorers in America formed part and parcel of the cultural baggage brought by Siberian big-game hunters at the end of the Ice Age. An early start was made in the search for New World hallucinogens, and seeds of the red 'bean', widely used to produce ecstatic-visionary effects among the tribes of the southern plains, have been found in the Amistad Reservoir area of Texas, dated to 7000 B.C. Far from losing their appeal, trance-producing plants were cherished by the Aztecs in the final period before the Spaniards: the sacred mushrooms were known as 'The Meat of the Gods', and the seeds of the morning glory (whose chemical properties are closely related to L.S.D.) were regarded as divine.*

Based on a common heritage of practical experience and ecstatic religion, myths from different places are so alike that Man's cultural history becomes a single story. The detailed aspects of the Greek myth of Demeter, Hekate and Persephone are strikingly similar to the Indonesian rites of Sätene, Rabin and Hainuwele – the result, as Sir James Frazer realized, of like causes acting on like minds under different skies. Basic to both mythologies is a trinity of goddesses, identified with the local food plants. In both Greece and Indonesia the maiden goddess is married, dies, and descends to the underworld where, after a time, her metamorphosis into food follows.

Myths retain a basic identity all the world over and can become adapted to any new environment. For instance, the image of the divine being whose body became a food plant is adjusted to the natural elements of Oceania and the role of the serpent is played by its closest counterpart, the monster eel.

Out of universalized myths, parallel ritual and customs have pervaded every continent. Human sacrifice, usually accompanied by ritual eating of human flesh, is almost universal, as well as the practice among primitive tribes of smearing the body with paint or clay and of covering corpses with red ochre.

Initiation rites follow the same pattern, whether in Africa, America, Australia or Melanesia: first the novices are taken from their parents, symbolically 'killed' and kept hidden in forest or bush, where they are put through different tests; and then they are 'reborn' as members of the society. Afterwards the initiates are returned to their parents, who proceed to simulate all the phases of a new delivery.*

Parallels even arise between peoples separated by vast stretches of time as well as distance. On the walls of palaeolithic caves in Europe and Asia, silhouette handprints have been found that often show a loss of several fingers; but such offerings are also made among Indian tribes of the North American Plains, and in many cases a man would be left with only enough finger joints to notch an arrow and draw a bow. Peculiar customs connected with the cult of the bear were already practised in 15,000 B.C. but have survived into modern times. Leo Frobenius, who recognized this cultural continuum, described a cave near Montespan, Haute Garonne, where a rough clay model of a young bear had been found: the head of the image had been cut off and placed between its forepaws. But among the Ainu, who still survive in northern Japan, an elaborate ceremony is performed which ends with the ritual killing of a young bear, whose head is then severed and revered as a sacred object.*

Studies in pre-Columbian links with the Old World are based more on parallels in art than in usage. But art was born of myth and ritual, both in our own Western civilization and among primitive peoples. And just as many ritual customs, forming part of Man's collective heritage from a distant past, appear in diverse places, so specific art forms, symbolic renderings of those rituals, recur in cultures thousands of years removed from each other.

The 'split-image' comprises a drawing in which an animal illustration is cut in two from head to tail; the two halves are then pulled apart and laid out on a flat surface facing each other, with the twin profiles joined together only at mouth and nose. This strange motif was used in archaic China in 1200 B.C. but survived into recent times among the Haida Indians of the north-west coast of America.

Another timeless and universal art form is the 'heraldic woman', the image of a female figure, flanked by two identical beings and holding her knees apart to expose the genital area. Clay statuettes of a woman giving birth, seated on a kind of throne, with a leopard on each side, already appear in Chatal Huyuk in Anatolia in the sixth millennium B.C.; females supported by identical serpents also occur in India in 3000 B.C. Figures in the distinctive posture of the heraldic woman with legs wide apart, flanked by two beings, first appear in Luristan about 1000 B.C. In Europe, the heraldic woman is to be found in Etruscan art, and subsequent Italian specimens include a carving on a Romanesque capital in Piacenza cathedral. In Asia, the design occurs in Han Dynasty times and in Oceania is present among the New Zealand Maori. In America, the heraldic woman reappears among the Indians of the north-west coast and a Haida slate pipe depicts a displayed female figure flanked by two enormous birds. The motif is also found in central Peru about A.D. 300, in the guise of a woman with legs spread apart, with felines on each side.*

Since prehistoric designs and rituals still survive, in a sense Primitive Man is our contemporary. The well of the past is deep, and the roots of civilization, including art, stretch far back into the Ice Age Millennia, perhaps centuries of millennia, lie between ourselves and those hunters of earlier days whose usages and customs live on in remote parts of the world. The whole human process, stemming from the human brain, is only starting to be examined. Some scholars are confident that neurologists will one day find out what part of the brain gives Man his capacity for language and even for art.

Alexander Marshak recently made a study of the complex markings scratched or engraved on animal bones in European prehistoric sites. By microscopic analysis, Marshak concluded that 30,000 years ago Man had already begun to develop a tradition of symbolic notation, perhaps connected with the phases of the moon, and the measurement of time.* These early hunters slowly increased their understanding and could adapt their rites and myths to very different conditions, as the ice melted and the face of the World changed. As yet, the cognitive steps that led from these post-glacial cultures to the beginnings of agriculture – and thence to higher civilization – are little understood.

Lévi-Strauss likens these successive stages in Man's ascent to a continuous card game: each human community is like a player who has taken his place at the table and picks up cards which he has not invented. Every deal in the game produces a particular distribution of the cards, unknown to the player at the time; he must accept the hand he is given and employ it as best he can. Obviously different players will vary their approach to the same hand, though the rules set limits to the different games that can be played with a given set of cards.

As between the chick and the hawk, so in human history a kind of lock–key relationship seems to exist. Age-long images from the subconscious may on occasion be unleashed upon the conscious mind of the group and trigger a given response. Artistic creation is not the product of a mere searching for pretty forms but, like an archetypal invader, swells up within the soul of diverse peoples and expresses their common fears and longings. Different in kind but subject to the rules of the same game, such peoples may be neighbours or may be separated by boundless seas.

The perennial problem takes us back to relations between archaic China and the civilizations of Ancient America and of New Zealand. Both questions were studied by the same eminent orientalist, Heine-Geldern, who arrived at similar conclusions in each instance. The purely artistic parallels were so close and numerous that in neither case could he attribute them to mere chance. Heine-Geldern thereupon applied his only yardstick to the problem and insisted that the art of both Olmec-Chavín and of the New Zealand Maori owed its inspiration to contact with Chou China. But such possibilities recede once it becomes clear that Olmec and Chavín beginnings precede Early Chou and that New Zealand was first inhabited one thousand five hundred years after Late Chou.

However, the lock–key parallel might apply in both instances. China has the best claim to rank as the point of departure both for the hunters who became the American Indians and for the seafarers who were the Polynesians' ancestors. In America and China the birth of higher civilization more or less coincided, after the stage had been set by the discovery of plant cultivation. The two peoples had then been separated for some three hundred generations – or about one-350th of the time since Man first began to develop – but they had once shared many like dreams, myths and rituals. Chinese and Americans might be compared to two players who sat at the card table at about the same time; they could not play identical games since each had different, if comparable hands, but in their manipulation of the cards they displayed a common touch, and uncanny parallels were visible in the outcome.

In the case of the Maoris, perhaps a small group left the coast of China in about 3000 B.C. and after many wanderings settled in Tonga and Samoa two thousand years later and became the first Polynesians, so distinct from the dusky Melanesians through whose lands they had passed. Since they were confined within the limits of their small islands, agriculture flourished but the cultural harvest was modest. These Polynesians, however, then hit upon the broader expanse of New Zealand and the scene was transformed. New vistas opened before them and a situation arose more comparable to archaic China; then only did the key fit the lock, and the latent talents peculiar to these Polynesian emigrants from China could be displayed on a much broader canvas. In New Zealand they rose to the occasion and created works of art recalling the genius of Late Chou China, whose people probably shared the same background and the same innate potential.

Neither duplicate invention nor historic contact suffices to account for all those strange likenesses, and science still lacks ways of determining whether certain forms are related: whether, for instance, Ecuadorians did or did not copy Japanese pottery, or whether Maori woodcarving was linked to the totem poles of the north-west coast or Maori tattooing to the body painting of the Brazilian tribes.

The science of anthropology is hardly a century old. Achievements have been so spectacular that we can barely guess what the coming era may bring forth; with the aid of the techniques of tomorrow, the pace of progress may even quicken. More attention is already being paid, not only to the growth of civilization, but to the burgeoning of its creators' minds. The 'history of mentality' is now a recognized subject of study, and in France a scientific journal bears the name *La Revue d'ethnopsychologie des peuples*.

But no breakthrough can ever spring from the sterile pursuit of mulling over analogies between Asian and American art inherited from our grandfathers, and then – as an alcoholic will reach for the bottle –

instinctively drawing the same banal conclusions and charting the same imaginary voyages between peoples that belong to different epochs as well as to different worlds.

Anthropologists face the challenge of probing deeper into those ties that seem to transcend time and space. The haze which clings to such enigmas will surely one day lift, dispelled with the aid of new facts and of new approaches that temper boldness with balance.

BIBLIOGRAPHY

Acosta, Padre Joseph de, *Historia Natural y Moral de las Indias* (Mexico City–Buenos Aires: Fondo de Cultura Económica, 1962).

Anales de Cuauhtitlan, *see Codex Chimalpopoca*.

Anderson, Douglas, 'A Stone Age Campsite at the Gateway to America', in *Early Man: readings from the Scientific American* (San Francisco, Calif., 1968).

Asimov, Isaac, *The Universe* (Harmondsworth: Penguin, 1971).

Ayres, William S., *Easter Island: an investigation in cultural dynamics* (Columbia, S.C.: University of South Carolina Press, 1975).

Beaglehole, J. C., *Exploration of the Pacific* (Stanford, Calif.: Stanford University Press, 1966; London: A. & C. Black, 1966).

Bellamy, H. S., *Built before the Flood* (London: Faber, 1943).

Bellwood, Peter, 'The Prehistory of Oceania', in *Current Anthropology*, vol. 16, no. 1 (Chicago, 1975).

Berlitz, Charles, *Mysteries from Forgotten Worlds* (New York: Doubleday, 1972).

Bernal, Ignacio, *El Mundo Olmeca* (Mexico City: Editorial Porrúa S.A., 1968).

Beyer, Hermann, *Complete Works*, vol. 1 (El Mexico Antiguo, vol. x) (Mexico City, 1965).

Bierne, Daniel Randall, 'Cultural Patterning as Revealed by a Study of Pre-Columbian Ax and Adz Hafting in the New and Old Worlds', in *Man across the Sea*, ed. Riley (Austin, Tex.: University of Texas Press, 1971).

Birell, Vera, 'Transpacific Contacts and Peru', in *Proceedings of the 35th International Congress of Americanists*, vol. 1 (Mexico City, 1964).

Bischof, Henning, 'The Origins of Pottery in South America', in *Proceedings of the 40th International Congress of Americanists*, vol. 1 (Rome, 1974).

Bosch Gimpera, Pedro, *Historia de Oriente* (Mexico City: Universidad Nacional Autónoma, 1973).

Braddon, Russell, *The Hundred Days of Darien* (London: Collins, 1974).

Brand, Donald D., 'The Sweet Potato, an Exercise in Methodology', in *Man across the Sea*, ed. Riley (Austin, Tex.: University of Texas Press, 1971).

Bronsted, Johannes, *The Vikings* (Harmondsworth: Penguin, 1965).

Campbell, Joseph, *The Masks of God: primitive mythology* (New York: Viking Press, 1959).

Capell, Arthur, 'Oceanic Linguistics Today', in *Current Anthropology*, vol. 3 (Chicago, 1962).

Caso, Alfonso, 'Relations between the Old and New Worlds: a note on methodology', in *Proceedings of the 35th International Congress of Americanists*, vol. 1 (Mexico City, 1964).

—, *El Pueblo de Sol* (Mexico City: Fondo de Cultura Económica, 1953).

Casson, Lionel, *The Ancient Mariners* (London: Gollancz, 1959).

—, *Ships and Seamanship in the Ancient World* (Princeton, N.J.: Princeton University Press, 1971).

Casteel, Richard W., 'The Relationship between Population Size and Carrying Capacity in a Sample of North American Hunter-Gatherers', in *Proceedings of the 9th Congress of Anthropological and Ethnological Sciences* (Chicago, 1973).

Castle, E. P. and Thiering, B. B. (eds), *Some Trust in Chariots* (Folkestone: Bailey Bros, 1973).

Cavalli-Sforza, L. L., 'The Genetics of Human Populations', in *Scientific American*, vol. 231, no. 3 (San Francisco, Calif., 1974).

Cavendish, Richard (ed.), *Encyclopaedia of the Unexplained: magic, occultism and parapsychology* (London: Routledge, 1974).

Ceram, C. W., *The First American* (New York: Mentor, 1972).

Charroux, Robert, *Lost Worlds* (New York: Walker, 1973).

Churchward, James, *The Lost Continent of Mu* (London: Futura, 1974).

Cieza de León, *Crónica del Peru* (Madrid: Imprenta Manuel Ginés Hernández, 1880).

Codex Chimalpopoca (Mexico City: Imprenta Universitaria, 1945).

Coe, Michael D., 'Archaeological Linkages with North and South America at La Victoria, Guatemala', in *American Anthropologist*, vol. 62 (1960).

—, 'San Lorenzo and the Olmec Civilization', Dumbarton Oaks Congress on the Olmec, Dumbarton Oaks Research Library, Washington, D.C., 1967.

—, *America's First Civilization* (New York: American Heritage, 1968, and Van Nostrand Reinhold, 1969).

Cook, Capt. James, *A Voyage towards the South Pole and Round the World* (London: William Strahan, 1784).

Coon, Carleton, *The History of Man from the First Human to Primitive Culture and Beyond* (London: Jonathan Cape, 1955).

Cottrell, Leonard, *The Tiger of Chi'in: how China became a nation* (London: Evans, 1963).

Däniken, Erich von, *Chariots of the Gods* (London: Souvenir Press, 1969, and Corgi, 1971).

—, *The Gold of the Gods* (New York: Putnam, 1973).

—, *Return to the Stars* (London: Souvenir Press, 1970, and Corgi, 1974).

Davies, Nigel, *The Aztecs* (London: Macmillan, 1973; New York: Putnam, 1974).

Díaz del Castillo, Bernal, *The Bernal Díaz Chronicles*, trans. and ed. Albert Idell (New York: Doubleday, 1956).

Dixon, Roland B., *The Building of Cultures* (New York: Scribner, 1928).

Dobrizhoffer, Martin, *An Account of the Abripones, an Equestrian People of Paraguay*, trans. from the Latin edn of 1784 by Sara Coleridge (London, 1822).

Donnelly, Ignatius, *Atlantis: the ante-diluvian world* (New York: Harper, 1880); ed. Egerton Sykes (London: Sidgwick & Jackson, 1970).

Doran, Edwin, Jnr, 'The Sailing Raft as a Great Tradition', in *Man across the Sea*, ed. Riley (Austin, Tex.: University of Texas Press, 1971).

Durán, Fray Diego, *Historia de las Indias de Nueva España e Islas de la Tierra Firme* (Mexico City: Editorial Porrúa S.A., 1967).

Easby, D. T., Jnr, 'Early Metallurgy in the New World', in *Scientific American*, vol. 204 (San Francisco, Calif., 1966).

Edwards, C. R., 'Sailing Rafts of Sechura: history and problems of origin', in *Southwest Journal of Anthropology*, vol. 16 (Albuquerque, N. Mex., 1960).

Ekholm, Gordon, 'Transpacific Contacts', in *Prehistoric Man in the New World*, ed. Jennings and Norbeck (Chicago University Press).

—, 'The Possible Chinese Origin of Teotihuacan Cylindrical Tripod Pottery and Certain Related Traits', in *Proceedings of the 35th International Congress of Americanists*, vol. 1 (Mexico City, 1964).

Ekholm, Gordon and Heine-Geldern, Robert, 'Significant Parallels in the Symbolic Arts of Southern Asia', in *29th International Congress of Americanists, Selected Papers* (Chicago, 1951).

Elbert, Samuel H., 'Internal Relationships of Polynesian Languages and Dialects', in *Southwest Journal of Anthropology*, vol. 9 (Albuquerque, N. Mex., 1953).

Eliseef, V., *Calcul et formalisation dans les sciences de l'homme* (Paris: Editions du Centre National de la Recherche Scientifique, 1968).

Emory, Kenneth P., 'Easter Island's Position in the Prehistory of Polynesia', in *Journal of the Polynesian Society*, vol. 81, no. 1 (Wellington, N.Z., 1972).

Erasmus, J., 'Patolli, Pachesi and the Limitation of Possibilities', in *Southwest Journal of Anthropology*, vol. 6 (Albuquerque, N. Mex., 1950).

Evans, Clifford and Meggers, Betty J., 'A Transpacific Contact in 3000 B.C.', in *Scientific American*, vol. 214, no. 1 (San Francisco, Calif., 1966).

Ferguson, Thomas Stuart, *One Fold, One Shepherd* (San Francisco, Calif.: Books of California, 1958).

Ferré, Ricardo, 'El Antropógeno de Siberia y el Hombre Americano', *Serie Investigaciones*, vol. 8 (Mexico City: Instituto de Antropología e Historia, 1965).

Florentine Codex, see Sahagún, Fray Bernardino de.

Foote, P. G. and Wilson, D. M., *The Viking Achievement* (London: Sidgwick & Jackson, 1970).

Fraser, Douglas, *The Many Faces of Primitive Art* (Englewood Cliffs, N.J.: Prentice-Hall, 1966).

Furst, Peter, 'The Olmec Were-Jaguar Motif in the Light of Ethnographic Reality', Dumbarton Oaks Congress on the Olmec, Dumbarton Oaks Research Library, Washington, D.C., 1967.

—, 'Morning Glory and the Mother Goddess at Tepantitla', in *Mesoamerican Archaeology, New Approaches*, ed. Norman Hammond (London: Duckworth, 1974).

Gladwyn, Harold S., *Men out of Asia* (New York: Whittlesey House, 1947).

Gordon, Cyrus, *Before Columbus* (London: Turnstone Press, 1972).

—, *Riddles in History* (New York: Crown, 1974; London: Arthur Barker, 1974).

Grobmann, A., Sevilla, R., and Mangelsdorf, P. C., *Races of Maize in Peru*, National Academy of Sciences and National Research Council publication no. 915 (Washington, D.C., 1961).

Haag, William, 'The Bering Strait Land Bridge', in *Early Man in America: readings from the Scientific American* (San Francisco, Calif., 1962).

Hahn, Albert, *see under* Hissink, Karin.

Harlan, Jack R., 'Agricultural Origins: centers and non-centers', in *Science*, vol. 174, no. 4008 (Lancaster, Pa, 1971).

Harrington, C. R., *see under* Irving, W. N.

Hawkes, Jacquetta, *The First Great Civilizations* (London: Hutchinson, 1973).

Heine-Geldern, Robert, 'Representation of the Asiatic Tiger in the Art of the Chavín Culture: a proof of early contacts between China and Peru', in *Proceedings of the 33rd International Congress of Americanists*, vol. 1 (San José, Costa Rica, 1958).

—, 'A Note on Relations between the Art Styles of the Maori and Ancient China', in *Wiener Beiträge zur Kulturgeschichte und Linguistik*, Band xv (Vienna, 1966).

—, 'Traces of Indian and Southeast Asiatic Hindu–Buddhist Influence in Mesoamerica', in *Proceedings of the 35th International Congress of Americanists*, vol. 1 (Mexico City, 1964).

—, *see also under* Ekholm, Gordon.

Heirtzler, J. R., 'Where the Earth Turns Inside Out', in *National Geographic Magazine*, vol. 147, no. 5 (Washington, D.C., 1975).

Hemmer, H., 'The Evolutionary Significance, Taxonomy and Environmental Aspects of the Upper Pleistocene, Neanderthal and Neanderthaloid Men of Europe, Asia and Africa', in *Proceedings of the UNESCO Symposium on the Origin of Homo Sapiens* (Paris, 1972).

Herm, Gerhard, *Die Phönizier* (Düsseldorf: Econ Verlag, 1973).

Heyerdahl, Thor, *American Indians in the Pacific: the theory behind the Kon-Tiki Expedition* (London: Allen & Unwin, 1952).

—, *The Ra Expeditions* (London: Allen & Unwin, 1972).

—, 'Inca Inspiration behind the Spanish Discovery of Polynesia and Melanesia', in *Proceedings of the 36th International Congress of Americanists*, vol. 1 (Madrid, 1964).

—, 'An Introduction to the Discussion of Transoceanic Contacts', in *Proceedings of the 37th International Congress of Americanists* (Buenos Aires, 1968).

Hissink, Karin and Hahn, Albert, *Die Tacana: Ergebuisse der Frobenius Expedition nach Bolivien, 1952 bis 1954* (Erzählungsgut, vol. 1) (Stuttgart, 1961).

Ho Ping-Ti, 'The Loess and the Origins of Chinese Agriculture', in *American Historical Review*, vol. 75 (1969).

Hopkins, D. M. (ed.), *The Bering Land Bridge* (Stanford, Calif.: Stanford University Press, 1968).

Imbelloni, J., *Fuegidos y Languidos* (Buenos Aires: Imprenta de la Universidad, 1937).

Ingstad, Helge, *Westward to Vinland* (London: Jonathan Cape, 1969).

Irving, W. N. and Harrington, C. R., 'Upper Pleistocene Radiocarbon Dates of Artefacts from the Northern Yukon', in *Science*, vol. 179, no. 4071 (Washington, D.C., 1973).

Irwin, Constance, *Fair Gods and Stone Faces* (London, 1963).

BIBLIOGRAPHY

Ixtlilxóchitl, Fernando de Alva, *Obras Históricas*, 2 vols (Mexico City: Editoria Nacional, 1952).

Jairazbhoy, R. A., *Ancient Egyptians and Chinese in America* (London: George Prior, 1974).

Jeffreys, M. D. W., 'Some Problems of Interpreting Transoceanic Dispersal of the New World Cottons', in *Man across the Sea*, ed. Riley (Austin, Tex.: University of Texas Press, 1971).

Jett, Stephen C., 'Diffusion versus Independent Invention', in *Man across the Sea*, ed. Riley (Austin, Tex.: University of Texas Press, 1971).

Jones, George, *The Original History of Aboriginal America* (London, 1843).

Jones, Gwyn, *A History of the Vikings* (Oxford University Press, 1968).

Kidder, A. V., *An Introduction to the Study of South Western Archaeology* (New Haven, Conn.: Yale University Press, 1962).

Kirchhoff, Paul, 'The Diffusion of a Great Religious System from India to Mexico', *Proceedings of the 35th International Congress of Americanists*, vol. 1 (Mexico City, 1964).

Klein, Richard D., *The Pleistocene History of Siberia* (Quaternary Research, vol. 1) (Seattle, Wash., 1971).

Knöbl, Kuno, *Tai-Ki* (Vienna: Verlag Fritz Molden, 1974).

Kolosimo, Peter, *Timeless Earth* (New Hyde Park, N.Y.: University Books, 1973).

Lanning, Edward, *Peru before the Incas* (Englewood Cliffs, N.J.: Prentice-Hall, 1968).

Las Casas, Bartolomé de, *Tratados* (Mexico City–Buenos Aires: Fondo de Cultura Económica, 1965).

Le Plongeon, Augustus, *Queen Moo and the Egyptian Sphinx* (New York, 1900).

Lévi-Strauss, Claude, *Antropologie structurale* (Paris: Librairie Plon, 1958).

—, *La Pensée sauvage* (Paris: Librairie Plon, 1962).

Lewis, David, *We, the Navigators* (Honolulu: University Press of Hawaii, 1972).

Lucas, F. W., *The Annals of the Voyages of the Brothers Niccolo and Antonio Zeno* (London: Stevens Sons & Styles, 1898).

Luce, J. V., *The End of Atlantis* (London: Thames & Hudson, 1968).

MacIntosh, N. W. C., 'The Aboriginal Australian: world's first mariner?', *University of Sydney News*, vol. 6, no. 7 (Sydney, 1974).

MacNeish, Richard, 'Investigation in the Southwest Yukon', in *Papers of the Peabody Foundation for Archaeology*, vol. 6 (Andover, Mass., 1964).

—, *El Origen de la Civilización Mesoamericana vista desde Tehuacán* (Mexico City: I.N.A.H. Departmento de Prehistoria, 1964).

—, *First Annual Report of the Ayacucho Archaeological–Botanical Project* (Andover, Mass.: Phillips Academy, 1969).

—, *Second Annual Report of the Ayacucho Archaeological–Botanical Project* (Andover, Mass.: Phillips Academy, 1970).

—, 'Early Man in the Andes', in *Early Man in America: readings from the Scientific American* (San Francisco, Calif., 1971).

Man across the Sea: problems of pre-Columbian contacts, ed. Carroll L. Riley and others (Austin, Tex.: University of Texas Press, 1971).

Marshak, Alexander, *The Roots of Civilization* (New York: McGraw-Hill, 1972).

Martínez del Río, Pablo, *Los Origines Americanos* (Páginas del Siglo, xx) (Mexico City, 1952).

Martir de Anglería, Pedro, *Decadas del Nuevo Mundo* (Buenos Aires: Edición Bajel, 1944).

Mastache de Escobar, Guadalupe, *Técnicas Prehispánicas del Tejido*, I.N.A.H. Publication no. 20 (Mexico City, 1971).

Matthews, Samuel W., 'The Changing Earth', in *The National Geographic Magazine*, vol. 143, no. 1 (Washington, D.C., 1973).

Millon, René, 'The Study of Urbanism at Teotihuacán, Mexico', in *Mesoamerican Archaeology, New Approaches*, ed. Norman Hammond (London: Duckworth, 1974).

Meggers, Betty J., *see* Evans, Clifford.

Mendieta, Fray Gerónimo de, *Historia Ecclesiástica Indiana*, 4 vols (Mexico City: Editorial Chavez Hayhoe, 1945).

Métraux, Alfred, *L'Île de Pâques* (Paris: Editions Gallimard, 1941).

Michener, James A. and Day, A. Grove, *Rascals in Paradise* (Greenwich, Conn.: Fawcett, 1957; London: Corgi, 1970).

Mochanov, Y. A., 'Early Migration to America in the Light of a Study of the Dyuktai Palaeolithic Culture in North-East Asia', in *Proceedings of the IXth Congress of Anthropological and Ethnological Sciences* (Chicago, Ill., 1973).

Morison, Samuel Eliot, *The European Discovery of America: the southern voyages, 1492–1616* (New York/Oxford: Oxford University Press, 1974).

Motolinía, Fray Toribio de Benavente, *Historia de los Indios de Nueva España* (Mexico City: Editorial Chavez Hayhoe, 1941).

Muller, Jon, 'Pre-Columbian Contacts. The Dryland Approach', in *Man across the Sea*, ed. Riley (Austin, Tex.: University of Texas Press, 1971).

Needham, Sir Joseph, *Science and Civilization in China*, 4 vols (Cambridge University Press, 1954–65).

Nekrasov, I. A., *see* Okhladnikov, A. P.

Nordensköld, Erland, *Origins of the Indian Civilizations of South America* (Göteborg: Erlanders Boktrykeri, 1931).

O'Gorman, Edmundo, *La Invención de América* (Mexico City: Fondo de Cultura Económica, 1958).

Okhladnikov, A. P., 'Ancient Settlements in the Main River Valley, Chukchi Peninsula', in *American Antiquity*, vol. xxvii (Salt Lake City, Utah, 1962), pp. 546–56.

Okhladnikov, A. P. and Nekrasov, I. A., 'New Traces of an Inland Neolithic Culture in the Chukotsk Peninsula', in *American Antiquity*, vol. xxv (Salt Lake City, Utah, 1959), pp. 247–56.

Parry, J. H., *The Discovery of the Sea* (London: Weidenfeld & Nicolson, 1975).

Paul, Günter, *Unsere Nachbarn im Weltall* (Düsseldorf: Econ Verlag, 1976).

Pearson, R., 'Migration from Japan to Ecuador: the Japanese evidence', in *American Anthropologist*, vol. 64 (Menasha, Wis., 1968), pp. 85–6.

Perry, W. J., *The Children of the Sun: a study in the early history of civilization* (London: Methuen, 1923).

Ping-Ti, Ho, *see* Ho Ping-Ti.

Pohl, F. J., *Prince Henry Sinclair* (London: Davis-Poynter, 1974).

Pörtner, Rudolf, *Die Wikinger-Saga* (Düsseldorf: Econ Verlag, 1971).

Prescott, William H., *History of the Conquest of Mexico* (London: Richard Bentley and J. M. Dent, 1963; Chicago, Ill.: University of Chicago Press, 1966).

Quevedo, Samuel A. Lafone, *El Culto de Tonapa. Los Himnos Sagrados de los Reyes del Cuzco según el Yamqui Pachacuti* (Lima, 1892).

Reiche, Maria, *Los Dibujos Gigantescos en el Suelo de las Pampas de Bazca* (Lima, 1949).

Rivet, Paul, *Los Origines del Hombre Americano* (Mexico City: Fondo de Cultura Económica, 1960).

Rowe, J. H., 'Stirrup-Spout Bottles from Central Africa', in *American Antiquity*, vol. xxx (Salt Lake City, Utah, 1965).

—, 'Diffusionism and Archaeology', in *American Antiquity*, vol. xxxi (Salt Lake City, Utah, 1966).

Sahagún, Fray Bernardino de, *Florentine Codex*, trans. from the Nahuatl by J. O. Anderson and Charles E. Dibble (Santa Fé, N. Mex.: University of Utah Press, 1950).

—, *Historia General de las Cosas de Nueva España*, 6 vols (Mexico City: Editorial Porrúa S.A., 1956).

Sahlins, Marshall, *Stone Age Economics* (London: Tavistock, 1972).

Sampaio, Fernando G., *A Verdade sobre os Deuses Astronautas* (Pôrto Alegre: Editora Movimento, 1973).

Santa Cruz Pachacuti, Juan de, *Tres Antiguedades Peruanas* (Madrid: Ministerio de Fomento, 1879).

Sauer, C. O., 'Cultivated Plants of South and Central America', in *Handbook of South American Indians*, vol. iv (Washington, D.C.: U.S. Government Printing Office, 1950).

Savoy, Gene, *On the Trail of the Feathered Serpent* (New York: Bobbs-Merrill, 1974).

Sharp, Andrew, *Ancient Voyages in the Pacific* (Harmondsworth: Penguin, 1957).

Shulter, Richard, Jnr, and Mary Elizabeth, *Oceanic Prehistory* (Menlo Park, Calif.: Cummings, 1975).

Sinoto, Y. H., 'An Archaeologically Based Assessment of the Marquesas as a Dispersal Center in East Polynesia', in *Studies in Oceanic Cultural History*, vol. i (Honolulu: Bernice P. Bishop Museum, 1970).

Simmons, R. T., 'Blood Group Genes in Polynesia and Comparisons with Other Pacific Peoples', in *Peoples and Cultures of the Pacific*, ed. Andrew P. Vayda (New York: Natural History Press, 1968).

Smith, Sir Grafton Elliot, *Human History* (New York: Norton, 1929).

Solheim, William C., 'An Earlier Agricultural Revolution', in *Scientific American* (San Francisco, Calif., 1972).

Spence, Lewis, *The Occult Causes of the Present War* (London, 1941).

Spengler, Oswald, *The Decline of the West* (New York: Alfred Knopf, 1926–8; London: Allen & Unwin, 1932).

Stephens, John Lloyd, *Incidents of Travel in Yucatan* (Oklahoma City: University of Oklahoma Press, 1962).

Stephens, S. C., 'Phaseolus: Diffusion and Centers of Origin', in *Man across the Sea*, ed. Riley (Austin, Tex.: University of Texas Press, 1971).

'The Strange Case of the Vinland Map', in *The Geographic Journal*, vol. 140, no. 2 (London, 1974).

Suggs, Robert C., *Lords of the Pacific* (New York: Geographic Society, 1962).

Suzuki, I., 'Chronology of Prehistoric Human Activity in the Kanto District, Japan', in *Proceedings of the IXth International Congress of Anthropological and Ethnological Sciences* (Chicago, Ill., 1973).

Tarrifi, Natalia Rosi de, *America, Cuarta Dimensión* (Caracas: Editores Monte Avila, 1969).

Taylor, Sir E. B., *Anthropology: an introduction to the study of Man and civilization* (London: Macmillan, 1881).

Taylor, E. G. R., *The Haven-finding Art* (London: Hollis & Carter, 1956).

Temple, Robert K. G., *The Sirius Mystery* (London: Sidgwick & Jackson, 1976).

Thompson, J. O., *A History of Ancient Geography* (London, 1964).

Torquemada, Fray Juan de, *Monarquia Indiana*, 3 vols (Mexico City: Editorial Chavez Hayhoe, 1943–4).

Vayda, Andrew P. (ed.), *Peoples and Cultures of the Pacific* (New York: Natural History Press, 1968).

Vega, Garcilaso de la, *Royal Commentaries on the Incas and General History of Peru* (Austin, Tex.: University of Texas Press, 1966).

Velikovsky, I., *Worlds in Collision* (London: Gollancz, 1950; Abacus, 1973).

Wallis, Helen, *see* 'Strange Case'.

Waterman, T. T., 'Some Conundrums in Northwest Coast Art', in *American Anthropologist*, vol. xxv (Menasha, Wis., 1923), pp. 368–91.

Watson, William, *China before the Han Dynasty* (New York: Praeger, 1961).

Wauchope, Robert, *Lost Tribes and Sunken Continents* (Chicago, Ill.: University of Chicago Press, 1962).

Whitaker, Thomas W., 'Endemism and Pre-Columbian Migration of the Bottle Gourd', in *Man across the Sea*, ed. Riley (Austin, Tex.: University of Texas Press, 1971).

Willey, Gordon, 'Olmec and Chavín: the early great styles and the rise of the pre-Columbian civilizations', in *American Anthropologist*, vol. 64.

Williamson, George Hunt, *Secret Places of the Lion* (London: Futura, 1974).

Wilson, D. M., *see* Foote, P. G.

Wuthenau, Alexander von, *Altamerikanische Tonplastik* (Holleverlag, 1965).

LIST OF SOURCES

CHAPTER 1. A PERENNIAL PROBLEM

1 Queen Moo: Wauchope, pp. 12–13.
2 Rowe, 'Diffusionism and Archaeology', p. 337.
2 Aztec emissaries: Davies, pp. 3–4.
4 Wauchope, chs 1, 2 and 6.
5 Viscount Kingsborough: ibid., pp. 51–2.
13 Traits in common: Birell, p. 36.
16 Chinese bronzes: Eliseef, p. 10.
16 Muller, pp. 70–2.
17 Voliva: Cavendish (ed.), *Encyclopaedia of the Unexplained*, p. 66.

CHAPTER 2. THE NORTHERN TRAIL

22 Continental drift: *National Geographic*, January 1973.
24 The Bering bridge: Hopkins, pp. 90–120 and 373.
24 Bridge characteristics: Haag, p. 11.
26 Siberian temperatures: Okhladnikov and Nekrasov, p. 248.
27 Hunting ground: Casteel, p. 1.
28 Malthus quotation: ibid., p. 10.
28 Sahlins, pp. 1–39.
28 Protection against cold: Klein, p. 99.
31 Ceram, p. 322.
34 Earliest human occupation: Irving and Harrington, pp. 335–40.
34 MacNeish, 'Early Man in the Andes', pp. 69–79.
35 British Mountain Tradition: MacNeish, 'Investigation', p. 376.
35 Onion Portage: Anderson, pp. 24–8.
37 Malta dating: MacNeish, 'Investigation'.
37 Dyuktai: Mochanov, passim.
37 Pekin area: Okhladnikov and Nekrasov, pp. 247–56.
37 Yuan Chu: Ferré, p. 35.
38 Suzuki, p. 3.
38 Projectile points: MacNeish, 'Early Man in the Andes', p. 73.
39 Migration from Siberia: Mochanov.
39 Early development of *Homo sapiens*: Hemmer, pp. 65–9.
41 Australian invasion: MacIntosh.

45 Racial characteristics: Cavalli Sforza, pp. 80–91.
46 Caucasoid tribes: Bosch Gimpera, p. 83.

CHAPTER 3. MAN AND MAIZE

51 Extinction of larger mammals: MacNeish, *El Origen*, pp. 9–22.
55 Valley of Ayacucho: MacNeish, *First Annual Report*.
56 Agriculture: MacNeish, *Second Annual Report*.
56 Increasing aridity: Lanning, p. 74.
58 Egyptian treasure: Hawkes, p. 368.
62 Varieties of maize: Grobmann.
63 Cotton: Sauer, p. 636.
63 Cotton in America: Mastache, p. 10.
63 Bird transfer: S. G. Stephens, p. 405.
64 The gourd: Whitaker, pp. 320–7.
65 Ho Ping-Ti, pp. 3–5.
65 Thai pottery site: Solheim, pp. 34–7.
66 Chukchi Peninsula: Okhladnikov and Nekrasov, p. 254.
70 Valdivia figures: Muller, pp. 66–78.
70 Colombian and Ecuadorian pottery: Bischof, pp. 269–81.
71 Fishing gear, Kyushu: Pearson, pp. 85–6.
71 Solo voyages: Jett, p. 17.
73 Arizona area: Kidder, *An Introduction*, p. 23.
73 Copper: Easby, pp. 75–6.
75 Agricultural 'non-centre': Harlan, p. 472.
76 Braddon, ch. 11.
77 Between Azuero and Guatemala: ibid., p. 76.

CHAPTER 4. AMERICA'S FIRST CAPITALISTS

81 Díaz de Castillo, p. 139.
82 Sahagún, *Florentine Codex*, vol. x, ch. 29.
84 Hawkes, p. 10.
87 Chinese warrior poems: Cottrell.
88 Bernal, pp. 127–8.
88 San Lorenzo: Coe, *America's First Civilizations*, p. 67.
89 'Jaguarism': Willey, p. 62.
92 Black men in the Caribbean: Martir de Anglería, *Década* III, Libro I, p. 202.
92 Non-Africans: Bosch Gimpera, pp. 110–11.
93 Furst, 'The Olmec Were-Jaguar Motif', pp. 143–85.
94 Hissink.
94 Dobrizhoffer, p. 67.
95 Olmec and Chavín: Willey, p. 15.
96 Ecuador and Guatemala: Coe, 'Archaeological Linkages', pp. 368–9 and 383.
99 Hopewell mounds: Ceram, pp. 237–69.
101 Hawkes, p. 49.

LIST OF SOURCES

CHAPTER 5. THE EASTERN OCEAN

103 Needham, vol. IV, pt 3, p. 550.
103 Early Chinese voyages: ibid., vol. IV, pt 3, pp. 551–3.
104 Early Chinese navies: ibid., vol. IV, pt 3, p. 440.
104 Shih Chi quotation: ibid., vol. IV, pt 3, p. 552.
106 Chi'in wealth: Cottrell, p. 33.
109 Ekholm, 'Transpacific Contacts', pp. 489–510.
110 Indian voyages: Heine-Geldern, 'Traces', pp. 48–9.
111 Mexico *versus* Cambodia: Ekholm and Heine-Geldern, 'Significant Parallels', p. 301.
113 Religious calendars: Kirchhoff, pp. 73–100.
115 Games: Erasmus, pp. 369–70.
115 Dice: ibid., p. 371.
116 Decorative designs: Caso, 'Relations', pp. 55–71.
117 Maize in China: Ho Ping-Ti, pp. 1–36.
119 First oceanic voyages: Needham, vol. V, pt 3, p. 178.

CHAPTER 6. WHITE GODS WITH BLACK FACES

126 Quetzalcóatl's journey: *Codex Chimalpopoca, Anales de Cuauhtitlan*, pp. 9–11.
126 Variant of above: Sahagún, *Florentine Codex*, bk III, ch. 13.
130 Hairlessness: Cottrell, p. 210.
133 Motolinía, p. 75.
133 Mendieta, vol. I, p. 100.
133 Ixtlilxóchitl, vol. II, pp. 23–4.
133 Beyer, p. 334.
136 Viracocha: Quevedo, ch. xv.
137 'Sons' of Viracocha: Cieza de León, pp. 6–10.
138 Heyerdahl, *American Indians*, pp. 225–343.

CHAPTER 7. PHARAOHS AND PHOENICIANS

141 Ten Lost Tribes of Israel: Wauchope, pp. 59–61.
145 Verrill quotation: ibid., pp. 74–5.
146 Ibid., pp. 81–2.
147 Gladwyn, pp. 224–5.
150 Phoenician voyages: Casson, *The Ancient Mariners*, p. 71.
151 Circumnavigation of Africa: ibid., pp. 130–1.
151 Carthaginian voyage: Herm, p. 298.
157 Gordon, *Riddles*, p. 76.
158 Gordon, *Before Columbus*, p. 137.
158 Kolosimo, p. 168.
163 Egyptian vessels: Herm, p. 73.
163 Voyage to Punt: Casson, *The Ancient Mariners*, pp. 11–13.
164 Keels: ibid., pp. 14–16.

CHAPTER 8. WORLDS IN CONFUSION

167 Mu: Churchward, p. 35.
169 Haeckel: Cavendish (ed.), *Encyclopaedia of the Unexplained*, p. 132.
169 Madame Blavatsky: ibid., p. 45.
171 Thompson, p. 91.
173 Akashic Record: Cavendish (ed.), *Encyclopaedia of the Unexplained*, p. 22.
173 Lemurians: ibid., pp. 235–99.
173 Atlantis theories: ibid., pp. 45–6.
176 Mid-Atlantic ridge: Heirtzler, 'Where the Earth Turns'.
182 Von Däniken, *Gold of the Gods*, p. 10.
182 Airstrips for spacecraft: Reiche, *Los Dibujos*.
183 Moving of a megalith: Durán, vol. II, ch. LXVI.
183 Aztec carving: Sahagún, *Florentine Codex*, bk x, chs 8 and 24.
185 Planets' distance from earth: Sampaio, p. 219.
185 Green Bank formula: Paul, pp. 50–5 and 82.
187 Sirius B: Asimov, pp. 189–91.

CHAPTER 9. POLYNESIAN PERSPECTIVES

192 Polynesian and Malay languages: Heyerdahl, *American Indians*.
194 Accidental voyages: Doran, p. 135.
196 Tonga pottery: Shulter, pp. 59–81.
197 Lapita pottery: Green, *Auckland Star*, 1 July 1973.
197 Tonga *versus* Samoa: Sinoto, pp. 20–5.
198 East Polynesian settlements: Bellwood, pp. 11–14.
198 Stone masonry, East Polynesia: Capell, pp. 371–8.
198 Austronesian languages: Elbert, pp. 165–6.
198 East Polynesian split from Tonga–Samoa: Simmons, p. 62.
199 Blood group genes: Coon, pp. 198–9.
199 Mongoloid blood: Nordensköld, pp. 16–23.
200 Oceanian elements: Jett, p. 27.
200 Sweet potato: Brand, p. 362.
201 *Cumar*: Beaglehole, pp. 39–57.
202 Solomon Islands: Sharp, pp. 66–7.
205 Manihiki–Ellice Islands voyage: ibid., pp. 76–7.
207 Voluntary expeditions: Jett, p. 10.
208 Polynesian sailing vessels: Lewis, p. 296.
209 West–east crossings: Heyerdahl, 'Inca Inspiration', p. 94.
211 Ocean-going rafts: Edwards, pp. 368–81.
211 Shape of raft sails: Métraux, p. 241.
214 Shulter, pp. 84–5.
215 Ayres, pp. 8–11.
218 Easter Island's position: Emory.

CHAPTER 10. THE VINLAND VIKINGS

219 Ship burial: Bronsted, pp. 140–1.
220 Gokstad vessel: Foote and Wilson, p. 248.

220 Length of voyages: Pörtner, p. 271.

220 Greenland–Iceland landfall: Taylor, p. 84.

221 Book of Land-taking: Jones, p. 165.

222 Pre-Christian human sacrifice: ibid., p. 288.

224 The Greenland base: Ingstad, p. 16.

225 Lief succeeds Eric: ibid., p. 45.

226 Crossness: Jones, p. 302.

227 Greenlanders' Saga: Ingstad, pp. 65–8.

232 Wallis' account: 'The Strange Case', pp. 183–214.

233 Pohl, *Prince Henry Sinclair*.

233 Zeno's narrative: Lucas.

233 Mahieu: *Excelsior*, Mexico City, 3 October 1975.

234 Celtic discovery: *Frankfurter Allgemeine Zeitung*, 4 September 1975.

234 Kin Hanna: *Excelsior*, 7 May 1975.

235 Ships' cargoes: *The Times*, 15 April 1976.

235 Henry the Navigator: Morison, p. 3.

236 Taylor, pp. 89–121.

CHAPTER 11. CAUSE AND EFFECT

242 *Time*, 6 January 1975.

242 Ceram, pp. 225–6.

245 A new world: O'Gorman, p. 30.

246 The Ming rising: Parry, pp. 81–6.

247 The will-to-power: Spengler, vol. I, p. 88.

247 The Norseman spirit: ibid., vol. I, pp. 333–5.

248 Intercourse with foreigners: Parry, p. 17.

250 Millon, p. 337.

251 Richard Parker, in the *Sunday Times*, 5 May 1974.

252 Heine-Geldern, *A Note on Relations*, pp. 53–9.

253 Lévi-Strauss, *Antropologie structurale*, pp. 282–3.

254 Nietzsche, *Menschliches, Allzumenschliches*.

255 Furst, *Morning Glory*, pp. 187–202.

256 Initiation rites: Lévi-Strauss, *La Pensée sauvage*, p. 264.

256 Cult of the bear: Campbell, pp. 334–9.

257 Heraldic woman: Fraser, pp. 36–99.

257 Marshak, p. 159.

INDEX

275